Life in the White House

Life
in the
White House

A Social History of the First Family
and the President's House

Robert P. Watson

State University of New York Press

Cover images:
Photo of the White House—Corel Stock Photo.
Background image—James Hoban's plan for the White House, 1792. Courtesy of the
Massachusetts Historical Society.

Published by
State University of New York Press

© 2004 State University of New York

For information, address State University of New York Press,
90 State Street, Suite 700, Albany, NY 12207

Production by Judith Block
Marketing by Jennifer Giovani and Susan Petrie

Library of Congress Cataloging-in-Publication Data

Life in the White House : a social history of the first family and the president's house /
    [compiled by] Robert P. Watson
        p. cm.
    Includes bibliographical references and index.
    ISBN 0-7914-6097-5 (acid-free paper) — ISBN 0-7914-6098-3 (pbk. : acid-free paper)
        1. Presidents—United States—History. 2. Presidents—United States—Family
relationships—History. 3. Presidents—United States—Biography. 4. White House
(Washington, D.C.)—History. 5. Washington (D. C.)—Social life and customs. I. Watson,
Robert P., 1962–

E176.1.L45 2004
973'.09'9—dc22   2003059081

10 9 8 7 6 5 4 3 2 1

For Alessandro and Isabella

Contents

Tables

Preface

In the fall of 2000, the White House celebrated its 200th anniversary. After two centuries, the White House remains the most recognizable residence in the nation and the most open and accessible home of a head of government in the world. It stands as an eternal symbol of popular government and is the national inheritance of the American public. Thanks largely to the efforts of first families occupying the building ever since John and Abigail Adams unpacked their luggage in late 1800, the White House has been preserved as a living museum.

The historic occasion of the 200th anniversary of the building known originally as the "President's House" was marked by celebrations and the publication of several books, including a popular volume by then-First Lady Hillary Rodham Clinton. In spite of the existence of several fine books on the White House in the trade market, very little effort has been made to integrate the building and its social history into the study of the presidency.

In addition to serving as the "people's house," the White House is also the private residence of the first family for four or eight years or so. It benefits scholars and the public alike to take a closer look at what went on behind the walls of the White House, for the story of the White House is the story of the nation and, in the stories of the families who inhabited this most famous building, one finds everything from inspiration to tragedy to family life played out on the public stage. Learning more about the experiences of those who lived in the White House gives us further appreciation of the trials and tribulations of our first families as well as what was simultaneously the extraordinary privilege and extraordinary challenge of calling the place home.

So too does the study of the social history of the first families and their lives in the White House inform the discipline of presidential studies. As the editor of the journal *White House Studies* and someone who has studied and taught courses on the presidency since 1992, I have been struck by the lack of attention in mainstream presidential scholarship given to the presidents' wives, marriages, children, home front, and other important aspects of presidential social and family life. In my capacity as an editor of a journal, I frequently found myself searching the field with no luck for scholarship on such topics and soliciting scholars to write on these topics for the journal.

As such, the initial goal of this book project was to provide an array of scholarly essays examining the social history of the first family and life in the White House. Another founding goal of the project was to provide a volume that would help integrate the social history of first families into mainstream presidential studies.

The study of the social history of the first families and White House should be approached from an interdisciplinary perspective and have cross-disciplinary applicability. In an effort to realize this goal, I invited a broad collection of scholars from political science, history, communication, law, and other fields to contribute to the book. This capable group of scholars offers a variety of perspectives and experiences as librarians, journalists, political advisers, attorneys, researchers, and professors. This is a real strength of the book. Most of the contributors met at the annual conference of the Western Social Science Association in 2002 to exchange ideas and fine-tune the project. I offer my sincere appreciation to each author for their contribution and for embracing the project.

A final goal was to produce a highly readable account of the social history of first families and life in the White House. Although the book has a scholarly foundation, the topic lends itself well to a lively assessment. In these pages, I believe you will find both a careful evaluation of the first families and fascinating examples of how first families coped with scandals, tragedy, the loss of privacy, and their attempts to bring a sense of normalcy and home to their lives in the White House. Perhaps most important, I believe the book illustrates how family life in the White House has impacted the presidency, presidential decision-making, and a president's performance.

The book is divided into four sections: (1) Introduction: The "First Home," (2) Private Lives in a Public Home: Media Coverage of First Families, (3) Profiles of First Families in the White House, and (4) Preserving the President's House. Each of the four sections opens with a brief overview to introduce the reader to the basic topics covered in that section. The fourteen essays that comprise the book examine such topics as the history and building of the Executive Mansion; efforts to decorate, rebuild, and preserve the home; the lives, roles, and media coverage of presidential wives, siblings, and children; the day-to-day lives of first families; the state of presidential marriages; and efforts by the First Family to balance their public and private lives.

I wish to acknowledge Michael Rinella, Judith Block, Jennifer Giovani, and the staff at the State University of New York Press for their interest in this project. It has been a pleasure working with them. Thanks also to my wife, Claudia Pavone Watson, for her support and for Celeste and Julio Pavone for being grandparents only too happy and willing to lend their services as baby-sitters, which allowed me to devote time to this project!

I hope you find the book informative and interesting.

Robert P. Watson
Boca Raton, Florida

Part I

Introduction:
The "First Home"

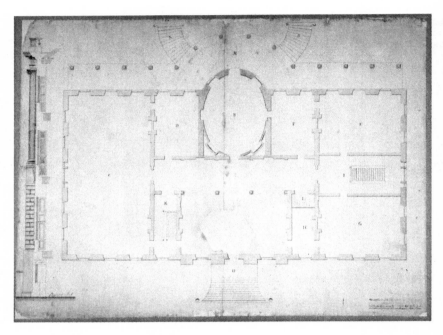

James Hoban's plan for the President's House, 1792. Ink wash, with some pencil sketch lines (courtesy of the Massachusetts Historical Society)

Overview:
Welcome to the White House

The White House is many things. It is a vast office complex housing the leader of the United States and many of the president's senior political advisers. It also functions as a living museum of architecture, politics, and history, and is the national inheritance of the American public. A monument to the nation, the White House is a powerful symbol of democracy to the world. But, in addition to being the "people's house," it is also the president's home. As such, it is where presidential families eat, sleep, and carry on their lives amid the monumental events surrounding them.

There is a human side to the building. Within the walls of the White House and surrounded by the buzz of the nation's business, first families must create a private space for the business of the family. This is done on the second and third floors of the building, which house the private living quarters.

The public used to be able to walk in to the President's Home on a whim and, up through 1933, during the final months of Herbert Hoover's presidency, the first family hosted a large "open house" reception on New Year's Day at the White House. Another similar reception was open to the public on Independence Day. Today the public is still able to visit their building, but they need a permit or authorization and public tours run several days a week (typically Tuesdays through Saturdays when the nation is not at war). Such accessibility has been balanced with the first family's need for privacy in their home and the burden of living in such an open and public residence. It has also been balanced with the constant threat to the safety of the first family. Starting with Abraham Lincoln, a special protective service has guarded the president. The modern equivalent of this protective service began in 1901 with Theodore

3

Roosevelt as a result of the assassination of President William McKinley earlier that year. Today, the Secret Service accompanies the president all hours of the day and night and protects the first family. In 1917, with U.S. involvement in World War I, that protection was extended to other members of the first family. Ultimately, Secret Service protection has been extended to include presidential family members, former presidents, and the family of former presidents, including widows and children. A separate, uniformed police force guards the White House itself.

The president and his family move into the White House after the inauguration, which is now held on January 20, just over two months after the election. Historically, this event was held on March 4. After Rutherford B. Hayes was elected in 1876, the controversy surrounding the election—Hayes lost the popular vote, but carried the Electoral College after a questionable arrangement with three southern states—raised the question about when and how he would be inaugurated. In the end, the transfer of power was peaceful and completed almost according to custom. Because the day of the inaugural—March 4, 1877—in this particular year fell on a Sunday, Hayes was secretly sworn in by the chief justice on the evening of March 3 at a private dinner with outgoing president, Ulysses Grant. The formal inaugural ceremony was held on March 5.

There are exceptions to how first families move into the White House. For instance, after a president has died in office, the vice president becomes president and moves into the President's House soon after being sworn in. In such cases, the incoming president has customarily given the grieving family of the deceased president additional time to move out of the building. Chester A. Arthur, Theodore Roosevelt, and other vice presidents who ascended to the presidency from the vice presidency after the death of the president allowed Lucretia Garfield, Ida McKinley, and other presidential widows ample time to depart the building.

Jane Pierce, the wife of Franklin Pierce, did not accompany the president-elect to his inaugural and did not move into the President's House with him. Grieving over the recent loss of her son, Benjamin, Mrs. Pierce delayed her travel to the nation's capital and, even after arriving in the area, delayed moving into the building. William Henry Harrison's wife, Anna, never did have the opportunity to live in the Executive Mansion. Her concern over the long journey, mixed with her marginal health and lack of enthusiasm for her husband's new job, led Mrs. Harrison to delay her trip. She had planned on traveling to Washington shortly after his inauguration. However, Harrison gave an excessively long inaugural address in bad weather, contracted a cold, and died only one month into his presidency. Anna Harrison had been dismayed at the prospect of moving to the capital city and, by a tragic twist of events, she was relieved of that burden.

Even the spouse of the first president did not attend her husband's inaugural. Martha Washington made the long trip from Virginia to New York City—the first location of the President's House while the building we now know as the White House was under construction—shortly after George Washington's inauguration.

FROM HUMBLE BEGINNINGS

The White House was not always the building of splendor it is today. Although it was the largest home in the country through much of the nineteenth century, the completion of the building ran late and it lacked many amenities necessary for habitability. The city had been carved out of a swamp and was sparsely populated in its early days, lacking the cultural and social amenities of most capital cities. Winters in the President's House were chilly and damp, while the humidity in summers was unbearable. Mosquitos and disease plagued the city's inhabitants in summers, causing many—including several presidential families—to vacate the area in summer, a custom practiced into the twentieth century.

John and Abigail Adams were the first to live in the President's House, arriving in late 1800 and living in the building for only the last four months of John Adams's term in office. The couple found only six rooms completed, the yard a clutter of construction supplies and workers, and less staff than was needed to run the home. Such hardships, inconveniences, and the pressures of the office hardly made living in the building a pleasant experience for some of the early presidential families. President and Mrs. Adams, as well as other first families living prior to the twentieth century, would hardly recognized the structure today.

Today the most famous residence in the country employs a large staff of ushers, chefs, and other professionals, trained to assist the first family in everything from protocol, to preparing meals, to entertainment; there is even someone to shop for the family members. An intricate system of bells has been used historically to summon the staff, who are on duty twenty-four hours a day, 365 days a year. First families enjoy some of the finest food and entertainment

served anywhere, priceless artifacts, and first-class service while
living in the first home.

One of the reasons for such a large domestic staff at the White
House is the first family's role as the nation's hosts. Even though it
is not specified in the Constitution, first families have been expected to represent the nation. Throughout the country's history,
they have played host to a variety of events and individuals, including kings and queens, world leaders, Nobel laureates, and politicians.
These social events can range from informal receptions for an individual receiving an award to formal state dinners for hundreds.

The extensiveness of planning and the intricacies of protocol
surrounding official events necessitate having a staff trained for
such events. For example, special guests are often welcomed at the
north entrance of the White House, while other guests often arrive
at the east entrance. Uniformed officers and ushers meet the guests
and members of the first family generally receive their guests and
escort them to the Yellow Oval Room on the second floor of the
building. Formal events call for the president and first lady, along
with their guests, to descend the grand marble stairway to an-
nouncements of their names. Special guests for years have been
met by a band performing such recognizable tunes as "Ruffles and
Flourishes" and "Hail to the Chief." By custom, the president
accompanies the ranking woman to the State Dining Room, followed by the first lady on the arm of the ranking man. Only the
finest foods and entertainment are offered the White House's guests
and individuals are afforded the opportunity to meet and shake
hands with members of the first family in an official receiving line.

All first families have entertained at the White House, although the style, frequency, and tone of these events has varied
from informal (the Carters) to regal (the Reagans). Even presidents
like Thomas Jefferson, who frowned on such royalist customs, did
provide ceremonies and receptions and served an assortment of
fancy dishes and wine. Even first ladies like Eleanor Roosevelt,
who disliked serving as hostess and who served during the turbu-
lent years of the Great Depression and World War II, found herself
fulfilling this "public duty." Members of the first family unable for
health reasons to stand for long receiving lines or shake hands with
hundreds of guests resorted cleverly to being seated on a dias for
such occasions or holding a bouquet of flowers in their hands. At
times, these same first ladies even had younger family members—
typically daughters, daughters-in-law, or nieces—stand in for them
at social affairs. The President's Home and responsibilities that

come along with living in the first residence are bigger than any single president or member of the first family, as the affairs of state transcend the particular first family presiding over them.

Most receptions have been memorable affairs for guests and enjoyable—if a bit taxing—for the first family. A favorite moment of many historians dates to a famous toast President John F. Kennedy made to a group of Nobel prize winners gathered for a reception in 1962 at the White House. The President extended a toast to "the most extraordinary collection of talent, of human knowledge, that has ever been gathered together at the White House, with the possible exception of when Thomas Jefferson dined alone."

The White House has also served as a showcase for the arts, American culture, and an array of design styles. Throughout its history, the building and rooms have featured the very latest gizmos and gadgets, including a showcase of such new technological wonders as gas lighting, indoor plumbing, electricity, telephones, and other inventions and social amenities. These have not always been met with success. When the Polks brought a new system of gas lighting to the home in 1848 to replace oil lamps and candles, it failed to work during an important social event. Fortunately, First Lady Sarah Polk had decided to leave the old candle chandelier in place, which ended up providing light for the occasion. Concerned about being shocked, President Benjamin Harrison and members of his family would not use the new electric lights installed in the home.

A HOME WITH A HISTORY

The chapters is this opening section of the book are designed to introduce the reader to life in the White House for the first family, the building's history—including the planning and construction of the original structure—and some of the historic rooms and their uses. The influence of the first family on the design and use of the building and its rooms is quite evident. This might come as some surprise. But it should not. The building is, after all, also their home for a few years.

One

At Home with the First Families

ROBERT P. WATSON

In the history of the White House are the stories of first families. The study of the establishment of a home for the president and two-plus centuries of changes to the President's House offer insights on the occupants who lived there. So too does the study of the social history of family life in the White House provide a useful lens by which to assess the presidents and presidency. What explains why first families made certain changes to the building? What activities and hobbies were a part of family life in the White House? How did the presidential marriage and first family cope with the demands of living in this public home? The answers to these questions promise to inform our understanding of an array of issues surrounding the presidency, from character to decision making.

For instance, Warren Harding's poor choice in friends and minimalist work ethic might be better understood through his preoccupation with playing cards and gambling in the White House. Many of those who shared his card table and bets were involved in the Teapot Dome scandal and other downfalls of the Harding administration. The mind of Thomas Jefferson is revealed in part in his passions for botany, architecture, literature, and science, all of which he brought to the President's Home, indulging his intellectual and creative interests through such means as technical and aesthetic improvements to the building and the Lewis and Clark expedition. Insights to Herbert Hoover's character and style of governing might be gleaned from the distance with which he treated the White House staff, while Richard Nixon's practice of bowling alone in the White House while wearing dress clothing says a lot about the man.

Families have been a part of the presidency for nearly all of its history and many family members have been a viable part of the

9

institution of the presidency. The social history of the presidency and President's Home reveal the central role of members of the first family in both the institution and building. Edith Roosevelt regularly visited her husband in his office, Rosalynn Carter attended Cabinet meetings, and Sarah Polk followed closely the legislative business of the Congress. Dolley Madison's elaborate socials and popularity brought the Madison presidency political support. And the presence in the White House of their spouse, children, or grandchildren comforted the presidents during what was easily the most difficult times of their lives.

A Building "For the Ages"

A Great Privilege and Responsibility

In spite of the challenges of the presidency and loss of privacy coming from living in the White House, it is a special privilege for all who have called the building home. The White House is the most famous residence in the country, if not the world. On entering the White House, first families become a part of the building's powerful symbolism, whether they want to or not, and must be mindful that they are occupying a living museum. Living in the centerpiece of the nation's government and political system, it is not surprising that Nancy Reagan echoed the sentiments of many other first families when she said, "Nothing can prepare you for living in the White House."[1]

Monumental decisions have been made within the building's walls. This is a part of the history of the White House that challenges each new occupant, yet is a part of the institution of the presidency from which each president draws strength and esteem. It was in the building that Thomas Jefferson made the decision to acquire from Napoleon the Louisiana Purchase, greatly expanding the nation's borders, providing access to the important Mississippi River delta, and doubling the size of the young country at the bargain price of 15 million dollars. It was here that Abraham Lincoln wrestled with the weight of the nation and her people being torn apart by civil war. Franklin D. Roosevelt crafted his response to the Great Depression within the walls and hosted Winston Churchill to discuss the status of World War II. From the White House, Harry Truman managed the end of the war and the reconstruction of Europe under the Marshall Plan, John F. Kennedy took

the country to the brink of another world war during his showdown with the Soviets over the Cuban Missile Crisis, and the
forty-first president, George Bush, watched the demise of the Soviet Union and decades of the Cold War come crashing down with
the Berlin Wall.

A Grand Vision

Known simply as *The President's House* upon its establishment—
the name preferred by George Washington—the building has also
been called the Executive Mansion throughout its history. It was
not until Theodore Roosevelt decided to place the name *White
House* on official letterhead in 1901 that the now-popular term
become commonplace.[2]
     The initial plans for a presidential house within a larger capi-
tal city date to the founding of the nation and reflect both the
internal struggle over the vision of the new nation by its founders
and the democratic principles embodied in that founding. These
plans sought to erect a building unlike the ornate palaces of European leaders: An unpretentious home for the new democracy, yet
one mindful of the need for legitimacy and befitting the aspirations
of the new nation.[3]
     George Washington, for whom the capital city was named,
played a fundamental role in selecting the site and approving the
plans for both the city and president's home. Authority for selecting a site for the capital city and president's house had been established in the Constitution and delegated to Congress. However,
Congress authorized George Washington to make the decision with
the support of a committee. Three commissioners were appointed
in this capacity, all with ties to Washington and, interestingly, to
the Potomac River as well. Essentially, it was George Washington's
project from the start. The Resident Act of 1790 authorized the
president to determine the site of the capital city and presidential
residence. The same legislation relocated the seat of government
from New York to Philadelphia.
     Even though it was a region of swamps and sparsely populated
forests, George Washington grew up and lived along the banks of
the Potomac River and preferred this site to any other. New York
and Philadelphia had lobbied hard to sway the committee and president, even building mansions in an attempt to become the permanent capital. But, by July 1790, Washington had selected the location
near the Potomac River. In 1800, legislation would transfer the

location again to what is now known as the city of Washington in the District of Columbia.

The General wisely selected this neutral location, one neither north nor south, on lands ultimately ceded by Maryland and Virginia. Having lived in a mansion in New York City during the inaugural presidency, and later in a stately home owned by Robert Morris on Cherry Street in Philadelphia, Washington recognized the need for a spacious structure. Although the homes in both temporary capitals were large, comfortable, and considered to be grand residences, they were far too small for the needs of family, staff, office space, and social hosting. Washington would eventually approve the design for a large building, expand on the original size, and later even inspect the pace of construction.[4]

Washington had been working with the celebrated architect Charles L'Enfant to design the capital city and its public buildings. L'Enfant had arrived in the colonies in 1777 and joined the Revolutionary cause, even serving under Washington. During the encampment at Valley Forge, L'Enfant had even painted the General's portrait. Egotistical and arrogantly sure of his abilities and of his selection as the capital's architect, L'Enfant used his personal connection to Washington to promote himself. He even proceeded with his plans for the capital and president's house before final approval had been bestowed on him. With visions of grandeur, L'Enfant intended to carve out of the rural marshes a Roman-inspired city of wide avenues connecting to a central political mall. But by 1792, the French architect had succeeded in making enemies of most everyone he encountered, including a reluctant Washington, and was summarily relieved of his duties.[5]

L'Enfant's grand city "for the ages" remained a guiding influence for the design and construction of both the capital city and president's home. It was Washington, however, who selected the current location of the White House on account of the small hill and view it afforded.

At the urging of Thomas Jefferson, an open, democratic contest was held, inviting designs for the presidential home. The competition and design prize of 500 dollars drew a handful of applicants from the small pool of capable architects in the young country. Even if the contest was not truly democratic, as Washington used his influence to select his preference for the building, the symbolic nature of the establishment of what would become the White House sent a powerful message. Washington's choice from the entries was the plan submitted by Irish architect, James Hoban. Hoban had a reputation as a competent designer of public buildings and his work in the city of Charleston, South Carolina, had caught the attention of many, including Washington. Hoban's design for the presidential house was a simple but elegant structure modeled after an estate in Dublin, Ireland, known as Leinster House.

Washington's vision for the city and home was on a grand scale and, from a contemporary perspective, proved to be practical and prophetic. Where Washington favored a large, stately stone structure, Thomas Jefferson—true to his vision of democratic simplicity for the young nation—made known his preference for a basic structure made of brick and hoped the competition would promote his plan.[6]

George Washington further extended his influence by amending Hoban's original design to include a larger, fancier house. However, with costs already too high for the cash-strapped nation, compromises were made in the plan and construction delayed by rain, mud, and a shortage of skilled workers and money. The number of floors was reduced from three to two and Washington's preferred stone structure was made of stone, along with brick and wood, the stone being used only for the bottom level and exterior façade. The building also incurred its share of criticism because of cost overruns and by those feeling the house was extravagantly large and undemocratic: "big enough for two emperors, one pope, and the grand lama," opined one sarcastic critic.[7] But with the considerable influence of George Washington, the sweat of slave labor, and skill of Scottish stonemasons, the cornerstone of the President's House was set down on October 13, 1792.

James Hoban continued to play a role in the building he designed, by supervising much of the construction. The General continued to monitor the progress of his vision during his second term in office in Philadelphia. The construction progressed slowly. At the conclusion of his presidency in 1797, Washington stopped at the construction site to inspect the building and city while on his way home from Philadelphia to Mount Vernon in Virginia. This would be Washington's last view of the unfinished site. Sadly, George Washington did not live to see his vision fulfilled. He died in December 1799, less than one year before John Adams moved into the home.

Although he was a visionary, it is doubtful Washington would recognize the home and city today. The cultural backwater of muddy streets, farms, and swamps has become a bustling city beyond even L'Enfant's dreams. In fact, most presidents serving prior to the start of the twentieth century would scarcely recognize the home. Gone are the stables, smokehouse, and old stone wall. In place of the 82-acre "Presidential Park" established in 1791 by Congress is a 500-acre estate of immaculate landscaping surrounded by fences and security, a vast White House complex, and a major urban center. But George Washington would appreciate the enduring symbol the building remains after over 200 years.

CALLING THE WHITE HOUSE HOME

Living over the Family Store

With the rare exception of times of war, threats of terrorism, and major renovation projects, the White House remains open and accessible to the public several days a week. Tuesdays through Saturdays the public is permitted to tour the home and grounds and dignitaries, public officials, and privileged individuals are frequently invited to the White House.[8]

What they tour is both a public museum and private residence. Accordingly, first families lead two lives in the building, one private and the other public. They must find a way to live among the tourists and employees in a highly public home that houses an extensive office complex and is the center of national government. As Ronald Reagan quipped, the experience of living in the White House is like "living above the family store."[9]

Living space and office space in the building have often been intertwined. Historically, both were also insufficient for the needs of first families and the president. For instance, stairways in the mansion were public and first families going about their daily business in their home routinely passed tourists, presidential advisers, and visiting dignitaries. Such invasions of privacy were especially taxing on spouses and children of presidents who shunned the public eye, for they found it inescapable while living in the President's House.[10]

When Benjamin Harrison moved into the President's House in 1889, he did so surrounded by a large, extended family. The President delighted in the company of his grandchildren, most notably his favorite grandson, nicknamed Baby McKee. Advances in photographic technology around the time of Harrison's presidency, coupled with the photogenic first family, made Baby McKee an overnight sensation. It is likely he was the most photographed and well-known child in the country. The media coverage of Baby McKee and public fascination with the first grandson ushered in a new relationship between the first family and the American public.

This intensive and personalized coverage of Baby McKee by the media brought a new human side to how the media covered presidents and, in this case, their families. The human dimension was newsworthy and the public clamored for more. They received it in 1901 with the arrival of Theodore Roosevelt and his large and lively brood in the White House. The charismatic president made for good copy with his bustling schedule of activities, quick wit, and willingness to engage the press. So too did his children, who were frequently seen wrestling with their father or romping through the White House with their veritable zoo of pets. Alice Roosevelt, the President's daughter from his first marriage, was deemed "Princess Alice" by the press. Headstrong, attractive, and not shy about sharing her opinions, Alice's every move was covered by the press and "Alice watching" became something of a nationwide pastime. This new human interest approach to reporting on the presidency was a two-way street, as President Roosevelt recognized the utility of reaching the public, enhancing his popularity, and crafting messages to his benefit through his intimate interaction with the press.[11]

The media's relationship with the president would never again be the same, as the proliferation of media outlets, media technologies, and intensity of coverage increased dramatically over the twentieth century. Franklin D. Roosevelt, much like Theodore Roosevelt, was media savvy and charismatic. He benefited greatly from the press coverage of both his message and himself. Roosevelt's wife, Eleanor, also became a media sensation and was easily the most widely covered first lady in history. The unprecedented fourth inaugural of FDR even showcased the President's thirteen grandchildren for the press and American public. First families since his time have also featured their family not only during inaugural festivities but the campaign as well.

Of course, with this new relationship, came a further erosion of any sense of privacy and anonymity afforded first families. The White House today houses within its complex of offices a large contingent of reporters representing the world's press. The media having been invited in to the home, first families are living their lives increasingly in the public fishbowl that the White House has become.[12]

Pets, Weddings, and Children

Because it is a home, the everyday activities, challenges, and special moments associated with family life are present within the

White House. Most first families brought with them to the residence their favorite furnishings, memorabilia and mementos, and hobbies. Such connections to their former lives helped first families establish some sense of normalcy while living in such a public home. The Hayes family, for instance, enjoyed the game of croquet and frequently played it on the mansion grounds. Lucy Hayes started the White House custom of the Easter egg roll for children, in part because of her own love of children and religious beliefs. Held on Easter Mondays, thousands of children gather for the fun event, which has been hosted by first families since the time of Mrs. Hayes. The Christmas holiday has always been a special time at the White House, where first families have celebrated with the nation by displaying numerous beautifully decorated trees and the official White House Christmas tree in the Blue Room, along with sparkling holiday lights and decorations in both the interior and on the exterior of the building.

Many families have pets. The same has been true for first families, who often brought pets with them to the mansion.[13] Several of these pets became popular with the press and public. Benjamin Harrison's grandchildren, for instance, had a goat named Whiskers and Caroline Kennedy, daughter of President John F. Kennedy, had a pony named Macaroni, who was photographed and reported on by the news media on a daily basis. Guests to the Jefferson home often saw the President's mockingbird, Curious, sitting on the presidential shoulder or eating from the same hand that penned the Declaration of Independence. Of the famous bird, Jefferson is reported to have said, "I tamed it and became its friend."[14] Lou Hoover had so many birds that the White House lawn appeared to be an aviary and, with the British army advancing on the President's House, intent on burning the structure, Dolley Madison not only saved priceless presidential artifacts and her husband's papers, but her pet parrot at the critical eleventh hour.

Many presidents have been dog lovers.[15] George Washington was an enthusiastic fox hunter who both bred hunting dogs and received dogs as gifts from diplomats knowledgeable of the General's interest in the sport. Among the most famous first pooches were Franklin Roosevelt's Fala, Kennedy's Charlie, Lyndon Johnson's two beagles Him and Her, Bill Clinton's chocolate Labrador Buddy, and George W. Bush's Spot. Richard Nixon's dog Checkers, a gift from a supporter, might even have saved the then-vice presidential nominee's political career thanks to a sentimental reference to the dog while giving a televised speech designed to allay allegations that Checkers' new owner was corrupt. George and Barbara Bush proudly showed the country the litter of puppies bore by their spaniel, Millie, and the First Lady penned the book *C. Fred's Story* as if it were written by her dog.

The two first families with the largest and most unusual assortment of pets were those of Abraham Lincoln and Theodore Roosevelt.[16] Lincoln's boys loved animals and collected the likes of rabbits, a pony, a turkey, and a goat who pulled a wagon around the mansion grounds. Theodore Roosevelt's boys had a badger, racoon, cats, dogs, snakes, rooster, and a pony, who was ridden inside the White House in an effort to cheer up one of the Roosevelt children.

One of the most celebrated events in the White House is the occasion of the wedding of a member of the first family.[17] One of the most storied of all White House weddings was the 1906 union of Theodore Roosevelt's daughter Alice to U.S. Representative Nicholas Longworth.

The first wedding to take place in the President's House was that of Lucy Payne Washington to Supreme Court justice Thomas Todd, which was arranged by and during the reign of First Lady Dolley Madison.

The first child of a president to marry in the President's House was first daughter Maria Hester Monroe who wed her cousin Samuel Laurence Gouveneur. A few years later, the son of John Quincy Adams wed in the mansion. Grover Cleveland remains the only sitting president to be married in the mansion. Cleveland wed Frances Folsom in 1886 in a ceremony that attracted more than its fair share of publicity. Not only was Cleveland the president at the time of the wedding, but Ms. Folsom was barely out of her teens and Cleveland had been acting as her god-father since the passing of Frances's father—Cleveland's former law partner—when she was a young girl. Not surprisingly, tongues wagged.

Among the many White House weddings were Elizabeth Tyler and William Walter, marking about the only event in which gravely ill first lady Letitia Tyler made a public appearance; Ellen "Nellie" Grant and Englishman Algernon Charles Satoris; both Wilson daughters—Jessie and Eleanor, the latter to William McAdoo, the Secretary of Treasury; Tricia Nixon and Edward Cox, married in the Rose Gardens; and Lynda Johnson to U.S. Marine Charles Robb, who would later serve as a U.S. senator from Virginia.

The White House has also experienced the births of many children over its 200-year history. The first baby born in the mansion was James Madison Randolph, son of Thomas Jefferson's daughter Martha

Randolph, born while Martha was visiting her father at the President's House in 1805. The child was named in honor of Jefferson's Secretary of State and fellow founding father, James Madison. The birth brought the President immense happiness, as he had lost his wife and all of his other children and was exceptionally close to his remaining daughter Martha. The first presidential child to be born at the White House was Esther Cleveland, the second daughter of Grover and Frances Cleveland. Esther was born during Cleveland's second—and nonconsecutive—term in office. An earlier daughter, Ruth, had been born to the first couple but not in the mansion. Baby Ruth, for whom the candy bar was named, had been born during the interim between Cleveland's two terms.

The press and public have always been drawn to children born or living in the White House and Baby Ruth was no exception, becoming perhaps the most popular child alive at the time and a source of joy to the mansion staff. Another daughter, Marion, would arrive during the second term in office, but was born at the Cleveland summer vacation home in Massachusetts. In part because of the interest shown in the Cleveland children, the First Lady was forced to have the building's gates closed and the South Lawn restricted from public access. Although acting in the best interests of her young children, Mrs. Cleveland was criticized for her precautions. Like the Clevelands, the Kennedys raised young children in the White House—Caroline and John, Jr. Stories of the Kennedy children were featured in newspapers across the country, while Mrs. Kennedy struggled to protect the privacy of her children. The First Lady even established a school in the White House for daughter Caroline and other children her age.

Stories of First Families

In addition to an assortment of first pets, elegant weddings, and the birth of children, the White House has housed over forty different presidential families. Their experiences in the building have covered the full range of possibilities, at times mirroring those found in homes of private citizens across the country. The first presidential couple to live in the building was John and Abigail Adams, who moved into the unfinished President's House in fall of 1800.

John Adams joined many other public officials residing in the temporary capital city of Philadelphia in departing the city during the summer months. Leaving the same brick mansion on Cherry Street inhabited by George Washington during his presidency, Adams traveled home to Quincy, Massachusetts, to escape the heat, humidity, and disease that plagued the city in summer.

On his way to Massachusetts, the President checked the status of construction at the President's House and was assured of its completion in time for his return in fall. Interestingly, Adams had demonstrated very little interest in the establishment and construction of the city and home, rarely visiting the site during either his vice presidency under Washington or his presidency to assess the progress. It was atypical behavior for Adams, who otherwise was engaged in most of the business of the founding period, but possibly a matter of him recognizing the centrality of George Washington in all matters pertaining to the creation of the federal city and president's house.

His furnishings shipped ahead of him to the President's House, Adams arrived in the new capital city on November 3, 1800 after a journey of roughly three weeks. His arrival coincided with the election, which he hoped would grant him a second term in office. The results of the election, however, were not the only disappointment to welcome Adams to the new mansion. As if the loss to rival Thomas Jefferson were not painful enough, construction in the city and on the home was running well behind schedule, and Adams found the residence far from completed. Only approximately half of the thirty-six rooms in the mansion were even plastered, the wall paper was still drying in others, and the President had only six rooms completed in which to enjoy.[18]

Abigail Adams had not accompanied her husband to the new residence and was planning on departing soon after him. The President, obviously understating matters, wrote to his wife of their new home, "The building is in a state to be habitable and now we wish for your company."[19] True to expectation, Mrs. Adams arrived to find the debris of construction strewn about the grounds, workmen coming and going, and the irritation of constant noise.[20] The unfinished building leaked when it rained, was cold and damp that first winter, had an insufficient number of fireplaces to warm its residents, and contained among the six finished rooms no place to hang the family's laundry. Abigail was careful not to voice her concerns in public, but did complain of the workers being lazy.[21] Likewise, the mansion's system of bells to summon servants was still under construction and the first couple had roughly half the staff of thirty they estimated it required to run the President's House.

With the sting of defeat from the election still lingering and the recent death of their son Charles, who died an alcoholic and in debt, the four months the inaugural first family spent in the mansion was not what they had hoped for. Still, Mrs. Adams enjoyed the scenic view the home offered and the promise of the building, commenting with mixed emotion and meaning on the "great castle" in which she resided.[22] After four months in the home, John and Abigail Adams vacated the building in the early hours of the morning, so as to not be seen and to avoid having to attend the inauguration of Adams's successor, Thomas Jefferson.

Unlike Abigail Adams, life in the Executive Mansion agreed with Julia Tyler, who thoroughly enjoyed the experience. This was reflective in her approach to hosting social events and her popularity. Other residents of the home also enjoyed their time in the building, including Dolley Madison, Julia Grant, and, more recently, Bill Clinton. On the other hand, several former residents spent perhaps the most trying times of their lives in the building, including Margaret Taylor and Jane Pierce.

The Lincoln home was one that ran the full gamut of experiences. The President and his wife embraced the opportunity to be the first couple and their children—Thomas ("Tad"), William ("Willie"), and Robert, who lived there only between terms at college—also contributed to a lively, happy home. Abraham Lincoln loved children and relished in the joys of fatherhood, while the Lincoln boys dashed through Cabinet meetings, explored the third-floor attic, and kept the domestic staff busy with pranks and youthful mischievousness. The boys also provided the President with a needed distraction from the pressures of the Civil War. The War weighed heavily on Lincoln and William's death in 1862 brought much grief to the family. The President also suffered through criticism of his handling of the war and his wife's constant scandals, from extravagant spending, to experimenting with the occult in an effort to communicate with her two deceased children, to her family's support of the Confederacy.[23]

The Eisenhowers used a quiet family room in the private residence to relax, established by Mamie Eisenhower in order that her husband might recover his declining health. Mrs. Eisenhower also brought to the home her signature color—pink—in the form of decorations and color scheme for the walls.

A number of presidential spouses sought to not only re-create a sense of home in the building, but to restore the mansion's history and integrity and to play an active role as the nation's hostess.[24] Because of the expectations of society, the role of housekeeper customarily fell to first ladies. Yet maintaining the home when the home in question is the President's House is quite a feat. First Ladies thus managed not only their own household affairs, but the mansion's staff, kitchen, and social events. Among those spouses most active in managing and preserving the White House or hosting social and state affairs were Julia Tyler, Abigail Fillmore, Mary Lincoln, Julia Grant, Caroline Harrison, and Edith Roosevelt.[25]

Julia Tyler sought to enhance the status and livability of the mansion, acquiring regal French furnishings and installing a new lighting system. The Tylers ended up covering much of the costs from their own pockets. The First Lady also offered elegant, grand social events on a scale rarely seen in the building's history. The Fillmores were successful in obtaining funds from Congress to establish a library on the second floor of the building and install improved plumbing, a new bathtub, and iron range in the kitchen.

Mary Todd Lincoln also desired to restore the mansion. Through elaborate redecorating and social events, Mrs. Lincoln reasoned that she could inspire pride in the Union and legitimacy in the presidency during the crisis of the Civil War. However, unlike other first ladies, her efforts toward those ends were merely seen as extravagant and wasteful. In part, the fault was her own doing. For instance, the First Lady's china service was extremely expensive and she ordered a second set, all the while her husband was encouraging thrift for the war effort. Mrs. Lincoln was also privy to an illegal plan to divert funds to cover her outstanding bills.[26]

Julia Grant used congressional funds to redecorate the Blue Room and East Room and install new gates on the mansion grounds. Mrs. Grant also purchased new china and fine art. Celebrated works of art have long graced the walls of the White House, making the building a center for showcasing American arts. Jacqueline Kennedy also brought performing arts to the building. Her "In Performance at the White House" series featured many of the nation's leading musicians, singers, and performers, along with acclaimed international performing artists. The Nixons, for example, marked George Washington's birthday in 1970 with a live performance of the Broadway musical 1776 in the White House. Jimmy and Rosalynn Carter, George and Barbara Bush, and Bill and Hillary Clinton all featured such distinctly American performances as jazz, country, gospel, and the blues.

Perhaps no other member of a first family has done as much to make the White House a living history museum and showcase for the arts and culture than First Lady Jacqueline Kennedy.[27] Accustomed to a life of great affluence and privilege, the First Lady was distraught when she first saw the condition of the White House. After poor design choices by previous first families and inadequate consideration to historical authenticity, Mrs. Kennedy found the building unsuitable to her tastes. She thus proceeded to catalog all items in the White House and building's storage areas and then set about collecting period furnishings. She restored the White House to its original vision, focusing on the quarter-century period from the arrival of John and Abigail Adams in 1800 to the end of the Monroe administration in 1825. The fruits of her work were unveiled to a nationally televised audience in 1962, with the First Lady leading a tour of the renovated home that would earn an Emmy Award and inspire record numbers of visitors to the White House in subsequent years.

The permanent preservation of the White House is her legacy.[28] The First Lady was the driving force behind the establishment of a Fine Arts Commission, the Committee for the Preservation of the White House, and the Office of the Curator of the White House. Because of her vision, any new furnishings or additions planned for the building must now be approved by the Committee for the Preservation of the White House and must reflect the history of the building. Existing furnishings cannot be sold or discarded, ending a practice that dated to the original construction of the building. In 1988, the White House was designated with museum status by the American Association of Museums.

THE PEOPLE'S HOUSE

Hosts for the Nation

Neither is it mentioned in the Constitution, nor is it found in statute, but one of the duties that has emerged for the first family is that of functioning as the nation's official hosts.[29] The first family represents the nation in meetings with kings and queens, prime ministers and presidents, while presiding over affairs in the White House. A first family's interest in hosting and their style of hosting have varied considerably. Thomas Jefferson, for example, was so informal at times that he stood at the door of the President's House to shake hands with anyone happening into the home.[30] Some guests even reported that the President greeted them "standing in slippers."[31]

Historically, presidential families were expected to cover the costs of hosting social affairs and the upkeep of the President's

House out of their own pockets.[32] The cost of food and wine, stables and horses, supplies and servants, drained many a presidential coffer. Indeed, presidents such as James Monroe and Thomas Jefferson experienced severe financial hardships as a direct result of their service as commander-in-chief, while other presidents including George Washington and Andrew Jackson saw their plantation businesses suffer in their absence while serving in the President's House.[33] Jefferson was known to serve bountiful feasts to guests at his state dinners and the cost of champagne itself threatened to bankrupt him. A presidential salary of 25,000 dollars might seem considerable for the time, but it more often than not proved inadequate.

Congress would eventually cover the costs of some of the repairs to the mansion and its furnishings, but it was not until the twentieth century that the problem was adequately addressed. During the presidency of William Howard Taft, Congress provided funding to cover the costs of maintaining and staffing the White House. By the time of Warren Harding's administration in the early 1920s, Congress expanded the funds and coverage to include the cost of entertaining, finally alleviating presidential families from that burden. Correspondingly, the presidential salary was increased from 25,000 dollars to 50,000 dollars in 1873, during the second term of Ulysses Grant. It was again raised to 75,000 dollars in 1909, to 100,000 dollars in 1949 during Harry Truman's presidency, and 200,000 dollars in 1969 under Richard Nixon. Today, the presidential salary is 300,000 dollars.

First families still pay for their own living expenses, which include everything from phone calls to weddings and birthday parties, to other family activities and consumption for personal use. The White House staff includes ushers, chefs, and an impressive array of individuals to assist with virtually every need that might arise. Nevertheless, the sometimes arduous task of constant entertaining remains a responsibility of the first families. One need only be reminded of the experience of Grover Cleveland, who claimed that he shook hands with roughly 8,000 people in one evening alone.[34]

Preserving History

In 1814, the British landed troops in Maryland and began an offensive that would take them to the President's House in the federal city. With President James Madison away with the American army and any resistance to the British crushed, the President's House sat unprotected. From her vantage point atop the mansion, First Lady Dolley Madison observed the British marching toward the building, but refused to abandon the home until the final moment. To the sound of cannon fire, she wisely and courageously collected priceless artifacts, her husband's presidential papers, and ordered the infamous Gilbert Stuart portrait of George Washington removed from its frame.[35] Her act of heroism in carting off these objects secured a link to the past and was perhaps the most dramatic effort to preserve the building and its history.[36] On August 24, 1814, the British burned the President's House. Only a timely rainstorm prevented complete destruction of the mansion. Mrs. Madison rallied the nation to rebuild the home and federal city. Shortly after the war, renovations of the mansion were under way. President James Monroe and his family were able to move in to the building in the fall of 1817.

Another dramatic threat to the building came in 1829 with the inauguration of Andrew Jackson, the popular "people's president" whose supporters literally wrecked the interior of the mansion during their wild, drunken celebration.[37] A little over three decades later, the building was again in imminent danger of destruction. During the Civil War, the Confederate army closed to within a few miles of the Executive Mansion and seemed ready to seize the Union capital. President Lincoln ordered the "Bucktail Brigade," a Company of Pennsylvania soldiers from the 150th Regiment, to be stationed on the building's grounds to protect not only the president, but the mansion as well.

The most enduring threats to the integrity of the mansion have come from the day-to-day use of the building by the first family, presidential advisers working in the offices, and the vast numbers of tourists coming through the President's House year after year. Furnishings wear out, carpets are stained, and drapery is torn. Sticky fingers of tourists eager for souvenirs also walk away with countless items from and pieces of the building. All need to be replaced.

All first families have added their own touch and tastes to the building, as historically there was no systematic approach for designing, redecorating, or preserving the building. Any efforts were largely left up to the individual families, along with the approval of Congress when public funds were utilized for the task.[38] Thomas Jefferson, the first occupant to serve a full presidential term in the building, began in 1801 to tinker with amenities and improvements for the building and its grounds. Working with the famous architect, Benjamin Latrobe, he had porticos on the north and south sides of the building designed, along with terraces on the east and west ends of the home.

Starting in 1815, the Madisons rebuilt the mansion after the 1814 fire and attempted to restore the structure to its original condition. They were assisted in this task by the Commission of the District of Columbia and the building's original architect, James Hoban, who reinforced the structure, replaced destroyed walls, and repainted the home. The restoration continued into the administration of James Monroe, who moved in with the project still under way. Like the mansion's first residents, John and Abigail Adams, James and Elizabeth Monroe found only a few rooms completed, but had a new south entrance constructed and revised the custom of hosting a New Year's Day reception for the public.[39] Later, Andrew Jackson added the large North Portico.

Lifelong bibliophiles Millard and Abigail Fillmore must have been shocked to find the absence of any books in the President's House when they moved to the building in 1850.[40] They promptly added a library on the second floor, a room used by the first family for entertainment and private family time. At times, the mansion fell into disrepair either from lack of funds, neglect, or the rapid change in residents. After a lifetime of living opulently and with expensive tastes, Chester A. Arthur refused to move into a building he deemed wholly unsuitable until he had the chance to completely redecorate and refurnish the home. Arthur ordered that the interior of the building be gutted and the items be hauled away by wagons so that he might improve on its delapidated appearance.[41]

Happily, not all of the decorating and renovating by first families was so drastic or done with so little regard for history. One of the problems most first families faced was the need for additional living and office space. The basement of the building housed employees, stairways crowded with tourists, aides, and members of the first family, and offices and private rooms figured into the second-floor scheme. So extensive were the renovations that the families of Chester Arthur, Theodore Roosevelt, Calvin Coolidge, and Harry Truman had to vacate the building in order that the repairs and improvements be completed. Two fires—the one in 1814 during the War of 1812, and another by accident in 1929— destroyed considerable sections of the mansion.

Perhaps the most ambitious and extensive plan for renovating the mansion envisioned by a member of the first family was that conceived by First Lady Caroline Harrison.[42] Working with

Congress and architects, Mrs. Harrison had plans developed for a complete renovation of the building, engaged in a publicity campaign to build support for the project, and undertook a comprehensive historical inventory of all items in the home. Her vision included the addition of wings coming off the sides of the home, a separate residence for the president, and an entirely new structure. Congress ultimately rejected the First Lady's bold plans, but did appropriate 35,000 dollars that enabled her to renovate parts of the building, replace worn furnishings, and install new electric lights. Moreover, her vision and efforts were later realized in the contemporary East and West Wings of the White House.

Another presidential spouse picked up where Mrs. Harrison left off. Shortly after the turn of the century, Edith Roosevelt also saw the need for extensive improvements to the building and campaigned for the work to be done. The Roosevelts oversaw a major renovation of the White House and employed the services of the prestigious New York architectural firm of Charles McKim. In one of the most comprehensive renovations of the building, the White House was made to be more livable for first families, a West Wing and presidential Oval Office were added, the size of the structure was increased, and an effort was made to return the mansion to the original vision of George Washington. The construction necessitated that the conservatories on the grounds be removed to make way for enlargements and the new wing, and internal walls be knocked down so as to increase the size of the State Dining Room.

By the 1920s, the ceiling was sagging due to the earlier removal of some of the walls to enlarge the building and cracks had appeared on the walls. President Calvin Coolidge ordered the second and third floors be rebuilt, with the attic redesigned to house guest rooms and additional living space for first families, and the walls and ceilings reinforced. In 1942, Franklin Roosevelt oversaw the construction of a new East Wing to the building, to match the earlier West Wing.

The 1920s renovations, however, had been poorly planned and soon took their toll on the building's foundation. By the late 1940s, the thick concrete poured for the third floor caused the ceiling to once again sag and the floors of the mansion creaked and groaned, indicating to Harry Truman that the whole structure was in jeopardy of collapsing. So, once again, extensive restoration of the building occurred from 1948 to 1952. This time the home was completely gutted and walls and floors removed. Rather than knock out all the walls, however, the Trumans ordered that a bulldozer needed for construction on the foundation be disassembled, taken inside the building piece by piece, and reassembled once again. Steel beams reinforced the structure, the third floor was expanded creating additional living space and apartments for the first family, and office space was expanded and better designed.

Another area of preservation has been the White House grounds. The "President's Park," the original 18-acre estate of lawns, gardens, and trees has changed considerably since John and Abigail Adams found it strewn with the debris of construction.

It did not take long for improvements to occur. The original wood fence was replaced by a stone wall designed by Thomas Jefferson, who also developed an intricate landscaping plan and gardens for the estate.[43] John Quincy Adams, an avid gardener, improved the grounds' appearance and practicality by adding flowers and an assortment of bushes along with vegetables and fruit trees. A lifelong horseman, Andrew Jackson had new stables erected on the grounds and provided a graveled pathway for carriages entering the estate. In honor of his late wife, Rachel, Jackson also planted a magnolia tree outside the President's House, which, as of this writing, still provides shade for presidential families.

Various landscaping plans, fences, and security measures have come and gone, along with meat houses, a wine cellar, and conservatories. Harriet Lane, niece and hostess for bachelor president James Buchanan enjoyed fresh flowers, so a variety of flowers were planted in a new conservatory. Today, a helicopter pad, jogging track, tennis courts, and elaborate underground security system can be found on the estate. The grounds are managed by the National Park Service and a staff of florists, gardeners, and groundskeepers.

With the building still unfinished and most of the servants and staff as well as his wife still en route to the new capital city, President John Adams had time for reflection. On his second night in the President's House, he composed in a letter the following words, which were later cut into the fireplace mantel of the State Dining Room by Franklin D. Roosevelt, that all posterity might heed the advice:

I Pray Heaven to Bestow
The Best of Blessings on
THIS HOUSE
and on All that shall hereafter
Inhabit it. May none but Honest
and Wise Men ever rule under This Roof.[44]

NOTES TO CHAPTER 1

1. Nancy Reagan, *My Turn* . . . , 1989, 22.

2. Lonnell Aikman, *The Living White House*, 1991, 2.

3. Donald R. Kennon, *A Republic for the Ages* . . . , 1999, 270–285.

4. Richard Norton Smith, *Patriarch*, 1993, 115–130.

5. Smith, 1993, 128.

6. John Whitcomb and Claire Whitcomb, *Real Life at the White House* . . . , 2000, 1–2.

7. Ibid., xvii.

8. An excellent source of information on public accessibility to the White House and the history of the "people's house," see the White House Historical Association's *The White House: An Historic Guide*, 1995.

9. Whitcomb and Whitcomb, 2000, xv.

10. See Tom Lansford, "Family Life in the White House," 2002, 394–403.

11. See the following helpful sources on the media's relationship with the president and press coverage of the presidency: Timothy E. Cook, *Governing with the News: The News Media as a Political Institution* (Chicago: University of Chicago Press, 1998) and Kenneth W. Thompson, *The White House Press on the Presidency: News Management and Co-option* (Lanham, Md: University Press of America, 1998).

12. See Lansford, 2002, 394–403.

13. Webb Garrison, *A Treasury of White House Tales* . . . , 1989, 192–197.

14. Ibid., 193.

15. For an insightful discussion of the first families' pets, see Carl Sferrazza Anthony, *America's First Families* . . . , 2000, 241–264.

16. Lansford, 2002, 402.

17. For an insightful discussion of weddings in the White House, see Anthony, 2000, 188–196.

18. Page Smith, *John Adams*, 1902, 1050.

19. Phyllis Levin, *Abigail Adams*, 1987, 387.

20. Ibid., 387–388.

21. Aikman, 1991, 15; Charles Hurb, *The White House Story*, 1966, 30.

22. Aikman, 1991, 15; Hurb, 1966, 30; Levin, 1987, 387.

23. See Jean Baker, "Mary Lincoln," 2002, 113–119.

24. Robert P. Watson, *The Presidents' Wives . . .* , 2000, 80–84.

25. See Robert Dewhirst, "White House Manager," 2002, 341–348.

26. See Baker, 2002, 113–119.

27. See Gil Troy, "Jacqueline Kennedy," 2002, 250–258.

28. Robert P. Watson, *First Ladies of the United States . . .* , 2001, 237–243.

29. Watson, 2000, 76–78.

30. Garrison, 1989, 188–190.

31. Paul F. Boller, Jr., *Presidential Anecdotes*, 1981, 34–35.

32. Watson, 2000, 76–78.

33. Garrison, 1989, 215–221.

34. Ibid., 191.

35. Dewhirst, 2002, 341.

36. Aikman, 1991, 39–41.

37. Ibid., 33–35, 43–44.

38. Dewhirst, 2002, 341–348; Robert P. Watson, "Nation's Social Hostess," 2002, 349–356.

39. Dewhirst, 2002, 342.

40. Elizabeth Lorelei Thacker-Estrada, "The Heart of the Fillmore Presidency . . . ," 2001, 83–98.

41. Garrison, 1989, 234–237.

42. Watson, 2001, 151–157.

43. Margaret Baynard Smith, *The First Forty Years of Washington Society . . .* , 1965, 18–20.

44. As quoted in Aikman, 1991, 29.

Two

Political Architecture: The Building of the President's House

RUSSELL L. MAHAN

INTRODUCTION

Architecture is politics by other means,[1] a lasting memorial to the country bequeathed by those who have gone before. Public buildings are the mortar and brick manifestation of political philosophy, revealing by their style and scope the designer's conception of the role of government in society. Wooden, stone, or brick in material, palatial, minimal, or functional in size, on a hill or in a valley in location, in the North or in the South in region, and whether constructed in the center of a new city or reconstructed from an existing building in an old one, are all issues ultimately decided upon the basis of a political agenda.

One of Britain's great architects, Sir Christopher Wren (1632–1723) put it well: "Architecture has its political Use; public buildings being the Ornament of a Country," he wrote. "It establishes a Nation, draws People and Commerce; makes the People love their native Country, which Passion is the Origin of all great Actions in a Commonwealth."[2] On the extreme was Albert Speer, the architect for Adolf Hitler's Nazi Germany. After discussing Hitler's consuming desire to construct public buildings, he admitted that "I, too, was intoxicated by the idea of using drawings, money and construction firms to create stone witnesses to history, and thus affirm our claim that our works would survive for a thousand years."[3]

The political nature of architecture was painfully evident when it came to the issue of locating the new American capital city. In 1789 and 1790 it became an extremely volatile political battle.

31

"The two great questions of funding the debt and fixing the seat of government have been agitated, as was natural, with a good deal of warmth as well as ability," President George Washington wrote later. "These were always considered by me as questions of the most delicate and interesting nature . . . They were more in danger of having convulsed the government itself than any other perils."[4]

THE COMPROMISE OF 1790

A Capital City

The decade of the 1790s brought clearly into focus the fact that while the Revolutionary War was fought to establish an independent nation, there were widely varying ideas of just what this new America ought to be. Men who had worked and fought shoulder-to-shoulder against the English now found themselves deeply and often bitterly divided. Whether the federal government ought to be strong or weak, whether the presidency within that government ought to be strong or weak, and where that government ought to be located, were issues about which Revolutionary brothers were in considerable disagreement.

The authors of the Constitution in 1787 had addressed the issue of a capital city in Article I, Section 8, paragraph 17 of that document. "The Congress shall have Power . . . To exercise exclusive Legislation in all Cases whatsoever, over such District (not exceeding ten Miles square) as may, by Cession of particular States, and the Acceptance of Congress, become the Seat of Government of the United States, and to exercise like Authority over all Places purchased by the Consent of the Legislature of the State in which the Same shall be, for the Erection of Forts, Magazines, Arsenals, Dock-Yards, and other needful Buildings." In other words, Congress had the authority to establish a national capital of up to ten square miles and to construct such public buildings as were needed there. Sequentially, of course, the question of the location of the capital had to be determined before the design of a home and office for the president could be seriously considered.

Various cities were advocated as the permanent capital city, and each had its good and bad points. George Washington was sworn in as president in New York City in April 1789, and some felt that city ought to be the permanent site for the government. Others wanted to go back to Philadelphia, which had been the capital from 1775 to 1789. Many wanted a more southerly site, and Baltimore was suggested. Still others wanted a brand new city to be constructed somewhere along the Potomac River between Virginia and Maryland. To facilitate a Potomac site, the state legislatures of Maryland and Virginia offered to the federal government any ten square miles it might want for its capital.

Three of the men who wanted the Potomac site, all from Virginia, had impeccable credentials and vast influence within the country. President George Washington was "the father of the country," Secretary of State Thomas Jefferson was the author of the Declaration of Independence, and Congressman James Madison was "the father of the Constitution." Even in the face of such worthies as these, however, the issue was in fair debate and in a state of suspense.

The ultimate decision of where to locate the federal capital was part and parcel of one of the earliest examples of political logrolling in Congress. The national legislature was deeply divided over the financial plan of Secretary of the Treasury Alexander Hamilton, who proposed several measures designed to put the new American government on a secure financial footing. Among other things, Hamilton proposed that the United States assume the existing debts of the states. This was a good deal for states that had not paid their Revolutionary era debts, but a bad bargain for Virginia, which had been faithful in its payment of obligations.

On the one hand, support for Hamilton's financial plan was centered primarily in the Northern states where commerce was more developed. On the other hand, support for a capital on the Potomac was strongest in the South. In this divergence Hamilton saw an opportunity for compromise.

On June 18, 1790, according to Secretary of State Jefferson, Alexander Hamilton came to him with a proposal consisting of three main components. First, Hamilton would convince key Northern congressman to support the location of the capital on the Potomac to be constructed over the next ten years and ready by November 1800. Second, Jefferson and Madison would shift votes in Virginia and Maryland to support the assumption of states' debts by the federal government. Third, effective with the next session of Congress, the federal capital would be moved to Philadelphia for the interim until 1800. This became known as the Compromise of 1790.[5]

And so it was done. Both Hamilton and Jefferson delivered on their commitments. On July 1, 1790, the Senate narrowly approved the Potomac site, and the House agreed a few days later. Before the end of the month assumption was also approved.

"An Act for Establishing the Temporary and Permanent Seat of the Government of the United States," usually referred to as the Residency Act, was signed by President Washington on July 16, 1790. Perhaps the most interesting part of the new law was that Congress effectively transferred a power granted to it in the Constitution over to the president. The act provided for a federal district of ten square miles to be located on the Potomac, the specific locale of which was to be selected by the president. He was also to appoint three commissioners to survey and define the limits of the district. The president was to oversee the construction of the city. The federal government was to be transferred there prior to the first Monday in December 1800, and in the meantime to adjourn from New York to Philadelphia, where the December session of 1790 was to open. There was no provision for paying for the construction of the new capital city.[6]

George Washington's City

George Washington was vastly pleased with the approval of the Potomac site. He had spent a lifetime working to develop that area, and was a major investor and landowner within the Potomac watershed. He had a personal interest in the matter, but also felt that it was in the best interest of the country. Such perceived convergences of the private and public interests are common in history.

On October 14, 1790, Washington set out from Mount Vernon on a trip up the Potomac River for the supposed purpose of reviewing potential sites for the capital city in conformity with the Residency Act.[7] It is likely that he already knew where he wanted the district to be located, but the particulars had to be worked out and courtesies needed to be extended to the citizens of other towns within the total area designated by Congress. He arrived back in Philadelphia on November 27. During the next four months he engaged in a flurry of activity connected with the new capital. He formally appointed the commissioners, announced the exact location of the federal district, sent out surveyor Andrew Ellicott, and engaged in indirect negotiations with landowners in the area. In March 1791 he went to the site again to take personal control of developments.[8]

After discussing the matter several times with the President, Thomas Jefferson drafted the proclamation announcing the selection of the site.[9] It was issued on January 24, 1791, as follows:

Proclamation. By the President of the U. States of
America. . . . Now therefore, In pursuance of the Powers to
me confided, and after duly examining and weighing the
advantages and disadvantages of the several situations within
the Limits aforesaid, I do hereby declare and make known,
that the location of one part of the said district of ten mile
square, shall be found by running four lines of experiment
in the following manner. . . .

And the said four lines of Experiment being so run, I do
hereby declare and make known, That all that part within
the said four lines . . .is now fixed upon, and directed to be
surveyed, defined, limited and located for a part of the said
district accepted by the said act of Congress for the permanent seat of the Government of the United States. . . .

And I do hereby direct the said Commissioners, appointed
agreeably to the Tenor of the said Act, to proceed forthwith
to run the said Lines of experiment, and the same being
run, to survey and by proper metes and bounds to define
and limit the part within the same which is herein before
directed for immediate location acceptance. . . .

George Washington[10]

The described district included Georgetown, Maryland, went
eastward to the Potomac's eastern branch, and crossed the river to
include Alexandria, Virginia. It was ten miles square but geographi-
cally was tipped with points in the four directions of the compass,
with Alexandria at the south point and Georgetown at the west
point. In 1846, the portion of the district south of the Potomac was
ceded back to Virginia at the request of that state.[11] The site actually
chosen went a little south of the area permitted in the Residence
Act, so it had to go back to Congress for some minor amendment.[12]

POLITICAL ARCHITECTURE

From the Ground Up

Europe had offered the example of establishing national capitals in
existing large cities where commerce, culture, and population were
centered. The republican government of the new United States,
however, opted for another experiment—construction of a new

capital out of whole cloth, a center of government hacked out of the wilderness, created solely as the seat of government, independent of and far from the existing centers of business, culture, and people.

Once this was determined, whole new vistas of possibilities opened up. Rather than being limited to existing buildings and streets, the layout of the city and public buildings could be anything within the possibilities of architecture and geography. Nothing would need to be modified or retrofitted; all would be new from the ground up.

This, of course, is where political philosophy and architecture came together and posed a dilemma for the country. Anyone who has studied the lives and principles of George Washington and Thomas Jefferson well knows that they sometimes held sharply divergent views of what America should be. Not surprisingly, these divergences resulted in different opinions of how the capital city and presidential home ought to be constructed.

Jefferson's "Town"

In brief, Jefferson believed in the virtue of the yeoman farmer and the agrarian life, with a limited government based on simple republican principles. When he worked out the Compromise of 1790, Jefferson accomplished two things close to his heart. First, he brought the federal city to the borders of his beloved Virginia. Second, he put the capital into the comparative wilderness, far away from the evils of the big cities and the corrupting influences of the commercial interests.

Now, with the location of the capital city settled, the question of what sort of public buildings ought to be constructed had to be addressed. The Secretary of State was not a novice in such matters. Plantation owners in general had a great interest in the architecture of their mansions, and such matters were like a hobby among the gentry. Jefferson's interests went beyond that, however. When the capital of Virginia was moved from Williamsburg to Richmond he proposed a layout of brick buildings that reflected his republican political philosophy. In March 1785, while he was U.S. Minister to France, Jefferson was asked by the directors of public buildings in Richmond "to Consult an able Architect on a plan fit for a Capital, and to assist him with the information of which you are possessed."[13] Jefferson undertook the assignment, speaking with an architect and drawing up suggestions of his own, but all to no avail. With the travel time required his answer did not arrive until after the directors had to act. In fear of the capital being moved back to Williamsburg, they moved ahead without the advice of Jefferson. When he saw it later, he was dissatisfied with what they did.[14]

In 1791, Jefferson proposed a national capital "town"[15] on a rural rather than an urban scale. Houses were to be far apart, interspersed among public buildings and parks. The capitol building and the presidential home were to be next to each other, facing the same direction, and constructed of brick. The proposal reflected his republican philosophy of agrarianism, simplicity, and limited government. As Peter Nicolaisen described it, "Jefferson was probably considering early in 1791 a relatively small town of no more than 2000 lots, laid out on a grid, with low buildings, light and airy, and with a few public edifices on a somewhat larger scale, based either on classical or approved modern models." The town was to consist of about 1500 acres, 300 of which would be devoted to public buildings and 1200 to private quarter acre lots.[16] The "president's house" was to be a modest brick structure, befitting Jefferson's ideology.

L'Enfant's Grand City

At this time in history, the conception of the role of the federal government and the magnitude of the presidency varied widely between the republicans and the high federalists. On the other architectural extreme from Jefferson was a Frenchman by the name of Pierre Charles L'Enfant. L'Enfant had come to America in 1777 to help in the Revolution, and had painted a portrait of Washington while at Valley Forge. He was educated as an architect and as an engineer. Washington had asked him to design the badge of the Society of the Cincinnati, and then sent him to France to present the badges to the French officers who had served in America. In 1789, he had converted the old New York City city hall into the elaborate neoclassical "Federal Hall," considered by many to be the grandest public building in the country.[17]

L'Enfant had his sights set on doing something much greater than merely renovating a building. He wanted to design and construct an entire, grand federal city that would be on such a scale as to last into the coming centuries. He boldly proposed himself for the job even before the project was approved by Congress or the President.

In a letter to the President on September 11, 1789, L'Enfant requested that he be permitted to draw up a plan for a capital city "of this vast empire." His ego could not be contained, and he stated that Washington "will not be surprised that my ambition and the desire I have of becoming a useful citizen should lead me to wish to share in the undertaking." He proposed that "the plan should be drawn on such a scale as to leave room for that aggrandizement and embellishment which the increase of the wealth of the nation will permit it to pursue at any period however remote . . . I now presume to sollicit [*sic*] the favor of being employed in this Business."[18]

The President granted that favor by inviting him to submit a proposal. Few architects were available in the United States, and Washington already liked what L'Enfant had done with Federal Hall. L'Enfant went to Georgetown in March 1791 and by August had a comprehensive plan devised.

L'Enfant's federal city was to consist of the usual grid of ordinary streets intersecting at right angles. Superimposed over this, however, was the novel idea of a system of wide avenues, crossing diagonally across the grid. Parks and heroic monuments would be placed where the avenues met. The two main public buildings to be located in the city, the legislative capitol building and the presidential home, were placed a mile apart, with a mall of parks and fountains between them. (Apparently no one at the time considered the Supreme Court to be a co-equal with the other two branches of government.)

L'Enfant's conception of the American capital city was, at the time, grandiose. He wanted to construct a city that went far beyond the needs, size, and wealth the country warranted in 1790, one that would grow as the nation developed, accommodating needs as time passed. At the time, Philadelphia was the largest city in the country with about 68,000 people located within about one square mile. London had approximately one million people in nine square miles. The proposed district, therefore, was gigantic at ten square miles.

The Principles of the New Republic

President Washington, then, had the two contrasting proposals in hand. Like Jefferson, he had architectural experience of his own, though not as much. But under the Residence Act the federal city was his to build as he saw fit, and inevitably his choice came down to his own political philosophy. Washington wanted the capital to unify the country and to boldly express the noble principles of the new nation. Although he had never seen one, he wanted something like a European capital that would symbolize the great nation established by the Constitution. He wanted an oversize federal city that could grow as the nation grew.

With his conception of government and the role of the president within it, Washington in August 1791 bypassed Jefferson's plan and selected L'Enfant's. This was not because he accepted L'Enfant's proposal, but because the proposal matched the President's conception of what ought to be done. Of the Frenchman the President wrote, "I have received him not only as a scientific man, but one who added considerable taste to his professional knowledge. . . . He [is] better qualified than any one who [has] come within my knowledge in this country, or indeed, in any other, the possibility of obtaining whom could be counted upon."[19]

THE CONSTRUCTION OF THE PRESIDENT'S HOUSE

A Presidential Palace

It is probably fair to say that people now are, as Washington wanted them to be, in awe of the presidency and the presidential home, the power of the presidential office, the fame of the people who live there, and the importance of the work that goes on there. With such goals in mind, how shall it be housed? The answer for L'Enfant was easy: a presidential palace. Washington agreed. In a letter L'Enfant indicated by his wording to Washington just what he had in mind. "I determined the seat of the presidential palace," he wrote. He explained that he had:

> the object to adding to the *sumptuousness of a palace* the convenience of a house and the agreeableness of a country seat situated on that ridge which attracted your attention at the first inspection of the ground.[20] (Emphasis added.)

His proposed palace was huge, running 700 feet east to west, and 350 feet north to south, and nearly five times larger than the home that was ultimately constructed. In a letter dated August 19, 1791, L'Enfant wrote Washington that "the grand avenue connecting both the palace & the federal House will be most magnificent and most convenient."[21]

The President's Project

George Washington was extremely interested in the building of both the presidential home and the federal city in general, and was personally involved in all of the important details of their construction. Rather than follow the advice of the three commissioners, he appointed men who did as *he* directed.[22] Washington personally selected the exact site of the ten square miles of the federal district, inspected the ground himself, and personally negotiated with the landowners to get their cooperation. He reserved for himself the power to decide where the presidential palace and other public buildings would go. There was no mistaking it, George Washington himself was building the city.

The diary of President Washington furnishes proof of his personal involvement and determination to have it the way he wanted it. The following entries demonstrate his hands-on involvement in matters:

> *March 28, 1791.* [B]reakfasted at George Town about 8 ... having appointed the Commissioners under the Residence Law to meet me ... I examined the Surveys of Mr. Ellicot [*sic*] who had been sent on to lay out the district of ten mile square for the federal seat; and also the works of Majr. L'Enfant who had been engaged to examine and made a draught of the grds [i.e, survey]. In the vicinity of George Town and Carrollsburg on the Eastern branch making arrangements for examining the ground myself to morrow with the Commissioners.[23]

> *March 29, 1791.* Finding the interests of the Landholders about George Town and those about Carrollsburgh much at variance and that their fears and jealousies of each were counteracting the public purposes and might prove injurious to its best interests, whilst if properly managed they might be made to subserve it, I requested them to meet me at six o'clock this afternoon at my lodgings, which they accordingly did.[24]

> *March 30, 1791.* This business being thus happily finished and some *directions given to the Commissioners, the Surveyor and Engineer with respect to the mode of laying out the district - Surveying the grounds for the City*

and forming them into lots, I left Georgetown, dined in Alexandria and reaching Mount Vernon in the evening.[25] (Emphasis added.)

The President's determination was illustrated in his dealing with a local landowner named David Burnes, who owned property in the area between the capitol and the president's house. Burnes was uncooperative in making his land available, and Washington simply flattened him. "I have been authorized to select the location of the National Capital," he wrote the farmer. "I have selected your farm as part of it, and the government will take it at all events. I trust you will, under the circumstances, enter into an amicable agreement." Burnes thereafter found a way to cooperate.[26]

With respect to the presidential palace, Washington noted in his diary for June 28, 1791, "Whilst the Commissioners were engaged in preparing the Deeds to be signed by the Subscribers this afternoon, I went out with Majr. L'Enfant and Mr. Ellicot to take a more perfect view of the ground, in order to decide finally on the spots on which to place the public buildings."[27] Washington accepted the general site selected by L'Enfant, but changed the exact location and orientation somewhat. Construction began and proceed with painful slowness. The cellar for the presidential palace was dug and the foundation began to go up.

A Design Contest

Unfortunately, Pierre L'Enfant was a prima donna, temperamentally unsuited to a system where funds were limited and his work was subject to the review of others. Very early on, on February 27, 1792, for reasons beyond the scope of this essay, Washington reluctantly instructed the Secretary of State to terminate the employment of the prickly and difficult L'Enfant.[28]

Jefferson undoubtedly did not share Washington's reluctance, and was surely glad so see the Frenchman go. His departure opened up another opportunity for Jefferson's conception of the capital city to be adopted. Construction had not progressed too far; a different course was still possible.

When Washington later considered rehiring L'Enfant, Jefferson convinced the unenthusiastic President to have competitions for the designs of the president's house and the capitol building. Although he knew Washington wanted stone on the president's house, Jefferson advertised for brick. On March 14, 1792, advertisements were published in major newspapers offering a prize for the winning design of the president's house:

> A Premium of 500 dollars or a medal of that value at the option of the party will be given by the Commissioners of the federal buildings to a person who before the fifteenth day of July next shall produce to them the most approved plan, if adopted by them for a President's house to be erected in this city—The Site of the building, if the artist will attend to it, will of course influence the aspect and outline of his plan and its destination will point out to him the number, size and distribution of the apartments—It will be a recommendation of any Plan if the Central Part of it may be detached and erected for the present with the appearance of a complete whole and be capable of admitting the additional parts in future, if they shall be wanting—Drawings will be expected of the ground plots, elevations of each front and sections through the building in such directions as may be necessary to explain the internal structure, and an estimate of the Cubic feet or brickwork composing the whole mass of the wall. March 14, 1792. The Commissioners.[29]

In the end, George Washington proved again that only he was in charge of this project. The advertisement for brick notwithstanding, the president's house would be made of stone. Regardless of the competition that Jefferson promoted, Washington would choose his own architect, tell him what he wanted, then select him as the winner of the competition.

In April 1791, President Washington went on a triumphant tour of the South. In the course of his travels he went to Charleston, South Carolina, where on the northwest corner of Meeting and Broad Streets he saw a structure that he very much liked. Its architect was James Hoban. Hoban had trained under the famous Irish architect Thomas Ivory at the Royal Dublin Society's school in Ireland, and had a thorough knowledge of Anglo-Palladian design and construction in stone.

Washington had Hoban meet him in Philadelphia in June 1791, when the President told the architect just what he wanted in a presidential house. Hoban then went to Georgetown, inspected the actual ground where the palace had been begun and abandoned, and drew up a plan. The next month Washington went again to the district, reviewed the nine entries in the competition, and not surprisingly selected Hoban as the winner. One can only hope that the other entrants did not spend a great deal of time or money in preparing their hopeless submissions. Hoban decided to take the medal instead of the cash award for winning the competition.

A comment made at this time by Washington is interesting. When he had received the first two competition entries to review, he was not at all pleased. "If none more elegant than these should appear . . . ," he wrote, "the exhibition of architecture will be a dull one indeed."[30] Certainly, architecture is politics by other means.

The Hoban plan was very substantially based on the home of the Duke of Leinster on Kildare Street in Dublin, Ireland. Hoban had brought the scope of the presidential palace down to a mere president's house, but Washington upsized it by 20 percent and added artistic carvings and architectural details. Washington went with Hoban to the site and personally drove in the stakes indicating the location.

Vivat Respublica

The cornerstone of the White House was laid on October 13, 1792, the 300th anniversary of the landing of Columbus in the Western Hemisphere. This area, after all, was to be called the District of Columbia. A brass plate was laid at the cornerstone, stating:

> This first stone of the President's House was laid the 13th day of October, 1792, and in the 17th Year of the Independence of the United States of America.
>
> George Washington, President.
>
> Thomas Johnson, Doctor Stewart, Daniel Carroll, Commissioners.
>
> James Hoban, Architect.
> Collen Williamson, Master Mason.
>
> Vivat Respublica[31]

As the decade of the 1790s progressed, the walls of the president's house were constructed and the roof installed. The rooms began to take shape. A ramshackle construction village surrounded the building. There were many alterations to the house as it went up, and the building that now stands is not the same one that Hoban submitted for the competition. The President, the commissioners, and financial limitations all required some changes. Washington periodically checked on progress by personally visiting the site.

Major financing of the federal district and the public buildings was originally expected to come substantially from the sale of lots in the new city. That effort turned into a failure and an embarrassment. Washington, Jefferson, and Madison were all personally in attendance at the first ill-fated sale of lots at auction in Georgetown. Unfortunately, the weather was bad that day and maps of the proposed lots were not available. Only thirty-five lots sold for a mere $2,000 in immediate cash.[32] A second sale later was also a disappointment.

Washington and Hoban were undeterred. They looked to cutbacks and other means of financing and proceeded. Hoban's estimate of the cost for the president's house was $400,000 in gold, which Washington knew was too much to be raised. As a concession to financial constraints, Washington agreed to reduce the number of storeys in the president's house by one. Solid stone was used only on the first floor, and the rest of the house had brick faced with stone.

Washington maintained a keen interest in the project for the remainder of his presidency, which ended on March 4, 1797. He continued monitoring the progress of the city and the president's house even after leaving the presidency, though he tried not to be intrusive. He intervened with his successor, John Adams, only when the new President proposed having the executive offices located near the Capitol. In the face of Washington's protests, Adams relented and had them placed by the President's House instead.[33]

He continued to regularly visit the district. Washington's diary records that he "went up to the Fedl. City" on July 17, 1797, and was "in the City all day" on the 18th. He was there on May 19, 1798 with his wife, Martha Washington, who played no known role whatever with respect to the design or construction of the White House. On September 21 and 22, 1798, Washington "examined in company with the Comrs. [commissioners] some of the Lots in the Vicinity of the Capital and fixed upon No. 16 in 634 to build on." This was on the west side of North Capitol Street between B and C streets, about in the middle of the block. Washington was to pay $535.71 for it in three annual installments, and made the first payment in 1798. The house was not finished before Washington's death a year later, and it was torn down about 1908 for an expansion of the capitol building grounds.[34]

Washington was back the next month, October 9 through 11, 1798, and again on May 31, 1799. Six weeks before his death, Washington visited the federal city for the last time, on November 9, 1799 and again the next day: "Viewed my building lot in the Fedl. City," he wrote.[35]

Unexpectedly and with virtually no warning, Washington died in December 1799, at Mount Vernon. He was not just "the father of his country," but was indeed the father of the city that bears his name. It became the city that he hoped it would be, the seat of government for a great nation of the world. It grew as the country grew, sufficient for the generations to come. The president's house, which he placed physically and fostered in the image he wanted, has inspired the awe and respect which he felt it, and the presidency, deserved.

THE PRESIDENT MOVES IN TO THE PRESIDENT'S HOUSE

On the afternoon of Saturday, November 1, 1800, President John Adams rode in his carriage into the federal city, now called "Washington" by everyone. A day earlier than expected, he found no fanfare and no reception committee. As he passed through the town, the streets were not only unpaved but obstructed in places by bushes, holes, and tree stumps. The capitol building was unfinished. The city then had just 372 houses, 109 of them made of brick.[36] The census of that year showed a population of 3,210 (not including Georgetown or Alexandria), consisting of 2,464 whites, 123 free blacks, and 623 slaves.

Adams rode on to what the people were calling simply "the President's House." In size it was the grandest home in America until 1870, but on that day just half of the thirty-six rooms had been plastered, and only the main ones had wallpaper. The President entered the house unannounced. He was greeted by two commissioners and some workmen who happened to be present at the moment.

The next day John Adams wrote a letter to his wife Abigail. "The building is in a state to be habitable," he wrote optimistically, "and now we wish for your company." Turning reflective, he wrote, "I pray heaven to bestow the best of blessings on this house and on all that shall hereafter inhabit it. May none but honest and wise men ever rule under this roof."[37]

NOTES TO CHAPTER 2

1. This, or course, is a paraphrase of the famous statement by Karl von Clausewitz that "War is diplomacy by other means." It is acknowledged that the precise language is in German, and that there are various translations into English.

2. Allan Greenberg, *George Washington Architect*, 1999, 95.

3. Albert Speer, *Inside the Third Reich*, 1970, 82.

4. Richard Norton Smith, *Patriarch*, 1993, 42–43.

5. Ibid., 41–42.

6. John C. Fitzpatrick, *The Diaries of George Washington*, 1925, 142–143.

7. Dorothy Twohig, *The Papers of George Washington*, 1998, 7:2.

8. Ibid., 7: 162.

9. Ibid., 7: 162.

10. Ibid., 7: 278–280.

11. Bernard A. Weisberger, *The District of Columbia . . .*, 1968, 39.

12. Twohig, 1998, 7: 163.

13. Boyd, *The Papers of Thomas Jefferson*, 1954, 9: 45.

14. Donald R. Kennon, *A Republic for the Ages . . .*, 1999, 277–281.

15. Twohig, 1998, 7: 549.

16. Lothar Honingshausen, *Washington, D.C.*, 1993, 109.

17. William Seale, *The President's House . . .*, 1986, 2–3.

18. Honingshausen, 1993, 118.

19. Wendell Garrett, *Our Changing White House*, 1995, 3.

20. Twohig, 1998, 8: 290.

21. Ibid., 8: 440.

22. Washington selected three commissioners, whom he appointed on January 22, 1791: (1) David Stuart of Alexandria, Virginia, was Washington's main voice. He was a medical doctor and married the widow of John Parke Custis, the late son of Martha Washington; (2) Thomas Johnson of Frederick, Maryland, had been in the Continental Congress and had nominated Washington to be Commander in Chief of the army in 1775. He was governor of Maryland from 1777–1779 and a member of the

U.S. Supreme Court in 1791; (3) Daniel Carroll was a delegate to both the Continental Congress and the Constitutional Convention and was the founder of the town Carrollsburg, which was within the southeastern part of the district. He resided in a mansion known as Duddington, which was located on ground roughly bound by First, Second, E, and F streets. Carroll was a congressman from Maryland. All three of these men held stock in the Potomac Company.

23. Fitzpatrick, 1925, 151–152.

24. Ibid., 153–154.

25. Ibid., 154–155.

26. John Whitcomb and Claire Whitcomb, *Real Life at the White House*, 2000, 6.

27. Ibid., 200.

28. Smith, 1993, 128.

29. Seale, 1986, 26–27.

30. Ibid., 28.

31. Frank Freidel and William Pencak, *The White House* . . . , 1994, 19.

32. Dumas Malone, *Jefferson and His Time*, 1951, 2: 377.

33. Kennon, 1999, 62.

34. Fitzpatrick, 1925, 284.

35. Ibid., 257, 277, 284–286, 305, 317.

36. Constance McLaughlin Green, *Washington* . . . , 1962, 4.

37. David McCollogh, *John Adams*, 2001, 551.

Three

Rooms of Their Own:
First Ladies and Their Impact
on Historic White House Rooms

ELIZABETH LORELEI THACKER-ESTRADA

INTRODUCTION

The domain of the president is the United States of America, but the realm of the first lady is the White House. Although portraits of presidential wives grace White House walls, many of the millions of visitors who have passed through the first floor state chambers and the ground floor Library and China Room might not realize that all of these rooms are largely the legacies of the women, some famous and some not-so-well-known, who presided at the White House as first lady.

This chapter will briefly describe how certain first ladies influenced the development of specific White House rooms and collections. The impact of first ladies on the use and development of White House rooms has been continuous and cumulative ever since Abigail Adams (1744–1818), the first presidential wife to reside in the White House, hung laundry in the unfinished East Room.[1] As long-time presidential aide William Crook recalled, "As a general thing one of the first duties that the wife of an incoming President has to attend to, and one which she usually enjoys heartily, is that of making such rearrangement and refurnishing of the White House as may be necessary or advisable, according to her personal taste, the size and customs of her family, etc."[2] Or as the ambitious and inventive first lady Helen Taft (1861–1943) more bluntly stated, "Each new mistress of the house has absolute authority, of course, and can do exactly as she pleases."[3]

In the days of the Early Republic, legendary hostess Dolley Madison (1768–1849) presided over the state chambers that later became known as the State Dining Room, the Red Room, and the Blue Room. In the mid-nineteenth century, Abigail Fillmore (1798–1853) established the library in President's House, and in the early twentieth century, Edith Wilson (1872–1961) created the China Room featuring a collection preserved by previous first ladies including Caroline Harrison (1832–1892) and Edith Roosevelt (1861–1948). In the nineteenth century, Lucy Hayes (1831–1889) initiated the collection of first ladies' portraits.

In her essay, *A Room of One's Own*, published in 1929, the British novelist Virginia Woolf contended that for a woman to be successfully creative, she needed not only artistic inspiration, but economic security and a room of her own. Woolf also illustrated that each creative step a woman takes paves the way for greater endeavors by the women who follow her. First ladies, demonstrating the truth of this assertion, have through personal resourcefulness obtained expert assistance, congressional funding, and valuable donations to create "rooms of their own" in the White House. These famous and historic White House rooms have attracted the interest of Americans and people from around the world to the Executive Mansion and have been a lasting legacy of the first ladies of the United States.

DOLLEY MADISON AND COLORFUL RECEPTION ROOMS

In the days of the early Republic, a "Virginia dynasty" of wealth and privilege held the presidency during four of the first five administrations, beginning with that of George Washington in 1789. These American aristocrats established the earliest presidential traditions. Although he never lived in the White House, Washington was instrumental in selecting its architect. (See chapter 2.)

In 1794, the President and his wife, Martha Washington (1731–1802), blessed the marriage of their young, vivacious Philadelphia relation, Dorothea Payne Todd, to the prominent statesman, James Madison. As Mrs. Madison, Dolley became a Virginia plantation mistress and "served a hard social apprenticeship." This proved useful preparation for running the Executive Mansion where she came to embody legendary "Southern hospitality." Although her

Quaker father had freed his slaves, Dolley now oversaw the management of enslaved Americans on her husband's estate and the Madisons would, like most early presidents and first ladies, rely on slave labor in the White House.[4]

A Social and Political Power Arises

Dolley Madison would become a social and political power for decades in Washington, beginning in 1801 when her husband became Secretary of State to President Thomas Jefferson, another Virginian. Soon after becoming president in March, Jefferson, a long-time widower, requested Dolley's presence as hostess to welcome women guests to the President's House. On May 27, 1801, the President invited her to dine with him "to take care of female friends expected."[5] Dolley was thus one of the first in a long tradition of "surrogate" or "proxy" first ladies to act as hostess at the White House for widowed or bachelor presidents and invalid first ladies.

During his tenure, Jefferson lived in only a corner of the great residence.[6] He was the first to introduce the color blue to the future Blue Room upholstery and the color green in the painted canvas floor cloth and table covers in what is now the Green Room, the chamber he employed most frequently and where he held stag dinners.[7] In the later nineteenth century, what became known as the Red and Blue Rooms tended to attract women whereas the Green Room would continue to possess more masculine associations especially with the installation of gas lighting in 1848. According to White House historian William Seale, the color green was not considered flattering to women's complexions in artificial light.[8]

From the beginning of her husband's term of office in March 1809, the extroverted Dolley became an innovator, holding the very first inaugural ball. To this now traditional event she wore plumes, pearls, and a yellow gown, this cheerful color being her favorite.[9] Dolley also oversaw the renovation and redecorating of the White House.[10]

As an architect, Jefferson "had done everything structurally necessary" to the Executive Mansion, but "the fashionable Madisons decided to improve the plain interior that Jefferson preferred."[11] When Mrs. Madison became the first presidential wife to occupy the White House in eight years, her occupation of "the bare President's House emphasized the necessity of furnishing it."[12] Dolley led congressmen on a tour of White House to demonstrate the need for funding and initially received $5,000 as a congressional appropriation.[13]

REFURBISHING THE WHITE HOUSE

In what would become a commonsense practice, the first lady received expert advice. President Madison designated the English-born architect Benjamin Latrobe as "the agent for expending the furniture fund."[14] Already on the congressional payroll, Latrobe easily retained his position in the new administration since his wife was a close friend of Dolley Madison. "Latrobe acted primarily as an interior decorator to the President and Mrs. Madison, who planned to refurbish the building in a manner befitting the residence of the Chief Executive." President Madison "informed Latrobe that he would receive instructions from Mrs. Madison on all domestic arrangements, and was to render accounts to her."[15]

Relying on European precedents, Latrobe planned neoclassical decor, known as "Grecian" style, for the future Blue, Red, and State Dining Rooms, referencing the antecedents of democracy in Ancient Greece, as well as employing a popular style of the era. According to her biographer Katharine Anthony, Dolley contributed harmonious taste and judgment to the redecoration.[16]

The first result of this collaboration was a drawing room (now called the Red Room), which became Dolley's domain as "Mrs. Madison's sitting room." Dolley's special color, sunflower yellow, dominated the room with satin draperies and satin-covered sofas and chairs of that color. Dolley held her first weekly "drawing room" here on May 31, 1809.[17] The return of drawing rooms for female guests established a new tone for presidential entertaining and a feminine influence asserted itself in the Executive Mansion.[18] Dolley provided women with access to power in other ways. "She returned all calls made her by her own sex, and the 'dove parties' composed of the wives of Cabinet Officers and foreign Ministers, when their lords were engaged in formal dinners, were exceedingly popular and lively."[19]

The redecoration of what is now the Blue Room had begun about the same time, but the project was more ambitious with "new furniture designed by Latrobe in the Greek style, probably based on drawings in Thomas Hope's *Household Furniture and Interior Decoration* and created in Baltimore, Maryland.[20]

The State Dining Room had been Thomas Jefferson's office and "library."[21] The portrait of George Washington by Gilbert Stuart hung here, the first, according to Latrobe, of a planned presidential portrait gallery. "The dining room is properly the picture room, and in speaking to the President as to the furniture of the room, I

understood it to be arranged that not only the Genl. but the succeeding Presidents should have a place there." Dolley often received in the Dining Room on levee nights.[22]

Dolley Madison, who remains one of the most famous hostesses in American history, usually employed what are now known
as the State Dining Room, the Red Room, and the Blue Room for
her celebrated parties. Her portrait, which was also painted by
Gilbert Stuart, hung in her special room, the future Red Room. In
1813, Elbridge Gerry, the son of Madison's Vice President, described
these rooms. The State Dining Room was:

> very spacious, and twice the height of modern parlours and
> three times as large. This is furnished in the most elegant
> manner . . . At the head of the room, General Washington is
> represented as large as life. [This opened] . . . by a single
> door into Mrs. Madison's sitting-room [the current Red
> Room] which is half as large. This is furnished equally as
> well, and has more elegant and delicate furniture. Her por-
> trait is here seen. This room, in the same way, enters into
> the drawing-room, which is an immense and magnificent
> room [now the Blue Room], in an oval form, and which
> form is preserved in those above and even to the cellar . . .
> The windows are nearly the height of the room, and have
> superb red silk velvet curtains . . . The chairs are wood
> painted . . . and each has a red velvet large cushion . . . These
> three rooms are all open on levee nights.[23]

The newly decorated rooms attracted favorable notice, and
during the Madison administration the President's House, which,
being a mile and a half from the Capitol, had been rather isolated,
at last became a magnet for visitors. As William Seale stated, "In
the 20-year history of the republic there had never been such easy
personal access to the President and his wife." The fascination and
identification of Americans with "their" house had begun.[24]

Creating a Nation and a National Symbol

Not just a private residence, the White House Dolley helped create
became a public space, a national symbol and a center of prestige
and power. Like Abigail Fillmore's library to follow, Dolley Madison's
reception rooms and parlors provided an oasis of civilization to

politicians far from home. Mrs. Madison's "crushes" were an asset in the political world of the early Republic, attracting Federalist as well as Democratic adherents and encouraging political and social contacts. The fame of "Mrs. Madison's levees" spread, attracting many notable visitors such as author Washington Irving. The sociability that animated the rooms were reminiscent of French salons, although Dolley had never traveled to Europe. Yet she stressed the power of the new nation through patriotic paintings and engravings. The French influence probably was heightened by the presence of another European [besides Latrobe] to whom Dolley entrusted the care of the President's House. The Frenchman Jean Pierre Sioussat, Mrs. Madison's loyal and valued steward, brought European manners to the Executive Mansion, and "He was a great help in running the domestic and social affairs of the President's House smoothly."[25]

More often a working housekeeper than a glamorous hostess, Dolley would transform herself whenever she switched from the plain Quaker garb of house manager to the elaborate dress of the President's lady for receptions. As biographer Katharine Anthony noted, Dolley changed from the practical to the symbolic, establishing a notable and influential presence for herself as consort to the president.[26]

During what is now called the War of 1812 between Great Britain and the United States, Dolley, who loved her years in the White House, would be forced to abandon the mansion she had so carefully decorated and developed. Her fame having crossed the Atlantic Ocean, Mrs. Madison, as a dominant, albeit "unofficial," member of the presidential administration, herself became a target. A British General predicted that he "would soon dine in Washington and make his bow in Mrs. Madison's drawing-room."[27]

On August 23, 1814, with British forces rapidly approaching Washington, Mrs. Madison determinedly waited for her husband to return to the White House from official business. According to Dolley, the President "left beseeching me to take care of myself, and of the cabinet papers, public and private." She filled wagons with "plate and the most valuable portable articles belonging to the house." Dolley wrote to Mrs. Latrobe that she had also saved some books. Most important in an era when the President's House served as an archive for state papers, Dolley secured public documents including the Declaration of Independence, and she rescued Washington's portrait from the State Dining Room. She famously recorded in a letter to her sister, "I insist on waiting until the large picture of General Washington is secured, and it requires to be unscrewed from the wall. This process was found too tedious for these perilous moments; I have ordered the frame to be broken, and the canvas taken out. It is done! and the precious portrait placed in the hands of two gentlemen of New York, for safe keeping."[28]

When Dolley finally vacated the Executive Mansion, she left behind a dinner intended for victorious American officers. Instead, British officers consumed the meal. Afterward, the British set fire to the White House, destroying all but its outer walls. Twenty years of effort, including that of Mr. Latrobe and Mrs. Madison, "literally went up in smoke."[29]

When Dolley returned to the ruined Executive Mansion following three days away from Washington as a refugee, the uninhabitable state of the White House left the President and First Lady homeless. Such was the destruction of Washington that a contemporary acquaintance of the presidential couple, Margaret Bayard Smith, thought Washington would never again be the seat of government. However, Dolley Madison has been credited with ensuring that the nation's capital remain in Washington, D.C., following much of its destruction during the War of 1812. Mrs. Madison actively continued the social and political life of the young capital by resuming in separate Washington lodgings the hostessing traditions she had established at the White House.[30]

Life After the Presidency

The Madisons and their successors, the Monroes, who were also members of the Virginia aristocracy, rebuilt and redecorated the White House. The structure itself was essentially completed in late 1817, and "plans for redecoration and furnishing began again in the spring of that year." After attending the inauguration of James Monroe, the Madisons retired to their estate, Montpelier, in Virginia.[31]

President James Monroe, formerly U.S. Minister to France, and his wife, Elizabeth, whom the French christened "la belle Americaine," brought French furnishings, including table china, to the rebuilt Executive Mansion.[32] "The fine quality of most of Monroe's acquisitions," from Paris in the then popular "Empire" style, prevented their sale during subsequent redecorations, and the "still numerous Monroe pieces are the earliest, most historic, and most valuable in the collection of authentic White House furniture."[33] The future Blue Room was still red under the Monroes with French furniture of crimson. Dolley's favorite sitting room remained yellow, and Washington's portrait which Dolley had rescued was placed here. (In 1930, First Lady Lou Henry Hoover had the portrait moved from the Red Room to the East Room where it remains.) The Monroes gave the Green Room its permanent name.[34]

Following her husband's death, Dolley returned to Washington in the fall of 1837. There she occupied a house on Lafayette Square near the White House, which the Madisons had left twenty years previously.[35] That same year, the first of the Martin Van Buren administration (1837–1841), the state floor oval room finally became the famous Blue Room.[36]

President Van Buren was a widower with four bachelor sons, and Dolley wasted no time establishing a feminine presence again in official Washington. On New Year's Day 1838 and later on the Fourth of July, people first paid their respects at the President's House according to tradition and then spontaneously developed the custom of visiting Dolley. Her presence in the city obviously filled a social vacuum. Like the White House itself, Dolley became an institution in a city where most people came and left according to election cycles. Dolley "fulfilled the role of arbiter of manners in the capital city," and powerful congressmen such as Daniel Webster were her guests.[37]

Dolley further strengthened her influence as an adviser, mentor, honored guest, and simply reassuring presence to new White House hostesses, some of them "proxy hostesses" as she had been for President Jefferson. She even became a White House matchmaker when she introduced her beautiful cousin, Angelica Singleton (1816–1877) from South Carolina, to the oldest Van Buren son, Abraham. The young couple married in 1838, and Angelica became the new White House hostess. Inspired by the example of the young Queen Victoria of Great Britain, Angelica, with Dolley's support, changed the manner in which White House guests would be received. In the Blue Room, Angelica and honored women guests stationed themselves atop a temporary dais as they greeted visitors. As members of the opposing Whig party criticized this Van Buren "court," these tableaux were short lived. Dolley, a product of the aristocratic Early Republic, witnessed a transition to a more democratic era of the "common man."[38]

Besides Angelica Van Buren, Dolley also mentored the women of President John Tyler's family. The former actress Priscilla Cooper Tyler (1816–1889), the wife of the president's son, Robert, became White House hostess in 1841 on behalf of her invalid mother-in-law, Letitia Tyler (1790–1842). Letitia became the first first lady to die in office. Priscilla relied on Dolley for advice as did

the young Julia Gardiner (1820–1889), who married President Tyler
in 1844. Julia even revived Angelica Van Buren's platform. Julia and
her successor, Sarah Polk (1803–1891), held weekly drawing rooms
at Mrs. Madison's suggestion, as Dolley had found them to be
politically useful to her husband. The first reference to Mrs.
Madison's yellow sitting room as the "Red Room" occurs during
the Polk administration (1845–1849).

In one of her last public appearances, Dolley, adorned in a
white satin gown, promenaded through the state rooms on the arm
of President James K. Polk. In these rooms she had presided as first
lady over thirty years earlier. Mrs. Madison, the doyenne of Washington society, passed away in 1849, during the brief administration of Zachary Taylor (1849–1850).[39] The following year another
first lady would create a different White House room.

ABIGAIL FILLMORE AND THE WHITE HOUSE LIBRARY

When Millard Fillmore suddenly became president upon the death
of Zachary Taylor in 1850, he noted the nearly complete absence
of books in the White House, a situation which he and his wife
Abigail (1798–1853), the new first lady, desired to remedy. Libraries
had always been important to Abigail, a former schoolteacher, who
as a child had educated herself in her father's library. As a young
woman she has been credited with helping to create a circulating
library in the Fillmores' home state of New York, to which the
young Millard purchased a subscription.[40]

Prior to establishing a library in the White House, the Fillmores
first had to obtain funding for the library from a Congress wary of
strengthening the executive branch of government. The presidential salary was still only $25,000 a year, the same as it was when
the Madisons occupied the White House four decades earlier. Although initial legislation to fund the library was defeated, it passed
on a second attempt following an effective appeal in the Senate
which noted, during an era of religious ardor, that the Executive
Mansion even lacked a Bible.[41]

The Fillmores established the White House library in the second floor oval room directly above the Blue Room. Originally intended as a ladies drawing room, the chamber has long been a favorite
of first ladies. Its feminine affiliation began early as it was the "only
room for which Abigail Adams had a kind word." Although no longer
a library, the room, now known as the Yellow Oval Room, "is still
the social center of the President's private quarters."[42]

A Room for Family and Social Functions

This room served both the president in his official capacity and his wife as the center of her duties and activities as first lady. Abigail converted the room into a library, a sitting room, and a music room with instruments brought from her home in New York. According to a family friend, "here Mrs. Fillmore, surrounded by her books, spent the greater part of her time, and in this room the family received their informal visitors."[43] In the library, Abigail established her own salon and served as hostess to important and powerful politicians including Secretary of State Daniel Webster.[44] Besides serving important political and social functions, the library demonstrated elements of what is now known as the "Cult of Domesticity" in which the president found an ideal refuge designed and maintained by his wife. "The President had but little time to give to this library, but he usually succeeded in leaving the executive chamber at 10:30 at night, and spending a pleasant hour in the library with his family."[45] The Fillmores played and sang music together, including a new Stephen Foster song.[46] Additionally, Abigail reflected the tastes of the average American of that time in her choice of the second-floor location and the mahogany bookcases, specially built to fit the oval shape of the room.[47]

Much as Dolley Madison benefited from the design expertise of Benjamin Latrobe, the Fillmores received assistance from librarian Charles Lanman of the War Department. Lanman, who was also Daniel Webster's secretary, purchased books for the Executive Mansion from, among other sources, publishers Little & Brown and George Putnam.[48]

Having met English author Charles Dickens when Millard was in Congress, Abigail expanded her circle of literary acquaintances when Washington Irving, a White House guest of the Madisons, and William Makepeace Thackeray, the British novelist, dined at the Executive Mansion with her and President Fillmore.[49]

A Legacy

Abigail would have been able to accomplish more if not for declining health and a short White House tenure.[50] She died less than a month after leaving the Executive Mansion in 1853. Still the Fillmores' success in creating a library and music room in the President's House illustrated the rise of American middle-class culture and values. Their tenure also reflected the growing tensions in the United States regarding slavery. Although most of their predecessors had depended on enslaved Americans to run the Executive Mansion, the Fillmores, who hated slavery, exhibited a more Northern attitude in the White House by paying "colored" and white servants equitable wages.[51]

The library Abigail bequeathed to the White House brought enormous pleasure to Abraham and Mary Lincoln during their tumultuous Civil War tenure (1861–1865). Mary Lincoln (1818–1882), who loved to shop, regularly purchased books with funds appropriated by Congress. According to William Seale, "The Lincolns read fewer sophisticated popular books than the Fillmores," but they also enjoyed the classics. To enjoy greater privacy, the Lincolns added a partition to create a closed passage between the president's office and the oval room library, the only Lincoln addition to the White House. The library became their private parlor, and Mrs. Lincoln read and sewed there while waiting for her husband to join her.[52]

Mrs. Lincoln not only purchased books for the library, she selected Haviland designed china decorated with a purple border, her favorite color. According to White House china expert Abby Gunn Baker, the Lincoln china "has always been greatly admired, and many consider it the handsomest of all." William Crook, who began his decades-long White House career during the Lincoln administration, made a study of the presidential china and noted that the china of the Ulysses S. Grant administration (1869–1877) also became known "all over the world" for "its beauty and elegance." This china, in its depiction of American wildflowers, indicated a developing interest in designs unique to the United States.[53]

Like the Fillmores and the Lincolns, Rutherford and Lucy Hayes, who succeeded the Grants, "collected books and shared many intellectual interests," and gathered in the oval library to enjoy music. Like Mrs. Fillmore, Mrs. Hayes (1831–1889) instituted memorable evenings mixing political company with musical entertainment. The unique Hayes china service would also be much commented on in a Gilded Age of conspicuous consumption and increasing publicity about first ladies.[54]

THE CHINA ROOM AND THE FIRST LADY PORTRAIT COLLECTION

A Story of Preservation and Patriotism

The collection of presidential tableware provides a lesson in the history of the United States. "The places of purchase, the types of china being used, the pieces which make up a dinner service and its design, tell much about the material culture and the social customs of our country."[55] A full set of White House china consists of breakfast, luncheon, and dinner services for the everyday needs of the presidential family as well as for official guests who gather at state entertainments.[56]

Early presidential porcelain for formal events reflected patriotic ties to France whereas much of the earthenware for more casual occasions was shipped from England. Not until the twentieth century did a first lady find a United States manufacturer who could produce a fine-quality service. Congress not only funded the acquisition of furnishings, including china, it also granted permission for furnishings to be sold. These public sales, often at auction, caused the dispersal of many White House china sets and thus greatly increased the challenges confronting subsequent first ladies in locating and obtaining historic presidential tableware.[57] Due to the efforts of several first ladies, many of them from the middle-class and late nineteenth-century "Ohio dynasty" of presidents and first ladies, this historical loss of presidential china was stemmed and a famous collection created. The preserved china also invites insights into the women who ran the White House. As First Lady Helen Taft, from Ohio, stated, "Perhaps nothing in the house is so expressive of the various personalities of its Mistresses as the dinner services which each has contributed."[58]

Lucy Hayes

In 1879, Lucy Hayes directed Theodore Davis to "create something especially American by using the flora and fauna of this country as decoration on the new china." Although produced by Haviland & Co. in France, this unique new china exemplified growing American nationalism. The service's unusual scenes and shapes elicited both positive and negative comments.[59]

Besides adding a distinctive White House china service, Mrs. Hayes began the first significant art collection in the Executive Mansion. The Hayeses augmented the gallery of presidential portraits that had begun with the George Washington painting rescued by Dolley Madison during the War of 1812. Perhaps inspired by a portrait of Julia Tyler the subject herself had given to the White House in 1870, Lucy Hayes initiated a collection of first lady portraits. According to William Seale, "No one before Mrs. Hayes seems to have had a desire to collect pictures of the past First Ladies" for the White House. Like Mrs. Madison, presidents' wives had usually hung their portraits in the Red Room, but only for the duration of their husbands' administrations, so few first lady likenesses remained in the White House. To address this lack, Eliphalet F. Andrews, a friend of the Hayeses from Ohio, painted a large portrait of Martha Washington. Using the strategy devised by Dolley Madison, Lucy Hayes held a dinner in 1880 for the Joint Committee on the Library to obtain funding for the portrait collection. She led the congressmen into the East Room where the Martha Washington portrait still hangs. First Ladies were finally receiving permanent, collective recognition in the White House.[60]

Mrs. Hayes herself received attention not only for the dishes she put on the table but for what she kept off of it, namely alcoholic beverages. "Banishing alcohol from the White House," according to Seale, "made Mrs. Hayes more of a celebrity than any President's wife since Dolley Madison." History subsequently bestowed on her the nickname "Lemonade Lucy." In gratitude, the Women's Christian Temperance Union raised funds for a full-length portrait of Mrs. Hayes, which was placed in the Green Room.[61]

Abby Baker credited Mrs. Hayes with planning a collection of White House china that "she could not complete" in time "to present it to the Government before her husband's term expired" in 1881.[62] That task fell to another first lady born in Ohio, Caroline Harrison (1832–1892).

Caroline Harrison

Benjamin Harrison, who became president in 1889, was the grandson of President William Henry Harrison. He and Caroline had visited the Hayeses in the White House. Presidential assistant William Crook recalled that "President and Mrs. Harrison were what may be styled 'home bodies,' a good deal like President Hayes and Mrs. Hayes, in this respect."[63] Caroline also shared much in common with Abigail Fillmore. Both women came from modest circumstances yet became well educated and cultured. Both were also practical, productive, and in poor health during their White House years, yet both managed to be actively domestic. Arguably, they displayed more inspiration and creativity than their dignified, methodical, and legalistic husbands.

The oval room beloved by Abigail Adams and Abigail Fillmore remained the family library and became the setting of a historical precedent in the White House. William Crook fondly remembered:

The first Christmas tree that ever lifted up its gift-laden green in the White House was placed there during the administration of President Harrison—and in my memories of many years' service within the walls of the Executive Mansion, this stands out as one of the pleasantest.[64]

The Harrisons found the presence of presidential offices and bedrooms together on the second floor "an impossible combination for their large family; an average of nine relatives stayed with them most of the time."[65] Bypassing the hostessing customs established by Dolley Madison, Caroline tried closing certain state parlors to the public so that her extended family would have more space.[66] As the plan did not work, she arranged for an architect with the Office of Public Buildings and Grounds to prepare plans for expansion, and Caroline actively lobbied for a larger White House. [67] Caroline Harrison presented her plans to friendly reporters in the Red Room and placed the plans on an easel in the entrance hall for visitors to see. Although ultimately unsuccessful in obtaining congressional funding for an expansion, Caroline Harrison had publicized the need for a White House renovation.[68] Frances Cleveland, who was both the predecessor and successor as first lady to Caroline Harrison, had married President Grover Cleveland in the Blue Room in 1886 during his first nonconsecutive term. Since Mrs. Cleveland had a growing family during her second stay in the White House, she too would promote Mrs. Harrison's plan.[69]

Although unable to expand the White House, Caroline did have it cleaned. The entire mansion was scrubbed and the Red and Green Rooms repainted. She redecorated the state rooms with solid middle-class respectability. In the Harrison White House "Women made more use of the state rooms than did men." Mrs. Harrison offered the prestige of the Blue Room as a meeting place to the founders of the Daughters of the American Revolution, a political organization for women before they enjoyed the right to vote. As first lady, Caroline received and entertained so many callers that "Sometimes, to speed the process, the hostess alternated her receiving among the three parlors."[70]

Caroline sought to make better use of space by cleaning out the White House basement. Irwin "Ike" Hoover, the future White House Chief Usher who began his career there as an electrician during the Harrison administration, remembered looking

about in what was then the basement. The floor was covered with damp and slimy brick; dust webs were everywhere. . . .

Everything was black and dirty. Rooms that are now parlors were then used for storage of wood and coal.[71]

According to architectural historians William Ryan and Desmond Guinness, "Mrs. Harrison's campaign, which involved complete renovation of the basement, was probably the most successful" in eliminating rats.[72] This basement, now called the Ground Floor of the White House, would later be the home of the Library, the China Room, and the first ladies portrait gallery.

Like Dolley Madison and Abigail Fillmore, Caroline Harrison possessed personal skills that were to serve her well in the White House. Displaying the "Victorian love for china," Caroline "was one of the growing number of American women who painted china as a hobby," and had taught china painting in Indianapolis. She continued these classes in the White House conservatory, providing, as had Dolley Madison, Cabinet wives and other Washington society women access to the Executive Mansion. Again, carrying on a tradition established by previous first ladies, Caroline enlisted the aid of an expert, German-born artist Paul Putzki, to assist in teaching the class. As had Abigail Fillmore, she transported supplies and equipment to the White house, in Caroline's case, her kiln and other art equipment.[73] According to one visitor,

> In the afternoons when we would need the President's signature or have some information for him, we would often find him seated at the window of his sitting-room reading. Opposite him would be Mrs. Harrison engaged in decorating china. Often he would be reading aloud to her while she kept on with her painting."[74]

In 1889, Caroline's first year in the White House, Theodore Davis, the designer of the Hayes china, reflected and promoted the "growing interest of the general public in the subject of presidential china" when he wrote two articles for *The Ladies Home Journal*.[75]

An emphasis on Americana would pervade the Harrison administration and reflect a growing interest in historic preservation. This upsurge in American patriotism echoed the Harrison "platform of 'America first,' advocating high tariffs to protect American industry while publicizing the superiority of America's products." Caroline had worn an American-made inaugural gown, and the formal china set designed by Mrs. Harrison and Mr. Putzki, although manufactured in France, displayed nationalism in the prominent depiction of cornstalks and goldenrod. Fond of flowers, Mrs.

Harrison, who cultured orchids, "wished to make the goldenrod a national emblem."[76] In the 1960s, Lady Bird Johnson's floral china design would be reminiscent of those of Julia Grant, Lucy Hayes, and Caroline Harrison.[77]

According to Smithsonian Curator Margaret Klapthor, "Mrs. Benjamin Harrison was the first presidential wife who was particularly interested in the china still to be found in the storerooms of the White House when the Harrisons moved there in 1889."[78] Caroline had the china washed, questioned staff regarding the history of the china, and planned to build china cabinets to display in the State Dining Room.[79] As Harrison biographer Harry Sievers stated, "Thus she began the White House collection of the china of past Presidents."[80]

Mrs. Harrison has been credited with preserving the old china of the White House and doing more to save it from destruction than any other first lady. "She repeatedly urged that the oldest of the china should not be used." Caroline even brought damaged White House china back to use. On a pantry shelf she found what was then thought to be a piece of the "Dolley Madison china" [actually from the Franklin Pierce administration 1853–1857]. It had been broken into three parts, but Caroline mended it "so deftly that the defect is almost imperceptible." The beautiful, two-foot-high punch bowl, upheld by figures of the three Graces, became one of the show pieces of the family dining-room.[81]

Like Abigail Fillmore, Caroline Harrison died in close proximity to the end of her husband's administration. "Mrs. Harrison . . . lay down . . . in one of the rooms of the White House, where she breathed her last between Monday night, October 24, 1892, and the following morning."[82] Unlike Dolley Madison, the tubercular Caroline Harrison had viewed the White House as an unhappy place. Still she had earnestly worked to improve the mansion. Her funeral was held in the East Room.[83] Fittingly, the last year of Caroline's tenure saw the publication of the book, *China Collecting in America*, by avid "china hunter" Alice Morse Earle. The book included a chapter on "Presidential China" and supported Mrs. Harrison's plan to display pieces of "state sets" of china "in a cabinet at the White House"[84]

Ike Hoover correctly observed that the Harrison administration "goes down in history as having accomplished nothing startling, yet which left its imprint everywhere around the White House."[85] William Seale echoed the same sentiment: "No one before Caroline Harrison had been so possessed by the desire to preserve the historic White House for generations to come."[86]

Ida McKinley

In the summer of 1901, the superintendent of public buildings and grounds suggested to Abby Gunn Baker, a journalist who specialized in historical subjects, that she write a story on the White House china. He hoped that such an article would engender interest in the preservation of the collection, and told Mrs. Baker that "If somebody does not do that pretty soon, there won't be any left to preserve."[87] First Lady Ida McKinley (1847–1907), a native Ohioan, gave Mrs. Baker permission to conduct a thorough study of the china at the White House that summer while the McKinleys were away. The assassination of President William McKinley in September 1901 ended her research, but fortunately she had gathered enough material to write the first definitive article on the subject of presidential china. Entitled "The China of the Presidents," the article appeared in the December 1903 issue of *Munsey's Magazine*. Baker warned that "The old White House ware, a historic treasure which can never be replaced, will practically disappear before long if steps are not taken to preserve it." She predicted that "The loss will be one that future generations will deeply but vainly regret." Perceptively she noted that "Unfortunately, the White House has never had a curator whose duty it was to care for its furnishing."[88] Until the appointment of an official curator over sixty years later, the protection of White House treasures was frequently the responsibility of the first lady. As Mrs. Baker noted in a 1908 article in *The Century Magazine*, "It can be said to the credit of the majority of the women who have held the high position that they have had a keen sense of the responsibility entailed upon them, and have lived up to it nobly."[89]

Edith Roosevelt

The new superintendent of public buildings and grounds showed the Baker article to Mrs. Theodore Roosevelt (1861–1948), the new first lady, who initiated the public display of the "White House China Collection." Like Caroline Harrison, whom she had visited in the White House, Edith Roosevelt had "always taken a great interest in American history and felt the obligation of being First Lady keenly." She ordered two glass display cabinets built for the lower east corridor of the mansion where visitors could admire the china, and requested that Mrs. Baker "come to the White House to choose the pieces of china to be displayed in the cabinets." Samples from several administrations were selected. Soon after the china was placed on shelves in the cabinets, President Theodore Roosevelt stopped by to admire the pieces. Enthusiastically he exclaimed to the superintendent, "this is a fine beginning; but it ought to be carried on until it contains some ware representative of every administration." Edith Roosevelt delegated the search to Abby Baker.[90] Mrs. Roosevelt also originated the plan "to gather together by means of patriotic loan or gift specimens of presidential china which had come into the possession of descendants of the original owners."[91] She ordered all chipped or broken pieces destroyed and forbid china sales at auction in the belief that the practice "cheapens the White House."[92] Along with the renovation of the Executive Mansion, Edith Roosevelt's legacies include the White House china display and the first ladies portrait gallery in the Ground Floor corridor for the enjoyment of White House visitors.[93] Certain first lady portraits still grace the vaulted Ground Floor hall.

Edith Roosevelt also enjoyed the legacy of Abigail Fillmore while continuing the tradition established by Dolley Madison of ensuring women entrée to the White House by inviting the wives of Cabinet officers to meet in the upstairs library. According to Ike Hoover,

> It was Mrs. Roosevelt who inaugurated the idea of the female cabinet meetings. Once a week at her invitation the wives of cabinet members would assemble in the library of the house and discuss affairs that pertained to the female branch of the Administration.[94]

Helen Taft

One of these cabinet wives was Helen Taft, the wife of Secretary of War William Howard Taft and Edith Roosevelt's successor as first lady. Mrs. Taft began a new tradition in 1909 by riding to the White House beside her husband on Inauguration day rather than following behind him in a separate carriage. She helped create the first lady dress collection at the Smithsonian by donating the first inaugural gown.[95] Perhaps inspired by the recent organization of the White House china collection, she had a closet built with divided compartments for the White House silver, after discovering the haphazard manner in which the silver had been kept in chests, boxes, and storerooms.[96]

Edith Wilson

Edith Bolling Galt Wilson (1872–1961), a successful jewelry store owner, became first lady and the second wife of Woodrow Wilson,

President Taft's successor, when she married the President in 1915. Concerned that heavy foot traffic might endanger the china collection still displayed in cabinets along the Ground Floor corridor, she created a separate China Room. Author Ada Camehl, who included a chapter on White House china in her 1916 book, noted that the separate room, which was then being planned, would also allow "a more satisfactory opportunity for observation and study." Mrs. Wilson "selected the room on the lower floor across from the foot of the stairway and had it equipped with built-in cabinets and glass doors." Fittingly, Abby Baker presided over the collection as unofficial curator. In 1918, Edith Wilson became the first first lady to order a presidential china service credited by American manufacturer, Lenox China, in Trenton, New Jersey.[97] Pieces of the state services ordered by the Woodrow Wilsons and subsequent presidents and first ladies have been preserved in the White House china collection as soon as they were received at the White House.[98]

Camehl observed that the White House collection of presidential china:

> is noteworthy in that perhaps to a greater degree than most other displays of historical relics in this country it bears interesting and intimate witness to the progress, halting and varying as it has been, in luxury and in taste of the American people throughout the century and more of national life.

It also contains "the choicest examples" from French, Dutch, English, and Oriental potteries.[99]

CONCLUSION

Throughout the remainder of the twentieth century and into the twenty-first century, first ladies have continued to make their mark on the White House by redecorating and redesigning these historic White House rooms. While still accepting congressional funding for changes to the rooms, first ladies have increasingly been able to seek donations of antiques and other historic items for these chambers. In the 1920s, First Lady Grace Coolidge (1879–1957) "persuaded Congress to permit the White House to accept gifts of appropriate furnishings," the first congressional and legal recognition that the White House functioned as a museum. Subsequent first ladies, notably Jacqueline Kennedy in the 1960s, have frequently relied on donations when restoring state rooms to the styles of specific historical eras.[100]

Another trend of the past 100 years has been the increased reliance on the support of professional associations in outfitting the White House. Professional organizations have assisted presidents and first ladies in providing expert advice on White House style and decoration and even supplying materials to the White House. However, increased observation of the White House and the actions of its occupants by formal organizations, official committees, and even the American public via the media has, on a number of occasions, restricted presidents and their wives in the changes that can be made to now familiar White House rooms.

The White House library illustrates the support that accompanies greater public and professional interest in the Executive Mansion. Since the Hoover administration (1929–1933) and during every subsequent administration, the American Booksellers Association has donated books to the White House library, which was relocated to the Ground Floor near the China Room in 1935 during the Franklin Roosevelt administration.[101] The library, although in a different location in the White House, continues to be popular with first ladies. During her 1961–1963 tenure, Jacqueline Kennedy (1929–1994) transformed the library with the expertise of interior decorator Jeanette Becker Lenygon, an associate of the American Institute of Interior Designers. Mrs. Kennedy also established a permanent collection of books based on the recommendations of a scholarly committee.[102] Appropriately, First Lady Laura Bush (1946–), herself a librarian, was interviewed on television in the White House Library in 2001.

The China Room has also continued to receive the care and attention of presidential wives. In the spring of 1952, following the Truman renovation of the White House, the chinaware of the presidents and first ladies was reinstalled in new cabinets in the China Room. As first lady from 1953 to 1961, Mamie Eisenhower (1896–1979) took a special interest in the China Room and, in 1974, wrote the Foreword to the book, *Official White House China; 1789 to the Present*. Mrs. Eisenhower had arranged for the china collection to be studied and cataloged in 1957 with assistance from the Smithsonian Institution, which also contains a White House china display as well as the famous exhibit on the first ladies.[103]

As William Seale stated, "Each presidential generation leaves an indelible mark on the house" and nearly all of the innovative first ladies and their husbands were quite conscious of their place in history.[104] Most of these practical presidential wives possessed managerial and organizational skills, an eye for beauty, decoration, and design, a sense of style, an appreciation of precedent, a knowledge of protocol, a desire for comfort and convenience, and not least of all, political savvy.

Many factors influenced these first ladies' expression and ultimate success in designing White House rooms, including their unique personalities and personal interests, the length of their husbands' tenure in office, and their and their husbands' relationships with Congress, the source of much of the funding for White House restoration and renovation. Public and social expectations for women, especially first ladies, during various historical eras both inspired and constrained these presidential wives as did the traditional roles, duties, and practices of previous first ladies.

The efforts of many of these first ladies may be more memorable and evident than that of their husbands. These women both reflected and set the trends of their eras in "the ultimate house," namely the White House.[105]

In the 1970s, First Lady Pat Nixon (1912–1993) oversaw the redecoration of the Red Room, Mrs. Madison's former sitting room and the room in which the much-admired First Lady Eleanor Roosevelt (1884–1962) held her first press conference in 1933. The wall covering was changed to the shade of red shown on the back of the chair in Mrs. Madison's portrait by Gilbert Stuart, which Dolley had rescued along with that of President Washington. Dolley would undoubtedly be pleased that her portrait, on loan from the Pennsylvania Academy of Fine Arts, again occupies a prominent place in the room where she once presided.[106] Evoking centuries of events, Seale notes that "The file of parlors—Green, Blue, Red—may well be filled tonight with the President's dinner guests."[107] In the historic White House rooms, the legacies of Dolley Madison and other first ladies live on.

NOTES TO CHAPTER 3

1. William Seale, *The President's House . . .* , 1986, 83.

2. William Crook, *Memories of the White House . . .* , 1911, 213–214.

3. Helen Herron Taft, *Recollections of Full Years*, 1914, 347.

4. Katharine Anthony, *Dolley Madison: Her Life . . .* , 1949, 83–84, 94; Seale, 1986, 121–122.

5. Lucia B. Cutts, *Memoirs and Letters . . .* , 1886, 28.

6. William Ryan and Desmond Guinness, *The White House . . .*, 1980, 122.

7. Seale, 1986, 91, 104.

8. Ibid., 268–269, 477.

9. K. Anthony, 1949, 193.

10. Catherine Allgor, *Parlor Politics . . .*, 2000, 59.

11. Ryan and Guinness, 1980, 124.

12. K. Anthony, 1949, 198.

13. Allgor, 2000, 60.

14. Margaret Brown Klapthor, *Official White House China . . .*, 1999, 34.

15. Ryan and Guinness, 1980, 111, 124.

16. Seale, 1986, 123; K. Anthony, 1949, 198.

17. Ryan and Guinness, 1980, 124.

18. Seale, 1986, 123, 125, 127.

19. Cutts, 1886, 71.

20. Ryan and Guinness, 1980, 124.

21. Seale, 1986, 91, 95.

22. K. Anthony, 1949, 199–200.

23. Elbridge Gerry, *The Diary of Elbridge Gerry, Jr.*, 1927, 180–181.

24. Allgor, 2000, 59–60, 62–63; Seale, 1986, 127.

25. K. Anthony, 1949, 196–197, 204.

26. Ibid., 202, 204, 250.

27. Seale, 1986, xviii; K. Anthony, 1949, 217.

28. K. Anthony, 1949, 230; Cutts, 1886, 106, 108, 110–111.

29. Ada Walker Camehl, *The Blue-China Book . . .*, 1916, 253.

30. Cutts, 1886, 117; K. Anthony, 1949, 230, 233; Allgor, 2000, 99.

31. Seale, 1986, xviii; Ryan and Guinness, 1980, 125; K. Anthony, 1949, 255.

32. Camehl, 1916, 254–255.

33. Ryan and Guinness, 1980, 128.

34. Seale, 1986, 148, 155–156, 901; Ryan and Guiness, 1980, 125.

35. K. Anthony, 1949, 338.

36. Seale, 1986, 215.

37. K. Anthony, 1949, 350, 357, 384–385.

38. Seale, 1986, 213, 223.

39. Seale, 1986, 241, 247, 263; K. Anthony, 1949, 369, 398; Elizabeth Tyler Coleman, *Priscilla Cooper Tyler* . . . , 1955, 87–88; Betty C. Monkman, *The White House* . . . , 2000, 101.

40. Kristin Hoganson, "Abigail (Powers) Fillmore," 1996, 155.

41. K. Anthony, 1949, 195; John C. Rives, *The Congressional Globe* . . . , 1850, 1926.

42. Seale, 1986, 80; Ryan and Guinness, 1980, 183.

43. Bess Furman, *White House Profile*, 1951, 156.

44. Laura Carter Holloway, *The Ladies of the White House*, 1870, 506–507.

45. Furman, 1951, 156.

46. Elise Kuhl Kirk, *Music at the White House* . . . , 1986, 70.

47. Elisabeth Donaghy Garrett, *At Home* . . . , 1990, 64–65.

48. Charles Lanman to Millard Fillmore, 12 and 13 December 1850, *Millard Fillmore Papers*.

49. Robert J. Scarry, *Millard Fillmore*, 2001, 109, 201.

50. Robert P. Watson, *The Presidents' Wives* . . . , 2000, 51.

51. Elbert B. Smith, *The Presidencies of Zachary Taylor and Millard Fillmore*, 1988, 198.

52. Seale, 1986, 377, 379–380.

53. Monkman, 2000, 124–125; Abby Gunn Baker, "The China of the Presidents," 1903, 324, 328; Crook, 1911, 94.

54. Seale, 1986, 490; Crook, 1911, 116.

55. Klapthor, 1999, 13.

56. Crook, 1911, 166–167.

57. Klapthor, 1999, 8, 19.

58. Taft, 1914, 351.

59. Klapthor, 1999, 67, 102, 104–105; Baker, "The China . . . ," 1903, 328; Seale, 1986, 744.

60. Seale, 1986, 472, 499, 500–503.

61. Ibid., 492–493.

62. Abby Gunn Baker, "White House Collection of Presidential Ware," 1908, 830.

63. Crook, 1911, 215.

64. Seale, 1986, 578; Crook, 1911, 205.

65. Ryan and Guinness, 1980, 144; Harry J. Sievers, *Benjamin Harrison . . .* , 1968, 52–53.

66. Seale, 1986, 580.

67. Ryan and Guinness, 1980, 144.

68. Seale, 1986, 587, 589–590.

69. Ibid., 566, 613.

70. Sievers, 1968, 53; Seale, 1986, 593–594; Charles W. Calhoun, "Caroline (Lavinia) Scott Harrison," 1996, 272.

71. Irwin Hood Hoover, *Forty-Two Years in the White House*, 1934, 5.

72. Ryan and Guinness, 1980, 176.

73. Seale, 1986, 582–583; Sievers, 1968, 54; Calhoun, 1996, 260, 269.

74. Henry L. Stoddard, *As I Knew Them . . .* , 1927, 175.

75. Klapthor, 1999, 8.

76. Calhoun, 1996, 268–269; Klapthor, 1999, 9, 67; Sievers, 1968, 54; Baker, "China of the Presidents," 1903, 328.

77. Seale, 1986, 1055.

78. Klapthor, 1999, 9.

79. Seale, 1986, 583.

80. Sievers, 1968, 55.

81. Baker, "China of the Presidents," 1903, 328–329; Camehl, 1916, 253.

82. Crook, 1911, 235.

83. Seale, 1986, xix.

84. Alice Morse Earle, *China Collecting in America*, 1892, 1, 256.

85. Hoover, 1934, 11.

86. Seale, 1986, 598.

87. Baker, "White House Collection . . . ," 1908, 828.

88. Baker, "China of the Presidents," 1903, 321–322, 329.

89. Baker, "White House Collection . . . ," 1908, 829–830.

90. Stacy A. Cordery, "Edith Kermit (Carow) Roosevelt," 1996, 299–300.

91. Camehl, 1916, 246.

92. Klapthor, 1999, 11.

93. Cordery, 1996, 309; Seale, 1986, 680.

94. Hoover, 1934, 37.

95. Stacy A. Cordery, "Helen Herron (Nellie) Taft," 1996, 336.

96. Taft, 1914, 358.

97. Klapthor, 1999, 153; Seale, 1986, 909; Camehl, 1916, 245.

98. Klapthor, 1999, 12.

99. Camehl, 1916, 247.

100. Ryan and Guinness, 1980, 162.

101. Seale, 1986, 867, 888, 957.

102. Betty C. Monkman, "The White House Collection . . . ," 2001, 54.

103. Klapthor, 1999, 7, 12.

104. Seale, 1986, xvii–xviii.

105. Ibid., xv.

106. Ibid., 935; Ryan and Guinness, 1980, 182; Allida M. Black, "(Anna) Eleanor Roosevelt," 1996, 435.

107. Seale, 1986, 1057; Allida M. Black, "(Anna) Eleanor Roosevelt," 1996, 435.

Part II

*Private Lives
in a Public Home:
Media Coverage
of First Families*

Tricia Nixon's White House wedding, 1971 (courtesy of the Library of Congress)

Overview:
On Stage in a Public Home

One of the most challenging aspects of being president is the extreme loss of privacy that comes from living in the White House. Whether it is the inconvenience of having one's daily routine interrupted or the embarrassment of having one's character criticized before the eyes of the world, such prospects have become part of the presidential relationship with the media. For instance, Calvin Coolidge had to end the practice of relaxing on the White House porch after dinners because the crowds that would gather to view him sitting on the North Portico interrupted traffic and disturbed the peace. Likewise, Harry Truman had to abandon his walks from the White House to the Capitol and around town owing to the security threat it presented. Richard Nixon and Bill Clinton suffered more than inconveniences in lifestyle during their presidencies, as their reputations were attacked publically in the media.

GETTING THE SCOOP ON THE FIRST FAMILY

A president's every day is chronicled by a professional but aggressive press corps eager to get the "scoop" not only on the latest policy initiative, but on a potential scandal and the activities of the first family. We insist on knowing what the first family eats, where they vacation, and how they live their lives. This intrusive coverage of everyday life must be even more difficult for first ladies, many of whom did not welcome the glare of publicity, none of whom ran for the office. Indeed, although first ladies generally withstood the pressures of living in the White House with great stoicism, several complained sorely of the highly public nature of living in the building. Eleanor Roosevelt, one of the least camera-shy presidential spouses, once quipped that she felt like she was "dressing a public monument" each day because of the constant attention paid to her clothing and taste in fashion.

While presidents such as Ulysses Grant and Calvin Coolidge, for example, were somewhat hesitant in their willingness to interact with the press, all presidents—even those ascending to the office from the vice presidency after the death or resignation of the president—have sought the presidency. It has still been difficult for many to forge a comfortable relationship with the press both in their official duties and in the coverage of their personal lives and families. Even George Washington, whose persona bordered the mythical, found himself battling opponents through the medium of the press and facing rumor-mongers within the media. But, such challenges "come with the territory" of being the president.

On the other hand, when the topic is the media's coverage of personal matters and family members, the issues are even less clear. Each presidential family has had to seek a balance between the public and private spheres of their existence in the White House. The act of defining the boundaries between public life and family has been made more challenging by a press corps seemingly bent on criticizing the president and gaining access to the most intimate details of each member of the first family. It has also been difficult for members of the first family who have been by nature very private individuals. For instance, such first ladies as Martha Washington, Margaret Taylor, Jane Pierce, Eliza Johnson, and Bess Truman wrestled with the loss of their privacy and anonymity during their husband's presidencies. Even these and other presidential spouses found themselves the target of the president's political opponents, the public, and press. Eleanor Roosevelt was depicted in ugly, comic caricatures with protruding, bucked teeth. Bess Truman was called "the last lady" for not championing political positions of her predecessor, Mrs. Roosevelt. First ladies from Abigail Adams to Hillary Rodham Clinton have been attacked in public for wielding too much political influential, or at least giving the impression of doing such.

FAMILY LIFE

At times, first families have included young children or grandchildren and presidents and their spouses have struggled to raise their families amid the demands of the office and the glare of publicity.

Franklin D. Roosevelt's children found themselves having to make appointments to meet with their parents. Amy Carter read about what presents she wanted for birthdays and holidays in the press and her older brother, Chip, saw his marital woes examined in print by the White House press corps. The media pondered where Chelsea Clinton would attend college and, later, whether it was proper for them to cover the underage drinking and partying of George W. Bush's twin daughters.

The families of Abraham Lincoln, Grover Cleveland, Theodore Roosevelt, John F. Kennedy, Jimmy Carter, Bill Clinton, and other presidents included children under the age of eighteen. George Washington, Andrew Jackson, Benjamin Harrison, Franklin Roosevelt, George Bush, and other presidents had grandchildren and other relatives visiting them or living in the Executive Mansion. The challenge for these families of balancing the public and private aspects of their lives were even more precarious. As shall be discussed in the chapters in this section of the book, family members of the president have been deemed newsworthy and have had the potential to both benefit and harm the president's image. So too have presidents and the media yet to resolve questions of what facets of family life are suitable for press coverage and how to cover the first family.

A RELATIONSHIP WITH THE PRESS

Media coverage of the first family is a two-way street. Presidents and their family members also take advantage of the press for political purposes. Whether it is orchestrating photo opportunities or utilizing the grandeur of the White House to advance their image in the press, presidents have attempted to manage or manipulate the nature of their press coverage. Living in the White House allows presidents advantages in press coverage that other politicians do not enjoy. Press conferences are held in the White House or its office complex, the press corps sits down the hall from the Oval Office, a staff of speechwriters and aides charged with media relations and communications serves the president, and the nation still enjoys watching the first family preside over the lighting of the White House Christmas tree and annual Easter Egg role on the lawn.

Theodore Roosevelt, one of the first presidents to truly understand the media and harness it to his advantage, benefited from a charismatic personality and large, vibrant family, both of which played out well in the press coverage he received. So too did John F. Kennedy's charm and attractive young family contribute to his generally positive press coverage. All recent presidents have tried with varying degrees of success to influence their relationship with the media. Changes in communication technologies and the advent of both the White House press corps and press office have shaped this relationship, as is discussed in the opening chapter of this section of the book.

Today, hundreds of newspapers, wire services, television outlets, and radio stations cover the White House. This was not always the case, as the nature and extent of coverage has changed over history. Many forces, from the individual personalities occupying the President's House to advances in the science of the news industry have influenced this relationship. Examples of this include the growth in number of newspapers and focus on national news occurring in the late nineteenth century, the advent of radio, film, and television in the first half of the twentieth century, and more recent developments such as the twenty-four hour news cycle, satellite broadcasting, and the Internet only heightened the already saturated coverage. In a highly competitive industry, the coverage is intense and often focuses on the human angle and social side of the presidency.

FINDING A BALANCE

This section of the book examines how first families have attempted to balance the public and private aspects of living in the White House and how has the press has viewed the social side of the presidency, including media coverage of the first family. The opening chapter provides an overview of how the media operates and of press relations with the White House. It also chronicles the advent of the White House press corps and press office. The next chapter in this section takes a broad look at the Carter family and the way they approached the issue of balancing public life with a "semi-private" life while living in the White House. The third chapter offers a case study of two presidential brothers, the media attention given to them, and how the presidents were impacted as a result of their brother's foibles and press coverage. Moving from siblings to children of presidents, the final chapter examines press coverage of presidential children and addresses the issue of whether the coverage is different on account of the child's sex.

Four

The Media in Their Midst

CAROL LYNN BOWER

A popular government without popular information or the means of acquiring it, is but a prologue to a farce or a tragedy, or perhaps both.

—James Madison, author of the First Amendment[1]

INTRODUCTION

Where once horse stalls were mucked out and, a hundred years later, a president swam, now swims a sea of sound cables, satellite links, and press credentials—a room that literally stands between the public and private realms of the presidency of the United States of America. Nowhere else in the world does a leader dare to live so precariously. The person who is elected to the most powerful political position on earth walks the few steps from his home to his office and back again each day under the scrutiny of the most powerful press corps that society has ever constructed. Adversarial and affectional at the same time, the White House Press Corps (WHPC) and the president live a symbiotic existence that has come to envelop the lives of the president's family and staff in a dichotomous system of visible secrecy that is, at times, incomprehensible to outsiders.

The WHPC is a part of the history: From the silences involving Franklin Roosevelt's paralysis, John Kennedy's dalliances, and Richard Nixon's missing minutes of audiotape, to the spectacular with Jacqueline Kennedy's White House Tour and the Nixon and Johnson daughters' weddings; from the minutiae of presidential pets and first lady fashion and hairstyles to the substantial in Betty

81

Ford's substance abuse recovery and Rosalyn Carter's mental health activism; from the Kennedy assassination and Reagan's assassination attempt. In this world that Gerald Ford called the "glass cage," a country is governed, a party is run, and a family is raised, all while the media watches.[2] In an effort to better understand this synergistic activity that has become a vital part of our cultural consciousness, this chapter examines the history of the White House Press Room and assesses how the White House Press Corps, the president, and the first family have become a combined effort in which the whole is far greater than its parts.

HISTORY OF THE WHITE HOUSE PRESS ROOM

From Ice, Horse Stables, and Swimming Pool

Nearly two hundred years of history constructs the different layers of what is known today as the Brady Briefing Room. At the beginning of the nineteenth century, President Thomas Jefferson began work on the first layer when his "ice house" was built just west of the White House in 1801. This structure was a sophisticated wine cellar that resembled a flowerpot. The ice house was dug into the earth, constructed of soft, absorbent clay bricks with a platform-style floor under which was the ice storage and on it were the wine racks that were covered by a wooden building. Ice was replenished every month by incoming ships.[3] Several years later in 1805, Jefferson covered the ice house with the first west wing addition that housed domestic quarters for White House staff.[4]

Architect James Hoban, working for James Monroe, added a 60-foot stable to the West Wing in 1819. The addition was built off the West Wing but stretched to the south, producing the "L" shape at the end of which stands the Oval Office. A courtyard paved in brick was situated in the area conjoining the West Wing and the new perpendicular extension.[5] Andrew Jackson was the next president to alter the structures that would become the home of the WHPC when he had his stables moved to the site. This is a part of the history behind Theodore Roosevelt's use, during his terms, of the phrase "muckrakers" in reference to reporters. The stables would remain until Franklin Pierce's presidency when, in 1855, John Blake, commissioner of public buildings, commenced plans to replace the stable with what was called the Treasury extension. Pierce ordered the construction but left office before it could start.

So when the stables came down in May of 1857, James Buchanan was president.[6]

At the completion of the Buchanan addition, future changes would never be as drastic as had been up to this point. Alterations to the existing structures or addition of smaller fixtures were undertaken mainly with the purpose of better handling the demands of particular presidencies. For example, in 1869, renovations by Ulysses S. Grant brought a billiard room to the west terrace.[7] The next most significant change in the history of the press briefing room was during the McKinley administration when the president allowed the newsmen into the White House building. Previously, the journalists milled about at the White House gates, often in freezing weather, querying visitors as they came and went. In 1897, William McKinley permitted them to attend the post-inaugural receptions in the mansion and during his term he allowed the reporters to wait in a warm reception room from which they could question passing Cabinet members and visitors.[8] When Theodore Roosevelt took office following McKinley's assassination, TR not only continued the openness practices of his predecessor but he established the first actual press room in the White House.

Structurally, an important change came with the construction of the swimming pool for Franklin Roosevelt over the old Monroe stable area. In 1933, a joint resolution of Congress was passed to authorize the refiguring of this portion of the West Wing, which housed makeshift laundry rooms, a bouquet room, black servants' dining room, and servants' rooms which were all in poor condition. This work required that the interior be gutted up to where the previous president, Herbert Hoover had installed his offices. The Roosevelt pool was a model of modern innovation for its time, with a complex steam and water heating system, underwater lighting, sterilizers, and circulation system. One problem arose. The mechanical works of the pool system could only be turned on after eleven o'clock at night because it required that the mechanical works of the executive offices next door be turned off.[9]

The Modern Briefing Room

The 1960s saw the creation of the modern White House West Wing briefing room when the Roosevelt pool was covered over.[10] Access to the swimming pool remains available through a hatch in the floor just in front of and to the right as one looks at the podium behind which the White House press secretary conducts regular briefings.[11] The room was renamed by Bill Clinton. Now called the Brady Briefing Room, it honors former presidential spokesman James Brady who was shoot and critically injured in the 1981 assassination attempt on Ronald Reagan by John Hinckley, Jr.

The Brady Briefing Room is separate from the space in which the journalists do their work. Longtime reporter Howard Kurtz recalls that the White House pressroom "wasn't really a room at all but an enclosed corridor connecting the main building with the West Wing."[12] Before the Roosevelt pool was floored over, the area had previously been home to a sauna, massage rooms, the old bouquet room, and a first family dog kennel. The first journalists granted space in the White House worked in cramped quarters just inside the entrance area. Theodore Roosevelt created this little press domain so they would not have to stand out in the cold while watching for presidential activity.

Herbert Hoover, who had the first presidential press secretary, moved the reporters' area across the hall, opposite the entrance into what was called a "ritzy loge."[13] Hoover's press conferences took place in his office in which reporters would assemble after the president "sounded a buzzer and a attendant clapped his hands twice to signal that it was time."[14] Franklin Roosevelt expanded the press quarters during a West Wing rebuilding in 1934. FDR provided card and chess tables for the journalists. Harry Truman continued the tradition started by his predecessor, of holding his press conferences in his office with the reporters standing about. However, this became cumbersome when the press corps assembled before the president, could number as many as the 348 who attended Truman's first conference. So the press conferences were moved out of the White House, across the street from the West Wing, to the fourth-floor Indian Treaty Room in the old State-War-Navy Building.[15] The regular presidential press conference would remain off White House grounds until the construction of the briefing room.

In 1969, Richard Nixon visited the still claustrophobic working conditions and ordered changes to improve the conditions. The initial plan was to relocate the press quarters out of the White House. The destination varied from the Old Executive Office Building to a sunken press room built into the White House lawn facing Pennsylvania Avenue. The alternatives were dropped and Nixon's own plan for converting the Roosevelt pool and the surrounding area where the dog kennels had been, was adopted. During this work, the formal briefing room was constructed between the press secretary's office and the area where the reporters had been. The new press facilities included forty writing desks and twelve broadcast booths.[16] The new location no longer allowed the media a view of the comings and goings of presidential visitors since the rooms were situated in a level of the West Wing lower than the Oval Office. The new facilities comprised three sections. The first section, which is called the upper press office and was able to be sequestered behind a sliding glass door, was the briefing room. Next was the start of what was called the lower press offices which also housed the lower-ranking White House communication assistants. Down a narrow hall, in the middle section were the offices for the more important wire services and newspapers. Here also was the staircase down to "The Dungeon" in which CNN, National Public Radio, Fox, and several foreign news agencies were housed. At the end of the corridor were the private booths of the big three television networks: ABC, CBS, and NBC.[17] The price tag for the renovation was a half-million dollars.[18] This configuration would continue through at least the next five presidencies.

THE PRESIDENT AND THE PRESS

Presidential-Press Relationships

White House correspondent-turned-scholar James Deakin identifies three types of relationships that exist between the press and the president: symbiotic, adversary, and permanent resident critic. The day-to-day relationship is symbiotic wherein the two institutions have a cooperative and beneficial relationship. However, as the issues become more important than the routine business or if they could become potentially embarrassing to the presidency, the relationship turns adversarial. Finally is the relationship that is ongoing regardless of who sits in the Oval Office in which the media acts as the permanent resident critic of government.[19]

   Those three relationships are played out in every presidency, in lesser or greater degree based on the West Wing occupants. But within each individual presidency, three phases—alliance, competitive, and detachment—are played out between a president and the press. Robert E. Denton, Jr., suggests that in the first stage of alliance, the president and the press are cooperative. They are in a honeymoon period with the president in which the chief executive receives positive media coverage. The competitive or second phase "begins when reporters start looking for conflicts within an administration, especially between Cabinet officials."[20] The media's behavior during this stage prompts White House staffers to attempt to counter the reporters' activities while the reporters become more openly hostile in their questioning. Finally, the relationship moves into a detached period. As the levels of frustration increase for the staffers, they tend to limit access by the national news agencies and the White House will pay more attention to the smaller or local media. In this stage, presidents tend to distrust the media and use surrogates to present their views. Hence, if presidents understand the adversarial relationship, handling the press with a "respectful-manipulative attitude," they will endeavor to keep maximum access and avoid the third stage of detachment.[21]

Presidents who have successfully maneuvered this relationship developed a reputation for handling the media and enjoyed substantial public popularity; such as TR, FDR, Truman, and JFK. In particular, JFK applied the principles found in Richard Neustadt's classic book *Presidential Power* to his handling of the media and found great success in the practice.[22] However, the presidents who moved into the detached stage of relations with the press find they have much more difficulty getting their message out to the public. Lyndon Johnson, Gerald Ford, and Jimmy Carter are modern presidents who experienced this situation wherein they had to work harder to gain the cooperation, respect, or both of the media.[23] Ford's offer to pardon Nixon in 1974 caused the public to turn against him. The press reflected this attitude change as it began covering presidential fumbles that under a "normal" political atmosphere would have been quick items buried three or four pages back, were now on the front page in excruciating detail or prized video clips repeated over and over again.[24]

Managing the Media

Handling the press has been a concern for presidents since George Washington. Federalist-era newspapers called Washington a "common defaulter," labeled John Adams a "ruffian," and wrote about Thomas Jefferson's "crimes of the deepest dies."[25] The Jacksonian era produced the first presidential interview, after which reporter "Joseph B. McCullagh, saw to it that the chief executive did not utter the 'right idea in the wrong words.' "[26] This symbiotic relationship helped to produce the grand oratory of the Jacksonian era. Andrew Jackson used to summon newspaper editor Amos Kendall to his office when the President wanted to make an address so that Kendall could write it down and help the president to edit it into what he "wished to say."[27]

The modern WHPC had its origins in the McKinley administration after Grover Cleveland's Secretary of War, Colonel Daniel Lamont, began to creatively manage reporters. McKinley's first personal secretary, John Addison Porter, began the institutionalization of the White House news procedures started by Lamont. Porter's successor, Secretary of Commerce and Labor George Cortelyou, produced the first "briefing papers" on complex issues. During this period, reporter W. W. Price wrote in the Washington *Evening Star*, "Newspaper men nowadays have access to the President but they do not intrude upon his privacy, except in cases of absolute necessity. They usually get all the information that is to be had by talking with the secretary or an assistant."[28] Cortelyou worked for both McKinley and TR, helping Roosevelt to become the inventor of the WHPC and presidential press conference. For the most part, TR enjoyed an open and friendly relationship with the press. He became the "first president to utilize the privately owned press as a means of frequent communication with the public . . . and the first to initiate close and continuous ties with reporters."[29] Controlling the WHPC was one avenue that TR used in an effort to make his office a "bully pulpit." Roosevelt is also credited with creating and enforcing the term "off the record" when dealing with reporters.

Ironically, as successful as TR was with the press, his successor, William Howard Taft, was not. Taft was reluctant to meet with reporters.[30] However, the next president followed in TR's example and, for the first half of Woodrow Wilson's first term, the President met regularly with the WHPC. Wilson relaxed the strident control that TR maintained in his press relations and that led to difficulties for Wilson that he worked, during his second term, to remedy. Wilson argued that journalists did not see the big picture of America.[31] He considered forming a publicity bureau but World War I intervened, enabling him to create "The Committee on Public Information," which watched over the nation's more than 2,600 dailies and even included a Bureau of Cartoons. This effort created a group of civil servants whose job it was to look over the shoulder of the press, "correcting" them.[32]

Warren Harding, also a former newspaperman, revived the press conference, making it a regular part of White House office activities and official duty. Harding also created the White House spokesman idea so that the president could be quoted without assuming full responsibility for his statements.[33] During this period, the WHPC sustained a vast increase in numbers. Calvin Coolidge continued Harding's practices while adding the practice of follow-up questions. Herbert Hoover followed his predecessors' traditions and began handing out statements after reading them during press conference. In Hoover's first 120 days, he held more frequent and regular press conferences than any president before or until 1982.[34] The stock market crash shortly into his term in office ended the positive rapport as Hoover began canceling his meetings with the WHPC.

The "Modern" Press Conference

Franklin Roosevelt reestablished good relations with the correspondents, going on to become one of the best media-managing presidents in American history. He is credited with having founded the "modern" press conference, of which he had many and was the first president to receive a standing ovation from the WHPC.[35] FDR's "fireside" radio chats during World War II became a vital connection between a war-time president and the public. Betty Houchin Winfield states that "FDR's rise to national prominence paralleled the growth of radio."[36] Roosevelt's presidency is highlighted by his ability to set and carry out his own agenda through his symbiotic relationship with the press.[37]

Taping and editing for later release began in the Eisenhower presidency, which cultivated its relationship with journalists with regular press conferences and informal dinners in the White House. However, that seemingly trusting nature was not held by his vice president, Richard Nixon. When Nixon became president, his paranoia about the press was evidenced by the fact that he held the lowest number of press conferences in the modern presidency with only thirty-nine in nearly six years in office.[38] Expanding on Eisenhower's efforts, Kennedy was the first to permit the press conferences to be broadcast live—an important step in the ability of the president to get his message out directly to the people. The era of the "Great Communicator" Ronald Reagan saw the beginning of the round-the-clock live cable news coverage of the White House.[39] Reagan was adept at causing the media to focus on the man who was president instead of the issues a president could place in the public discourse, causing Robert E. Denton, Jr., to state that Reagan was the president who operationalized Marshall McLuhan's concept that "the medium is the message."[40]

That medium can be a frustration for the president. Clinton, a throwback to the Kennedy communicative charisma, preferred:

... televised interview programs and electronic town meetings because of his distrust of what he deemed scandal-preoccupied reports ... in late 1994, President Clinton mused, 'Sometimes I think the president ... is least able to communicate with the American people because of the fog that I have to go through to reach them.[41]

The manifestation of this West Wing attitude in the handling of the media prompted the dean of the WHPC, Helen Thomas of UPI, to say:

[Presidents and staffers] feel we are expendable, and if they make an end run, they will get a better press ... with the people. Eventually, [the public] should realize the president has to be interrogated, and has to be accountable, and we're the ones to do it.[42]

A Changing Relationship

Campaign moments like the infamous "boxers or briefs" interview question on MTV created a guarded media that feared this candidate who was succeeding in delivering his message directly to the people. The backlash to Clinton's campaign successes was that the press gave Clinton no leeway or honeymoon period as a newly elected chief executive. An adversarial posture was taken on both sides of a relationship that had become mutually exclusive.[43] Clinton doggedly pursued his agenda while the media tenaciously dug into any aspect of the family's lives or his policy efforts. This heightened state of existence culminated in the suicide of White House staffer Vince Foster who, in his suicide note, blamed his death on journalists and political opponents who were conspiring to destroy the Clinton White House.[44] A rebounding economy tied to Clinton's ability to lower the national deficit continued to keep the public on his side despite the onslaught of negative press. Like the Clinton presidency, the administration of George W. Bush did not enjoy a positive relationship with the media during its campaign and the beginning of its White House efforts. However, the media's treatment of Bush during both the campaign and his presidency was far less aggressive and negative than that experienced by Clinton. At the outset, the confusion of the Florida vote counting and the legal battles between the Bush and Gore camps added fuel to an already contentious journalistic story. A public sentiment of political illegitimacy was reflected in the media at the beginning of Bush's term, but this would soon change. The tragedy of the World Trade Centers attack on September 11, 2001, resulted in a jump in Bush's public approval from a mediocre 50 percent to a remarkable 90 percent just a day after the bombing. Much like the public, the media seems to have responded to the "rallying effect"—whereby the nation supports the president during times of war—with a far softer treatment of the president than is usually the case during the months after the terrorist strikes and at the outset of the president's war on terror. Terrorism and the war against it repositioned the presidency, the public, and the press to such a degree that it could be years before the impact is understood.

However, a change in the relationship between the presidency and the media had already commenced—a change that was introduced in the Reagan White House, institutionalized with the Clinton administration, and appeared to persist with George W. Bush's arrival in the West Wing. This shift precludes any alliance stage or possibility of a symbiotic type of relationship. Instead, the affiliation of the press and the presidency begins in an adversarial type of relationship and in the second or competitive stage. This could have long-term effects on the president in a divided government who relies on the honeymoon or alliance stage of relations with the media to help secure some early policy accomplishments in Congress.

THE FIRST LADIES AND THE PRESS

The chapters in this section of the book examine the relationship between the president and the media as well as the interaction between the media and presidential progeny and siblings. But an understanding of the media—White House relationship would not be complete without some analysis of the connection between the first lady and the media. It could be argued that the president's wife, especially in modern times, is one of most powerful, unelected positions in American government. Her influence extends far beyond the fashion spectrum, although designer labels and hairstyles remain a constant source of journalistic fodder. How the modern first lady has interacted with the press will be the final element of this chapter's examination of the relationship between the White House and the media.

Approaches to Interacting with the Press

Betty Boyd Caroli notes that, with the advent of the twentieth century, presidents' wives began hiring their own separate staffs, creating the Office of the First Lady and involving themselves in policy issues and social reform movements as well as trying to maintain a family in the White House.[45] But the influence and the image of the presidential partners has never been more powerful than, when in the twentieth century, these women moved beyond the staid, flat newspaper etching or official portraiture to the intimacy and immediacy of the live broadcast media. The modern media first ladies were either strategic on their own or handled strategically by the West Wing staff in their relationship with the media.

In one of the first attempts to understand presidential wives and their interaction with the media, Myra G. Gutin found that modern first ladies have taken on one of three distinct stances as public communicators: Hostess/Ceremonial, Emerging Spokeswomen, and Political Surrogates/Independent Advocates.[46] In the first category, Gutin groups Elizabeth "Bess" Truman and Mamie Eisenhower. The emerging spokeswomen are Jacqueline Kennedy and Patricia "Pat" Nixon. Finally, Eleanor Roosevelt, Claudia "Lady Bird" Johnson, Elizabeth "Betty" Ford, and Rosalynn Carter are considered the surrogates/advocates. Gutin's work was completed during the Reagan era so, a complete picture of the Nancy Reagan's tenure was not yet available. However, Gutin called her a "First Lady in Transition" due to the rather large amount of media attention, both positive and especially negative press that Reagan drew to her White House role and her ability, over eight years, to transform herself in the public eye.[47]

This type of media transition is highly evident in the tenure of Hillary Rodham Clinton who went, in the media, from being a political pariah to a darling to a candidate in her own right.[48] Shortly after moving into the White House and against the advice of knowledgeable insiders, Hillary Rodham Clinton decided that her work and the president's work would be encompassed in a "zone of privacy." Her original plan, which was rejected, was to move the WHPC out of the West Wing to the Old Executive Office Building across the street.[49] She did go so far as to erect a wall in the hall that divided the rest of the West Wing from the press area.[50] This air of secrecy was to taint Rodham Clinton's health care reform efforts. Groups of interested parties such as doctors, were rumored to be excluded from the proceedings. Interviews were refused. The public was left in the dark about changes that would be integral to their lives. Behind the wall of confidentiality, her efforts to reform health care would die.[51]

This understanding of first ladies and their use of the media is also supported by Robert Watson's partnership typology. Of the five types of first ladies Watson constructed, four have relevance here. None of the modern presidential spouses falls into the fifth or "Nonpartner" category. A survey of presidential scholars named Roosevelt, Carter, and Clinton in the first type—or "Full Partners"—while Johnson, Ford, and Reagan were labeled type two—or "Partial Partners." The third category in the typology is the "Behind-the Scenes Partner," with Kennedy and Bush listed. The "Partner-in-Marriage," the fourth type, includes Truman, Eisenhower, and Nixon.[52] The depth of public awareness about the first ladies tends to decrease with the wives who are grouped in the lower levels of the typology.

Trailblazing Wives

Eleanor Roosevelt is arguably the most visible of the twentieth century presidential wives. Her husband's paralysis thrust her into a limelight for which she was not trained but learned, exceedingly well, how to use. First lady longer than any other woman has been or will be, Roosevelt had more time to develop her media savvy as the media itself learned about its own potential and power. She became the voice of hope in some of America's darkest days during the Depression and World War II and the conveyer of the public conscience throughout much of the twentieth century through her radio broadcasts, magazine articles, and daily newspaper column. Gutin estimates that Roosevelt gave some "fourteen hundred speeches, lectures, and radio broadcasts. . . . from 1933 through 1945," many of which were extemporaneous.[53] Her public discourse skills caused White House staffers to recommend the unprecedented beginning of the first lady press conference. The first took place on March 6, 1933, when 35 newswomen sat down with Mrs. Roosevelt in the Red Room of the White House. She held these Monday briefings whenever she was in residence for the next 12 years, for an estimate of between 353 to 500 press conferences.[54] Gutin writes:

> Eleanor Roosevelt's press relations stand as a watermark in the history of press relations between a First Lady and the fourth estate. Characterized by candor and total access, the

relationship benefitted both parties. Mrs. Roosevelt aired her views, and newspaperwomen were afforded a chance to further legitimize their work by covering a controversial and newsworthy public figure.[55]

The impact of the relationship with the media was never more obvious than when Jacqueline Bouvier Kennedy opened the doors of the White House and invited the nation in for a televised tour. Estimates are that almost one-third of the country was watching as Jackie showed off the newly renovated icon in February 1962. In that hour "more than a hundred thousand electronic pictures were broadcast."[56] The woman who made the pill-box hat a closet must-have and Oleg Cassini a household name, had made history and changed forever the power of the woman who stands just behind the nation's top political man.[57]

Already an accomplished political partner of nearly three decades experience, Claudia "Lady Byrd" Johnson, logged nearly 57,000 miles by herself on her husband's presidential campaign trail in 1964 while additionally helping other Democratic candidates. She is credited with "boosting" two senators who were in tight races. Johnson established a unique and highly strategic policy of being silent when appearing with Lyndon, while speaking out when on the road by herself. This procedure allowed the First Lady image to be one of a supportive spouse while capable partner.[58]

This tactic of strategic silence has been used effectively by the modern media first lady. Nancy Davis Reagan who convinced Ronald to run for governor of California and, although, reluctant to speak in public, became a proficient campaigner while continuing, behind the scenes, to be her husband's principal protector and adviser.[59] Professing to prefer that the limelight shine on her husband, Barbara Bush was a mainstay on the preelection road to victory. Although staying away from the campaign rhetoric on the hard issues, Bush was adept at subtly championing the softer social issues that were definitely political, such as, a meal program for the indigent, day care center, rehabilitation center, and after-school center.[60] Her success with the media during her husband's political career and her own strong positive public image were the impetus for her son, George W. Bush, to bring his mom out of electoral retirement to bring a final bang to his 2000 campaign. The *New York Times* reported that the "big guns" had came out and "the Bush campaign unleashed its silver-haired, pearl-draped howitzer" when Barbara began stumping for her son.[61]

As pundits and proficients began to strategically use this media power so did the first ladies. Rosalynn Carter went from having a "fuzzy" image to being "most powerful" when it was learned that she was attending the Cabinet meetings.[62] She said it never occurred to her not to accept her husband's offer to sit in on the high-level sessions because they had always been partners and advisers. Carter reported that even as a governor's wife—a state's first lady—she knew her position brought power and recognition to issues.

> A First Lady can pick and choose her projects and do almost anything she wants because her name is a drawing card, she is influential, and although legislators may not always support her, she can always get their attention, as well as the attention of other powerful people. She also has access to the press.[63]

The relationship between the modern media and the first ladies demands that these presidential wives become much more publically multifaceted than ever before. Expectations for a new White House hostess far exceed the mere ceremonial. A defining process takes place similar to that of a new presidency in which the spouse sets forth an agenda of work for her tenure in the White House. Hence, the first lady of the twenty-first century has developed into a political symbol with dynamics comparable to her husband's role. As a president is both a ceremonial and policy leader so too must the presidential spouse be both a ceremonial partner as well as policy advocate. This evolution in the partner's role allows for greater use of the media by the first lady as well as higher levels of scrutiny by the media.

CONCLUSION

The most powerful tool any president has available is the ability to symbolically use the presidency to set and carry out an agenda. As demonstrated in this chapter, the principle conveyer of those symbols to the public is the media. The growth of the media from penny papers during the Revolutionary War to the round-the-clock feeding frenzy of the newer cable news systems has both benefited and damaged the residents of the White House. The expansion of broadcast has moved the presidency from the potential of intimate connection with the nation's first family to the spectacle of celebrity.

Notes to Chapter 4

The author wishes to express her gratitude to Ryan Walker, Autumn Fehlhaber, and Deborah Koshinsky of Arizona State University for their dedicated research assistance; Elizabeth Thacker-Estrada of the San Francisco Public Library for her research support and friendship; Bernadette Adams, Reference Librarian of the System Reference Center BALIS at the Peninsula Library System—Silicon Valley Library System; and Dr. Robert Watson for his boundless mentoring.

1. James Madison wrote this following the presidency and was addressing the necessity in a democracy for a symbiotic relationship between the government and the press; Betty Houchin Winfield, *FDR and the News Media*, 1990, 3.

2. Amy Blumenfeld and Richard Jerome, "When Dad Is President," 2001, 52.

3. William Seale, *The President's House . . .*, 1986, 103.

4. Ibid., 109.

5. Ibid., 151.

6. Ibid., 343.

7. Ibid., 463.

8. Timothy E. Cook, *Governing with the News . . .*, 1998, 47–48.

9. Seale, 1986, 924–925; see also the White House Historical Association's (WHHA) History Timeline at www.whha.org.

10. See WHHA.

11. Associated Press photo, *Arizona Republic* (May 2, 2001), E2.

12. Howard Kurtz, *Spin Cycle . . .*, 1988, 33.

13. W. Dale Nelson, *Who Speaks for the President?*, 1998, 48.

14. Ibid., 49.

15. John Tebbel and Sarah Miles Watts, *The Press and the President . . .*, 1985, 458.

16. Nelson, 1998, 169.

17. Kurtz, 1988, 33–34.

18. Louis W. Liebovich, *The Press and the Modern Presidency . . .*, 1998, 77.

19. Frank Cormier et al., *The White House Press . . .*, 1983, 23.

20. Robert E. Denton, Jr., *The Primetime Presidency* . . . , 1988, 27.

21. Ibid., 27.

22. Brigitte Lebens Nacos, *The Press, Presidents, and Crises*, 1990, 18.

23. Denton, 1988, 28; Nacos, 1990, 18.

24. Liebovich, 1998, 94–98.

25. Thomas C. Leonard, *The Power of the Press* . . . , 1986, 142.

26. Ibid., 80.

27. Ibid., 78.

28. Seale, 1986, 691–692.

29. Blaire Atherton French, *The Presidential Press Conference* . . . , 1982, 3.

30. Ibid., 3–4.

31. Leonard, 1986, 166.

32. Ibid., 190.

33. French, 1982, 5.

34. Ibid., 6.

35. French, 1982, 6; Tebbel and Watts, 1985, 441.

36. Winfield, 1990, 17.

37. Ibid., 236.

38. Liebovich, 1998, 78.

39. See Theodore Bogosian, *Press Secretary*, 2001.

40. Denton, 1988, 59.

41. Cook, 1998, 134.

42. Ibid., 84.

43. Liebovich, 1998, 183–184.

44. Liebovich, 1998, 185; see also David Brock, *Blinded by the Right* . . . , 2002.

45. Betty Boyd Caroli, *First Ladies*, 1995, 117.

46. Myra G. Gutin, *The President's Partner* . . . , 1989, 2–4.

47. Ibid., 163.

48. See Carol Lynn Bower, Hillary Rodham Clinton . . . , 2001.

49. Kurtz, 1988, 82.

50. Gail Sheehy, *Hillary's Choice*, 1999, 226–228.

51. Ibid., 235–236.

52. Robert P. Watson, *The Presidents' Wives* . . . , 2000, 142.

53. Gutin, 1989, 97.

54. Gutin, 1989, 98; Tebbel and Watts, 1985, 440.

55. Gutin, 1989, 99.

56. Perry Wolff, *A Tour of the White House* . . . , 1962, 9.

57. Carl Sferrazza Anthony, *First Ladies* . . . , 1991, 40–41.

58. Gil Troy, *Mr. and Mrs. President* . . . , 2000, 140–141.

59. Anthony, 1991, 143–144.

60. Ibid., 412.

61. Frank Bruni, "Barbara Bush Joins G.O.P. Women . . . ," 2000, A30.

62. Rosalynn Carter, *First Lady from Plains*, 1994, 184–185.

63. Ibid., 93.

Five

The Carter White House: The Public and Semiprivate Lives of the First Family

Virginia A. Chanley

Introduction

W hen Jimmy and Rosalynn Carter moved into the White House on January 20, 1977, they brought an extended family with them. Along with nine-year-old daughter Amy came sons Chip, 27, and Jeff, 24, and daughters-in-law Caron and Annette. Their oldest son Jack, 29, and his wife Judy were in Washington for the inauguration, but afterward they returned home to Georgia where Jack was practicing law. President Carter had benefited from his family's support in each of his efforts to gain public office, from his first campaign for senator in the Georgia state legislature to his campaign for the presidency. Not surprisingly, the President had come to rely on his family for support and advice, and he would continue to do so in the White House. It is thus beneficial to assess the relationship of the Carter family during his presidency.

For the first time in nearly two years, the family was able to spend time together on a regular basis. Jimmy and Rosalynn had begun to make campaign trips outside Georgia early in 1975 in pursuit of the White House.[1] Before the campaign ended, family members Jack, Chip, Jeff, and their wives also campaigned across the country. The family relocated to key states such as New Hampshire and Florida and devoted themselves full time to the effort to gain the White House. Family members typically traveled separately in an effort to maximize the number of people they could reach. After all, not many people outside Georgia knew who Jimmy Carter was, and the efforts of the family helped address this problem. By the time of the general election in November 1976, the name Jimmy Carter was known across the United States. Victory in 1976 made the White House home to the Carter family. At the same time, members of the Carter family became the subject of news stories ranging from the front page to the Style section. Family members were not entirely pleased with the attention they received, but they knew that it came with their new position as first family of the nation.

THE WHITE HOUSE AS THE PEOPLE'S HOUSE

Setting the Tone for the Carter Presidency

Before moving into the White House, the Carters studied the history of the presidency and thought about the tone they wanted to set for the Carter administration.[2] Most important, they wanted the Carter presidency to be open and inclusive. They planned to revive some of the traditions of older and simpler inaugurals, wanting to ensure that all types of people felt welcome. They shared Andrew Jackson's view of the president as a direct representative of the people, but they did not want to replicate Jackson's opening of the White House at his inaugural, which by all accounts became rather raucous. Thus, they planned a number of events at different locations in Washington and limited the number of people who were actually invited to the White House in the first days of the new administration.

Among the first to visit the Carter White House were supporters from across the country who had opened their homes for members of the Carter family to stay while they were on the campaign trail.[3] Staying in private homes rather than hotels had helped defray campaign expenses and given family members the opportunity to learn more about voters' concerns. In return, these supporters were invited to the White House and given a plaque with the inscription "A member of the Carter family stayed in this house during the campaign of 1976." State governors, Democratic National Committee members, party leaders from across the country, and close to 2,000 supporters from Georgia also visited the White House in the first two days of the Carter presidency.

Social Events at the Carter White House

The number of visitors to the White House lessened after the events immediately following the inaugural, but the White House calendar remained full throughout the days of the Carter administration. Almost every day of the week, the White House calendar included a social function of one type or another. Fortunately for the First Lady, who was in charge of White House social affairs, there was a competent and hard-working staff on which she could depend to ensure that White House social events were well planned and executed. From official state dinners to informal picnics on the South Lawn, the President and First Lady wanted to ensure that everyone who visited the White House felt welcome.

The most formal events at the Carter White House, of which there were many, were state dinners with foreign dignitaries. In the first twenty months of the Carter administration, nearly 100 heads of state visited Jimmy and Rosalynn at the White House. In keeping with the administration's goals of reducing government spending and opening the White House to all citizens, the First Lady made some changes from the social functions of earlier White Houses. In a description of the first Carter White House state dinner, held for Mexican President Jose Lopez-Portillo and his wife Carmen, *Newsweek* reported that "[a] Carter state dinner is very much like the President himself—punctual, efficient and as unpretentiously homey as a White House affair can be."[4]

Although mocked by some, the President and First Lady chose to serve wine or vermouth rather than hard liquor at state dinners. The Carters also planned to end state dinners at 11:00 P.M., which was early enough that the White House staff could be gone by midnight and not have to be paid overtime. It was estimated that the Carters would save about a million dollars by serving wine and ending events before midnight, which the President judged to be significant enough to make the changes worthwhile.

When making out guest lists, Rosalynn made sure to include people who previous presidents and first ladies were unlikely to have considered adding to the guest list for a state dinner. At one of the first White House state dinners, for instance, Rosalynn included a couple from North Carolina who ran a small store.[5] Based on the Carter administration's "Peoples' Program" at the White House, the President and First Lady wanted to provide that citizens from across the country, regardless of their social status, had the opportunity to attend important social events at the White House. Not everyone appreciated the Carter's approach to putting together the White House guest list, however, as evidenced by the remark of a guest who lamented that she had not recognized any of the after-dinner guests following her attendance at one of the state dinners early in the Carter administration.

In addition to dinners for foreign heads-of-state, the First Lady and her staff were responsible for dinners, receptions, and other events scheduled for members of Congress, state governors, women's groups, senior citizens, and others who had legislative interests or who the White House wanted to honor. One of the President and First Lady's favorite social events was the annual dinner with state governors.[6] Jimmy and Rosalynn knew many of the governors and their wives from Jimmy's tenure as governor of Georgia, which made this event a welcome opportunity to renew old acquaintances.

Some Carter White House functions were arranged with politics in mind so as to help garner political support for legislation that was particularly important to the Carter administration.[7] One of the most important of these types of social functions took place when President Carter was working to build support for the Panama Canal Treaty. The administration asked U.S. senators to give them a list of influential leaders from their states, from which several thousand people were invited to the White House. The group included influential people from the media, educational institutions, the business community, elected officials, and a variety of interest groups. The visit to the White House gave the administration the opportunity to brief these community leaders on the background and justification for the Panama Canal Treaty, in the hope that these individuals would in turn pass the information along to others and contribute to building a base of support for the treaty. The administration felt that this effort on behalf of the Panama Canal Treaty was sufficiently successful that they used it as a model for future efforts to gain support for policy initiatives that were particularly important to the President.

In 1978, the Carter White House began a series of Sunday afternoon performances by renowned artists and entertainers. A relatively small group of people was invited to watch the actual performances at the White House. To reach the broader public, however, the performances were taped and shown on public television. In February of 1979, for example, approximately 130 people watched a performance by Mikhail Baryshnikov in person, while the entire public was able to view the event on PBS.[8] Pianist

Vladimir Horowitz, cellist Mstislav Rotropovich, soprano Leontyne Price, and classical guitarist Andres Segovia were among the other performers who participated in the series. In the fall of 1979, PBS decided they could not continue the series for political reasons— with the approaching election, there was concern that other presidential candidates would need to be given equal time on the public airwaves. The First Lady saw these events as an important way for the average person to be able to enjoy the quality of entertainment available in the White House, however, and she was particularly disappointed when politics interfered with the effort.[9]

Furnishings and Decor in the Carter White House

During the four years of the Carter administration, the President and First Lady made relatively few changes in the White House. As is discussed in the final section of the book, at various times in the history of the White House, presidents and first ladies have overseen major renovations or redecoration of the White House, but the Carters were relatively happy with things as they were. If they had been in the White House for another four years, they undoubtedly would have added a few more changes and personal touches, but this was not to be.

One of the Carter's first steps in making changes to the furnishings of the White House was to have White House curator Clement Conger organize a campaign to raise a $10 million endowment for the White House.[10] Congress appropriates funds to maintain the White House, but there were no government funds set aside for purchasing White House furnishings or works of art. The White House could accept donations, but the First Lady wanted to be able to make additions to the White House without having to rely on donations. Through the Committee for the Preservation of the White House, they developed a White House Trust Fund. During her time in the White House, Mrs. Carter worked to acquire a collection of paintings by American artists and obtain objects of historical interest. A necklace and brooch that belonged to First Lady Louisa Adams, the wife John Quincy Adams, were among such items added to the White House during the Carter presidency.

In making changes to the second- and third-floor living quarters of the White House, the first family focused primarily on redecorating the solarium. The bright yellow walls of the solarium were repainted off-white, and yellow-and-orange flowered drapes were replaced with off-white curtains. Using a yellow-and-blue color scheme, polka-dot chintz sofas were reupholstered with a light blue-, white-, and yellow-striped fabric. Easy chairs and a rug were similarly changed to fit the new decor. In one of the guest rooms on the third floor, the Carters paneled a wall with wood from a barn from Rosalynn's grandfather's farm in Georgia. In the third floor game room, the Carters covered the walls with family photographs.

The furniture in the White House dates to various past presidents, and a warehouse holds pieces not currently in use. The President and First Lady moved a sofa and chair set that had been given to Caroline Kennedy into Amy's bedroom. Jeff and Annette used a chair purchased by Mary Todd Lincoln in one of their rooms. Jimmy and Rosalynn brought a coffee table from the warehouse to use in their bedroom. Called the First Lady's bedroom, their room had a four-poster canopy bed and a glass cabinet with velvet-covered shelves. Although designed to display expensive curios, Rosalynn used the cabinet for items that Amy made for her, such as a small pottery bowl and a fan made with lollipop sticks.

For the most part, the President and First Lady were content to leave it to White House curator Clement Conger to ensure that the rooms were appropriately furnished and decorated. Rather, both Jimmy and Rosalynn focused on issues they saw as having greater importance to the nation and to the Carter administration.

THE WHITE HOUSE AS THE CARTER FAMILY HOME

The Occupants of the Carter White House

The President, First Lady, and other members of the first family participated in public events at the White House, but they also had private lives in the White House. The Carter White House was home to Jimmy, Rosalynn, Amy, Chip, Caron, Jeff, and Annette— along with two dogs, a cat, and a parakeet—all of whom tried to live, as the President described it, "a normal life as much as any presidential family could."[11] The President and First Lady were most often mentioned in the media, but as the first preteen in the White House since the early 1960s when Carolyn and John Kennedy, Jr., lived there, Amy also received significant attention from the press. Chip and Caron were in the news early in the Carter presidency with the birth of their son James, who came to live in the White House with them. Later, Chip and Caron became the subject of speculation about the status of their marriage. Jeff and Annette worked to maintain as much privacy as possible, largely avoiding the media spotlight. Ultimately, though everyone in the family would have preferred to have greater privacy, they found the White House a very desirable place to live.

The only family member who had to be persuaded that the move to the White House was a positive thing was Amy, who had not wanted to leave the family's hometown in Plains, Georgia.[12] Amy had already experienced time away from family and friends, first with a move to Atlanta when Jimmy became governor and then with the family's time away campaigning. Thus, the nine-year-old was not particularly pleased when her father won the presidential election. The family did what they could, however, to make the move as easy as possible. Rosalynn invited Amy's cousin Mandy and other friends and relatives to spend time with Amy during the transition and move to the White House. Then once Amy began school in Washington and her teachers and other students became used to having Secret Service agents around, the first daughter began to make friends and adjust to life in the White House. She often brought friends home from school and had sleepovers in the Lincoln Bedroom. It has long been rumored that Lincoln's ghost sometimes appears in the room, and Amy and her friends would try to stay awake listening for him. Jimmy and Rosalynn brought a sense of home to the White House by building a tree house for Amy on the grounds. On some summer nights, she and her friends spent the night there, guarded by Secret Service agents. Like other girls her age, Amy enjoyed roller skating and practiced diving. Unlike other girls her age, she was always under the watchful eyes of the Secret Service.

All of the members of Carter family tried to ensure that Amy was happy in the White House. As first lady, Rosalynn's schedule was always full, but she made certain that it included time to spend with Amy. Rosalynn had been able to spend more time with her sons while they were growing up, but she felt that her time with Amy was different.[13] With the boys, her attention had often been on other things, such as her work at the Carter family warehouse. With Amy, however, Rosalynn made certain that she took time for her and Amy alone. She woke Amy and had breakfast with her on school mornings, and she joined Amy in taking violin lessons.

Amy enjoyed reading, often taking a book to state dinners or other official events. Although some questioned the propriety of this, reading at the dinner table was something that Jimmy's family had done while he was growing up, and Amy continued the

Carter family tradition. Jimmy and Rosalynn did not want Amy to get bored, and they saw no harm in letting her do something she enjoyed. Rosalynn did not insist that Amy dress formally for every White House event, as she wanted Amy to be herself and live as normal a life as possible. From meeting the Pope and other foreign dignitaries to being the subject of national media speculation about whether she would transfer from a public to a private school, however, it was inevitable that life in the White House was quite a unique experience.

Compared to Amy, the media seemed less interested in first sons Chip and Jeff, although they too received at least some press coverage. Jeff and Annette tried to maintain as much privacy as they could while living at the White House. Jeff attended George Washington University and did not take an active role in public life. The press largely appeared to respect his desire to avoid the media spotlight. Chip took a position with the Democratic National Committee and played a more active role in public life, however, making it more difficult for him to avoid media attention. When Chip and Caron began having marital problems during the first year of the Carter presidency, it became national news.[14] Rosalynn and Jimmy encouraged Chip to try and work things out with Caron, but they were unsuccessful. Chip and Caron officially separated in November 1978, and Caron and James left the White House to live with Caron's parents in Georgia. Divorce was rare in the Carter family, and the failure of Chip and Caron's marriage was not easy for the President and First Lady to accept.

Living Quarters in the Carter White House

The living quarters of the White House are on the second and third floors. The second floor has a center hall that extends from the east to the west end of the building, which was arranged as a living room during the Carter family's time in the White House.[15] The hall included a stereo, television, and videotape set that the family used for entertainment and provided room enough for the extended family to congregate and spend time together. The Lincoln and Queen's bedrooms and sitting rooms are at the east end of the second floor. The president's suite, the president's dining room, a kitchenette, and the family bedrooms are at the West End, which is where Rosalynn and Jimmy and Amy had their bedrooms. The Yellow Oval Room, used as an after-dinner parlor for dinners in the president's dining room, is also located on the second floor, and the Truman Balcony, which was Rosalynn's favorite place in the White House, opens off this room.

The third floor of the Carter White House had two suites, two guest rooms, and a game room. Chip and Jeff each had a suite on the third floor. The game room had both pool and Ping-Pong tables, and family members and friends often enjoyed swimming in the pool and games of Ping-Pong. The third floor also included an ironing room, laundry room, and changing rooms for White House domestic staff.

There is a solarium accessible from the third floor of the White House, which first families have used in various ways. Jacqueline Kennedy used the solarium as a nursery school for daughter Caroline and her friends. President Johnson, who had two teenage daughters, had a soda fountain installed in the solarium during his time in office. In the Carter White House, the solarium became a favorite place for Chip, Jeff, and their friends. There was a small kitchenette off the solarium and when the President and First Lady had guests on the second floor the children often ate upstairs. The entire family sometimes spent Saturday afternoons in the solarium watching football. The First Lady used the solarium for the Spanish lessons she took in preparation for a trip to Latin America.

The roof of the White House is on the same level as the solarium, and the family also enjoyed spending time there. Hidden from view from the front of the structure, the roof allowed privacy for sunbathing during the day. Before their separation, Chip and Caron set up a playpen for their baby on the roof on days when the weather was nice. At night, the roof provided an excellent view of the night sky. Jeff was an amateur astronomer, and he had a telescope the family could use to look at the stars and planets. They could also borrow a larger telescope from the Naval Observatory.

The White House also has a movie theater and bowling alley. The theater, in particular, became a favorite place for the family to relax in the evenings. After his first few months in office, President Carter arranged his schedule so that he was up by 5:30 in the morning and on his way to the Oval Office by 6:30 A.M. He wanted to have time away from work in the late afternoon and evenings, and the movie theater or bowling alley provided welcome diversions. When the President and First Lady had schedules that were particularly full, they sometimes set up trays and had dinner in the theater.

Although the First Lady liked to cook, she did relatively little cooking after moving into the governor's mansion in Georgia. Then, after leaving the governor's mansion, she had been on the road campaigning for most of the time before moving to the White House. During the transition period, the President had used their home in Plains for meetings with potential Cabinet members, members of Congress, and a host of experts in various areas of domestic and foreign policy, giving Rosalynn more than ample opportunity to cook. When they reached the White House, however, she was ready for the relief provided by the White House kitchen staff. The family had the opportunity to cook on Sunday afternoons when the kitchen staff was gone, but the staff typically left food already prepared, leaving little need to cook.

The First Lady enjoyed spending time on the Truman Balcony, which was just off the Yellow Oval Room on the second floor.[16] The President and First Lady had rocking chairs on the balcony that were similar to chairs they had on the back porch of the governor's mansion in Georgia. Late in the afternoon or at night after dinner, the first couple liked to sit on the balcony and discuss the events of the day. In the summertime, they would eat lunch on a glass-topped table on the balcony. Gardeners at the White House kept the area supplied with blooming flowers, and the First Lady found the balcony to be a wonderful place for a quiet retreat.

The White House grounds include a swimming pool and tennis court, which various members of the first family made use of when the weather permitted, as had their predecessors. The President and First Lady enjoyed jogging and ran on the South Lawn of the White House grounds. Knowing the importance of exercise for good health, Jimmy and Rosalynn encouraged each other to be active and stay in good physical condition.

The First Lady typically began her day around 6:30 in the morning. She woke Amy and helped her get ready for school and the day. At 7:30 A.M., Rosalynn and Amy had breakfast together, and then Amy left for school. Rosalynn then began her workday. Most of the first ladies who preceded Rosalynn had their office in the living quarters of the White House, on the second or third floor. Rosalynn, however, wanted the living quarters to be someplace where she and Jimmy could escape from work. Thus, she chose to have her office in the East Wing of the White House, which is where the first lady's staff had their offices.

THE PUBLIC ROLES OF THE FIRST FAMILY

The First Lady

The position of first lady, though not formally defined in the Constitution or law, has developed into a position with a range of responsibilities, one of which is to oversee all official and social White House functions. Rosalynn took this responsibility seriously and she and her staff took special care to make sure that everyone who visited the White House, whether as a tourist or a visiting dignitary, felt welcome.

In addition to the traditional role of the first lady as White House hostess, Rosalynn Carter took on more political and policy activities than has been typical of most first ladies. She was widely recognized as a key political adviser to her husband in the 1976 presidential campaign,[17] a role she continued throughout the Carter presidency. President Carter valued his wife as someone with whom he could discuss issues and debate ideas to help form his own opinions and as someone who could help him understand what people in the country were thinking and feeling.[18]

Rosalynn took a leading role in formulating policy for the mentally ill, an issue with which she had first become involved as first lady of Georgia. Issues related to women, children, and the elderly were also prominent concerns for the First Lady. The Carters had become actively involved in their local community in Plains before Jimmy first ran for public office. As first lady, Rosalynn took a prominent role in community activities in Washington, D.C. Moreover, she advocated citizen involvement in community efforts across the nation.

One of the most controversial activities that Rosalynn Carter undertook on behalf of President Carter was traveling as an envoy to Latin America. The President was strongly committed to human rights and democracy, viewing the U.S. relationship to Latin American nations as particularly important. During his first year in office, both he and Vice President Walter Mondale had very busy schedules. The President did not want to delay addressing U.S. concerns in Latin America, however, and he saw the First Lady as the best person to convey his personal commitment to the area. Rosalynn spent weeks in preparation for her visit with the heads of state in seven Latin American nations, carefully studying the history of U.S. relations with these nations, current issues of importance, and President Carter's views on these issues. Ultimately, the First Lady's trip was widely seen as a success. The questions it raised about the appropriate role of the first lady remain today, however, as evidenced, for example, by the widespread criticism that First Lady Hillary Clinton faced when she took a leading role in health care reform during the early years of the Clinton presidency.

*Informal and Ceremonial Roles for Members
of the First Family*

Long before they moved to the White House, the Carter family
became accustomed to discussing their views on the issues of the
day. Family members did not always agree, but they respected
each other's views and were willing to express differences of opinion. In the White House, President Carter valued the information
provided by family discussions.[19] Chip's work with the Democratic party brought him in contact with a range of national,
state, and local elected officials and gave him unique opportunities to learn about events within the party. As a college student,
Jeff had a different set of experiences and observations. In one of
the debates in the 1980 election campaign, President Carter was
ridiculed when he referred to his daughter Amy's concerns about
nuclear weapons, but he saw Amy's concerns as a sign of the
importance of the issue.[20]

There are more than enough events and issues to fill a
president's day. During his time in office, President Carter tried to
minimize the number of ceremonial events that he attended and
often sent the First Lady or other members of the first family as his
surrogate.[21] When the President of India died, Jimmy asked his
mother Lillian Carter, who had served in the Peace Corps in India,
to travel there on his behalf. In June 1977, Chip and Caron Carter
hosted Britain's Princess Anne and her husband Mark Phillips at a
White House lunch. In September of 1978, amid attempts to gain
Arab acceptance of the Camp David Accords, Chip met Saudi
Arabian King Khalid with a presidential limousine when the king
arrived in Cleveland, Ohio, to receive medical treatment.

In addition to holding a part-time paid position with the
Democratic National Committee for a time during the Carter presidency, Chip Carter also served as an unpaid assistant to his father
on occasion. During the thirteen days of meetings at Camp David
that resulted in a peace agreement between Israel and Egypt, for
example, Chip was available to run errands and help President
Carter avoid interruptions that might have hindered the process of
negotiations. In February of 1977, Chip was sent to Buffalo, New
York, to show the Carter administration's concern after the area
was covered with more than twelve feet of snow. In April of 1977,
Chip accompanied a congressional delegation to China, reportedly
with a message to urge the Chinese to have one of their most
senior officials travel to Washington.[22]

President Carter had extensive help from his family in the campaigns of both 1976 and 1980. In the 1980 campaign, the President felt it inappropriate to engage in a partisan campaign when U.S. hostages were being held in Iran.[23] Rosalynn and other members of the family, however, did campaign across the country. The Carter's oldest son, Jack, had become the owner of a grain elevator in Georgia while Jimmy and Rosalynn were in the White House, enabling him to better understand the concerns of farmers in Iowa as he traveled across the state making the case for reelecting his father. Chip Carter had become an effective fund-raiser, which made him especially valuable in the reelection effort. Although they were ultimately unsuccessful in their effort to remain in the White House for another four years, family members remained Jimmy Carter's strongest supporters.

THE SEMIPRIVATE NATURE OF LIFE FOR THE FIRST FAMILY

Just as first families before and since, the Carters found that life in the White House was somewhat like, as one newspaper reporter put it, living in a fishbowl.[24] News reporters followed Amy Carter's first day at school in Washington, D.C., quite closely and later speculated as to whether she would continue to attend public school or transfer to a private institution. On a family ski vacation in 1979, photographers captured Amy skiing on the bunny hill, while reporters even noted her decision not to enter a slalom race.[25] When Chip and Caron Carter were having problems in their marriage, the whole family read about it in the newspaper. As the couple was trying to reconcile, the first son acknowledged to reporters that life in Washington had changed him and put strains on his marriage.[26] After Chip was divorced, the media began to speculate about a new romance when he was seen with a "darkly attractive woman" at a Democratic party miniconvention in Memphis.[27] Subsequent reports indicated that the woman was only a friend. As if these types of news reports were not sufficiently personal, when Rosalynn Carter went to Bethesda Naval Hospital for a "routine gynecological procedure," it was reported in a front-page story in the *Washington Post*.[28]

In addition to being in the media spotlight, family members from grandson James to President Carter were constantly monitored by Secret Service staff. Members of the security detail gave Amy Carter the nickname "Dynamo," signifying "the unpredictable comings and goings" of the President's young daughter.[29] When the Carters left the White House, curator Clement Conger regained access to the half of his office he had lost when the Secret Service commandeered the space so that they could effectively monitor the first daughter. Although Amy had not wanted to move to the White House in the first place, she came to see Washington, D.C., as home. Ultimately, it seems, the semiprivate nature of life in the White House, including media scrutiny and the watchful eyes of the Secret Service, was tolerable enough to lead the most reluctant member of the Carter first family to embrace the White House as home.[30]

NOTES TO CHAPTER 5

1. See Rosalynn Carter, *First Lady from Plains*, 1984, 106–134, for an account of the Carter family's role in the 1976 presidential campaign.

2. See R. Carter, 1984, 1–7, for a description of the President and First Lady's planning for the inauguration and setting the tone for the Carter presidency.

3. See R. Carter, 1984, 140–141, for information on the first visitors to the Carter White House.

4. Susan Fraker, "Making of a State Diner," 1977, 30.

5. Ibid.

6. R. Carter, 1984, 216–217.

7. Ibid.

8. Paul Hendrickson, "Light and Magic in the East Room," 1979, B1.

9. R. Carter, 1984, 219–220.

10. Sarah Booth Conroy, "Toward Comfort for Some . . . ," 1978, H1.

11. J. Carter, 1984, 29.

12. Edna Langford and Linda Maddox, *Rosalynn: Friend and First Lady*, 1980, 39–40; R. Carter, 1984, 146–147.

13. Langford and Maddox, 1980, 121–122.

14. For examples of media coverage of Chip and Caron's marital woes, see William Claiborne, "Chip Carter Moving Out of White House," 1977, A1; Mindy Fetterman, "Chip and Caron in Church," 1977, B3; Donnie Radcliffe, "Chip and Caron Carter . . . ," 1977, D1.

15. For accounts of White House furnishings and use during the Carter presidency, see R. Carter, 1984, 135–153; Conroy, 1978, H1; Langford and Maddox, 1980, 119–122.

16. R. Carter, 1984, 149.

17. See, e.g., "Betty vs. Rosalynn . . . ," 1976, 22; Fraker, "Plains Women," 1976, 39.

18. J. Carter, 1984, 31–32; R. Carter, 1984.

19. J. Carter, 1984, 29–34.

20. Ibid., 564–565.

21. Ibid., 30–32.

22. John A. Conway, "Diplomat in the Family," 1977, 21.

23. For an account of the 1980 presidential campaign and the family's involvement, see R. Carter, 1984, 296–324.

24. Michael Kernan, "Aswim in the Social Fishbowl . . . ," 1977, K1.

25. Barbara Graustark, 1979, 50.

26. "Chip and Caron Break Up Again," 1978, 11.

27. "Life in a Fishbowl," 1979, 5.

28. Claiborne, 1977, A1.

29. Bill Roeder, "The Busy White House Curator," 1981, 19.

30. For a report of Amy's reluctance to leave the White House, see "Washington Whispers," 1981, 14.

Six

A Tale of Two Brothers: Billy Carter, Roger Clinton, and the Media

CHRISTOPHER S. KELLEY

INTRODUCTION

The Office of the Presidency can be a difficult job for the president, his staff, and his family. Like many others who held the position, Jimmy Carter seemed to have aged considerably from the time he took office until the end of his term. Marlin Fitzwater, press secretary under Presidents Ronald Reagan and George Bush, noted that a staff member to the president often was left with only two hours each day devoted to his or her private life.[1] Equally important, yet largely understudied, are the pressures placed on the family members of the president.

Pressures placed on the family members are different from those placed on the staff. The staff are individuals who have been hired to assist the president and deal mostly with the institutional pressures that come with the office (congressional relations, foreign events, press management), while the first family face pressures simply because they are related to the president. In this regard, they often become public persons without their choosing, and for those who become famous, it is often because of something negative they have done. For instance, Abraham Lincoln served as Commander-in-Chief during the Civil War, while his brothers-in-law became known for fighting on the side of the Confederacy.[2] President Reagan had to contend with one child (Ron, Jr.) who wrote for *Playboy* magazine, another (Michael) who claimed he was adopted only because his sister wanted a brother, and a daughter (Patti) who wrote a critical, tell-all book about Reagan's wife, Nancy.

115

The brothers of presidents have also been a source of embarrassment. For instance, Sam Houston Johnson, the brother of President Lyndon Johnson, was constantly making headlines with lurid tales of his addiction to drinking and gambling.[3] Richard Nixon found himself having to defend the suspicious business dealings of his brother, F. Donald Nixon.[4]

This paper focuses on two recent presidential brothers who were very similar, yet had different impacts on the administrations of their brothers. This paper examines Billy Carter (brother to President Jimmy Carter) and Roger Clinton (brother to President Bill Clinton), and the impact that press coverage had on linking the actions of these brothers to the very legitimacy of the presidency. In the case of Billy Carter, he was seen as a political liability from the moment Jimmy Carter gained office, while Roger Clinton, even though he was seen as a liability from time to time, really had no lasting impact on President Clinton's approval ratings.

This paper will be divided into four sections, discussing: (1) the press accounts and the similarities that existed between the two brothers and the two administrations; (2) two in-depth case studies chronicling the various escapades and troubles that both brothers brought on themselves and their brothers' administrations; (3) the relationship between the press and the president, both from a theoretical perspective and from a practical one of image management; and (4) the conclusion that it was not the brothers that made the difference on popular approval of the president, but rather the way in which each administration handled the image in the media. For instance, Jimmy Carter paid very little attention to how he and his family were defined by the media and paid a price for it, while Bill Clinton, despite his slow start, paid a great deal of attention to his image.

COMPARISONS

At the outset of the Clinton administration, the comparison between the Clinton administration and the Carter administration was natural. The election of Clinton marked the first time a Democrat had been in the White House since the Carter administration. The two presidents were also former southern state governors. And both had brothers who were strikingly similar, both in their personal lives as well as in the type of media attention they attracted.

Both Billy Carter and Roger Clinton had struggled with addictions. Billy was an alcoholic who checked into a clinic to fight the addiction; Roger had battled a drug addiction and was sent to prison in Arkansas after a sting operation busted him with cocaine. That sting operation, ironically, was given the go-ahead by his brother, then-Governor Bill Clinton. Both Billy Carter and Roger Clinton used the connection with their brothers to make money. Roger used his connection to sign a record deal for his band, "Politics," and was earning $10,000 a shot for speaking engagements;[5] Billy made as much as $300,000 "judging beauty contests, speaking at rodeos," and personally hawking his own brand of beer, *Billy Beer*.[6]

It was the negatives that the press could not help but pay attention to when comparing the two brothers. In an interview that Roger Clinton gave to CBS's Connie Chung, Chung introduced the segment in this manner:

> Good evening. You've probably heard about the president's brother, Roger Clinton? You're probably saying, 'Oh, yeah, I know, he's just another Billy Carter.' Well, he's not. He's worse. I don't really mean that. But seriously, does President Clinton need more problems? This week he did finally pick a nominee for the Supreme Court. But everyone knows you can't pick your relatives.[7]

One writer, comparing the addictions of the two brothers, noted that Roger Clinton "more than matched the beery boorishness of Billy Carter, once spotted urinating on a runway."[8] And finally, regarding Roger's record deal, one recording executive found that Roger was "immature and unpredictable where Billy Carter has a confidence and a style, Roger seems like a dimwit out of control."[9]

The comparisons certainly were easy to make, and many tried. The Clinton administration, however, wanted to squelch any connection that his administration could have with the Carter administration, which continued to be seen as a low point in Democratic administrations. And even though both brothers seemed to be heading in the same direction as far as being a chronic sore spot in the administration of their brothers, in the end both were very dissimilar. Jimmy Carter was still explaining the actions of his younger brother Billy up to the end of his administration. Bill Clinton, with the exception of his first year in office, never had to deal with a "Roger" question. The exception to this was the President's questionable "midnight pardons" at the end of his administration, when it was alleged that Roger Clinton and Hillary Clinton's brother, Hugh Rodham, attempted to lobby President Clinton to pardon certain individuals. The answer to that had less to do with the behavior of the brothers and more to do with the way in which the president and his staff handled the president's image in the press. But before addressing image management, it is useful to get a detailed look at how the impact of the younger brother played out in the press depiction of the president.

Case Study: Billy Carter

There are two different stories to the Billy Carter era. In the first story, Billy is a wise-cracking "good ol' boy" who was always good for a quote on his brother, on politics, or on world affairs. In the second story, Billy is painted not just as a liability for his brother, but worse—as an anti-Semitic traitor to his country who was involved, along with several high-ranking officials in the Carter administration, in criminal behavior.

Billy Carter, along with Jimmy, ran the family peanut business in Georgia, which was fairly successful. Billy was thirteen years younger than Jimmy and barely had the chance to know his older brother while he was growing up. When Billy finished high school, he married his high school sweetheart, Sybil Spires, and then joined the Marines. After Billy finished with the Marines, he returned to Plains where he joined Jimmy and his mother, Lillian, as a minority partner in the family's peanut business.[10] Once Jimmy became Governor of Georgia, Billy ran the business until 1977, when he resigned after it was placed in a trusteeship to avoid any conflict of interest between President Carter and the business.[11]

When Jimmy Carter ran for president, Billy cashed in on the opportunity. In Plains, he held court both at a filling station and a bar at the Best Western hotel, which he referred to as his office.[12] He was consistently good for a colorful quote, and he played perfectly the caricature the press had of the South, that it was full of backwoods rednecks. As Jimmy Carter lamented in his memoirs over this caricature:

> When the hordes of news reporters descended on Plains during the final months of the 1976 presidential campaign, they found Billy to be hard-working, intelligent, well-read, witty, popular with the farmers in the area, and something of a country philosopher. Over the months he became carica-

tured, not unkindly, as an entertaining red-neck country bumpkin, always ready with a lively quip about government, politics, the press, or any other subject of current interest.[13]

Among Billy's more colorful statements were: "I got one sister who's a holy-roller preacher. Another wears a helmet and rides a motorcycle. And my brother thinks he's going to be president, so that makes me the only sane one in the family" and "I help make us an average family. It works out this way. Jimmy is 100 percent and I'm zero percent. So it comes out 50 percent because of me."[14] Billy was also known to tell reporters that his favorite seven-course meal consisted of "a six-pack of beer and a raccoon" and that he was tried and true *Red, White, and Blue*—"he was a *red*neck, he wore *white* socks, and he drank large quantities of Pabst *Blue* Ribbon Beer."[15]

When Billy resigned from the family business, it gave him the time to cash in on his newfound fame as "America's Hillbilly." For example, after the election, tourists who flocked to Plains made it a point to visit the gas station that Billy owned, where they could "see Billy and the boys sittin' and jawin', as if they were a theme park attraction."[16] Billy sold them gas "as if a shortage were imminent."[17]

Billy's entertainment stock was great in the first two years of the Carter administration. With an abundance of time on his hands, Billy devoted himself to touring the country in order to make money. Billy was a judge at the World Belly Flop and Cannonball competition, a position that got him into a scuffle with an audience member who threw a pie at him. The pie thrower felt justified in his actions, noting that Billy's popularity proved just "how sick our society is."[18] Billy had a walk-on part on the "country" variety show *Hee Haw*, in which he showed up wearing a vest made of pop-tops from beer cans. He also had a small role in the barely viewed movie *Flatbed Annie and Sweetie Pie: Lady Truckers*. Billy Carter often made drunken appearances with the spokes-model (Peanut Lolita) of a liqueur made with peanuts.[19] In 1978, toward the end of the first "Billy" period, he got into a public spat with Dolly Parton's sister, noting that her inferiority complex came from the fact that she was "flat chested." Ms. Parton retorted: "At least my situation can be remedied. But whoever heard of silicone for the brain?"[20] And in 1978, Billy launched the short-lived *Billy Beer*, a beer so bad Billy would later joke that it was the reason he quit drinking[21] and so awful that one tavern had a contest in which first prize was a six-pack and second prize was two six-packs, and neither winner would claim the prizes![22]

By 1978, going into the midterm elections, the antics of Billy Carter were wearing thin on many Democrats who felt that the inability of President Carter to control his brother was potentially going to cost them in the elections. Billy, who had been dubbed "the Clown Prince" by William Safire,[23] was now considered "an unguided missile" by the White House.[24] To make matters worse, when pressed, President Carter admitted there was very little he could do to influence the behavior of his younger brother. In fact, President Carter stated that if he told Billy to straighten up his personal life, Billy would tell him to "kiss my ass."[25]

By 1979, Billy's popularity had diminished to zero. He was spending "15 to 20 hours" a day drinking,[26] and the money that had been so readily available was now gone.[27] It was not unusual to find Billy at the bar in the Best Western Hotel—his office—early in the morning drinking beer, with a "cigarette in his trembling hand."[28] Billy recognized that he had a problem—that he had become "the world's most public drunk,"[29] and on March 6, 1979, he checked himself into a rehabilitation center in Long Beach, California. If Billy thought that his life had bottomed out—that his problems could get no worse—then he could not have imagined just how much worse things would become both for him and for his brother, the president.

The more damaging phase of the Billy Carter–President Carter relationship would now begin, which would in the end be referred to as "Billygate," a sordid affair involving a relationship that Billy Carter had with the Libyan government. Billy's wife, Sybil, claims that Billy became interested in Libya after he heard a speech by former Secretary of State Dean Rusk, in which Rusk indicted Libya, along with Cambodia, as being the "two worst terrorist nations on Earth."[30] In order to see what the Libyans were like for himself, Billy, along with an assistant and a group of Georgia businesspersons, traveled to Libya as guests of the Libyan government. Billy claimed to be very impressed both with the Libyan government and the Libyan people, and as a gesture of goodwill, invited a Libyan delegation to travel to Georgia in order to build business ties between Libya and Georgia.[31] The nature of these business ties involved the Libyans investing in a large convention center complex in Atlanta.

Billy was on hand to greet the Libyan delegation when they landed in Atlanta. While waiting for the delegation, Billy and a reporter went behind a building to "relieve" themselves.[32] Billy claimed that the building was away from the terminal and out of the sight of the public. The press immediately began raising questions about the propriety of the President's brother arranging deals with terrorists nations, as well as about the behavior of a brother who urinates in the outdoors at the Atlanta airport. This set Billy off: First, Billy readily acknowledged that he had "relieved" himself outdoors, but he claimed that it was out of the sight of the public and; second, he said that it was with the reporter who was writing the story, but that no one mentioned his involvement.[33]

The nature of the press coverage spooked the Libyans, and they withdrew their support for the center. Billy immediately criticized then-Mayor Maynard Jackson, whose early support for the project dissipated in the face of public pressure, for "bowing to pressure from the city's Jewish community."[34] Additionally, he also informed the press that "there's a hell of a lot more Arabians than there are Jews," a statement he said was "fact, not evidence of prejudice."[35]

The Libyans, who wished to make up for pulling out of the deal, arranged for Billy to secure a $500,000 loan, of which he would eventually receive $220,000. Two major problems now haunted Billy and the Carter administration—the first was that Billy was branded an anti-Semite. The second, and more damaging to the Carter administration, was Billy's acceptance of money from the Libyans and his failure to register as a foreign agent. Billy was required to register as a foreign agent due to his contacts with officials in the Carter administration regarding matters of foreign policy.

As to the first problem—the charge of anti-Semitism—Billy did not try to clarify his statements. Always frank in his discussions with reporters, he was now seeing the downside of being open with the press. When Billy was questioned by a Jewish reporter on the nature of his remarks, Billy told the reporter to "kiss his ass."[36] Press reports took this to be an expression of how Billy felt about all Jews.[37] President Carter did not come out and distance himself from his brother's remarks nor did he openly chastise his brother. This was now construed by prominent Jewish organizations to mean that the Carter administration was sympathetic to Billy's views. In fact, during the 1980 election campaign, President Carter was openly criticized by Mayor Ed Koch for the actions of his brother. Koch never missed an opportunity to criticize Billy as a "wacko" and an "alcoholic," or to blame the Carter administration for allowing Billy to have any connection with the Libyans.[38] President Carter wrote of this episode in his diary. In an entry on August 6, 1980 entry, Carter wrote that he gave Koch "hell" for stabbing him in the back with his comments.[39] And when Koch pulled out a list of things he wanted the President to do for him (to bring Koch back into the Carter camp), President Carter barked that having "friends like him, I didn't need any enemies—and with supporters like him, I didn't need any Republican opponents."[40] Billy's comments now were having a direct electoral impact on the President, who, as an incumbent, was having a difficult time securing renomination for 1980.

Billy's problems began on January 12, 1979, when the Justice Department sent him two letters asking for details of his connections with the Libyans and ordering him to register as a foreign agent if he received any money from the Libyans. Billy decided to ignore this request and any other requests coming from the Justice Department. In a nest of contradictions, Billy would deny receiving money from the Libyan government and then later admit to having received money. He would deny any business arrangements with the Libyans and then admit to having business arrangements.[41]

Remarkably, up to this point, the White House had successfully maintained distance between Billy's Libya connection and a connection to the White House. Billy continued to maintain that he was not being paid by the Libyan government[42] and that he was not lobbying on their behalf, and for these reasons continued to refuse to register as a foreign agent. Then in November of 1979, the United States Embassy in Tehran, Iran, was seized by Iranian students, marking the start of the Iranian hostage crisis. This crisis played a tremendous role in the downfall of the Carter administration for a number of reasons. One important reason was the role Billy Carter played in driving up the President's negative approval ratings on this issue in an election year.

The hostage crisis was a disaster for the Carter administration. In seeking every possible avenue to secure their release, First Lady Rosalynn Carter and National Security Advisor Zbignew Brzezinski asked Billy to use his connections with the Libyans in the hope that the Libyans might help bring a resolution to the crisis.[43]

The crux of President Carter's problems was rooted in the Justice Department investigation to determine the nature of the Billy–Libyan–White House connection. If there was a connection, then Billy would have to register as a foreign agent. Billy maintained that there were no payments and therefore was no reason to register.

On November 20, 1979, nearly three weeks after the fall of the Embassy in Tehran, Billy arranged a meeting (prompted by the earlier meeting with the First Lady and Brzezinski) between Brzezinski and the representative of the Libyan government to the

United States, Ali el-Houderi.[44] A week later, a meeting took place in which Brzezinski requested the Libyans' help in securing the release of the hostages.[45] On December 2, 1979, the Libyan radicals seized control of the United States Embassy in Tripoli, and President Carter called to the White House Libyan representative el-Houderi to condemn the attack on the United States Embassy. However, in addition to condemning the assault on the United States Embassy, President Carter also thanked el-Houderi for getting a message to Ayatollah Khomeini, in Iran, which requested help for the release of the hostages. On December 31, 1979, the Libyans deposited $20,000 into Billy Carter's bank account.[46]

In January 1980, Billy was still telling Justice Department investigators that he had received no money from the Libyan government—a claim he would maintain up until July.[47] On April 15, 1980, the Libyans deposited a $200,000 check into Billy's bank account, and on June 10, 1980—less than one month later—Billy requested a meeting with the Justice Department, Brzezinski, and Lloyd Cutler, the White House Counsel.[48]

During the course of the Justice Department investigations, the press began its own inquiry into the whole messy situation. The White House continued to assert this entire time that there was no connection between it and Billy Carter's dealings with the Libyans. Further, the White House was making statements, along with Attorney General Benjamin Civiletti, that it was not applying pressure to the Justice Department to relax its investigation of Billy Carter.

In July 1980, the entire episode blew up in the face of the administration. On July 14, Billy would register with the Justice Department as a foreign agent and finally, albeit reluctantly, admit he had received $220,000 from the Libyan government that he termed to be loans.[49] He continued to deny ever speaking to the White House on behalf of Libya. However, on July 17, President Carter admitted to discussing Libya with Billy "a few days ago." On July 22, the White House claimed that "at no time" did it ever have any contact with the Justice Department and its investigation of the Billy Carter–Libyan connection,[50] something that was reinforced on July 24 when Attorney General Civiletti told the press that the Justice Department did not make it a "practice of discussing investigations with the White House."[51] The next day, on July 25, Attorney General Civiletti held a news conference in which he admitted that he and President Carter did indeed discuss the investigation into Billy Carter.[52] It appears that Attorney General

Civiletti had a meeting on June 17, 1980, in which he told President Carter that if Billy would register as a foreign agent, the Justice Department would be unlikely to take any actions against Billy for lying about the money he had received from the Libyans and the access he had to the president.[53] This omission then caused a Justice Department investigation into a potential cover-up and tip-off by the Attorney General.[54]

As if this was not bad enough, on July 24, the same day that Attorney General Civiletti was denying any connection to the White House regarding a Justice Department investigation into Billy Carter and the Libyans, the White House admitted that Rosalynn Carter had used Billy's connection to the Libyans to arrange a meeting between Zbigniew Brzezinski and Mr. el-Houderi in November 1979, and that the president had in turn had a meeting in December 1979 in which he thanked Mr. el-Houderi for Libya's help in transmitting a message from the United States to the Ayatollah Khomeini.[55] This was in direct contradiction to earlier White House statements. Now the White House was admitting that Billy was approached and a meeting with the Libyan representative did take place. To make matters worse, on July 30, 1980, the President disclosed that he had discussed with Billy classified State Department cables regarding Billy's first trip to Libya in 1978.[56]

The release of all this information sparked a series of investigations into the White House by both houses of Congress. Jimmy Carter claimed that no new dramatic revelations would come, yet the press now smelled blood. Reports of Billy Carter securing the release of military transport aircraft to Libya, which had been frozen after the assault on the United States Embassy in Libya, appeared in most major newspapers in the United States. Additionally, wild tales about the subject of the cables that were shown to Billy were bantered about both in the newspapers and on the nightly news programs.[57]

On August 4, 1980, President Carter was forced to give a national press conference in which he answered a litany of questions on the influence that Billy Carter had on United States foreign policy, the propriety of the president's family setting up secret meetings with representatives of states deemed by the United States to be terrorist states, and the suspicious activities regarding White House influence over a Justice Department investigation. All of this before the Democratic Convention scheduled in New York for later that month.

In October 1980, the Senate special subcommittee investigating the Billy Carter incident reported that Billy had no influence over foreign policy, nor was there any improper or criminal activity on the part of the White House.[58] But even with that exoneration, and the relatively positive opinion the public gave the President's press conference, the damage had been done. The President, who never had good relations with the press, was now feeling the wrath of that poor relationship. The press had painted a caricature of the administration as incompetent, something the Republicans certainly relished so close to the election, and nothing that the administration did nor the results of investigations would convince otherwise. An opinion piece by the *Wall Street Journal* editorial board probably summed up the feeling of the press the best: "We're offended by the combination of this beer-swilling, Snopesian yahooism, on the one hand, and the born-again, moralistic preachiness, on the other, that pervades the Carter administration."[59]

Case Study: Roger Clinton

By the time that Bill Clinton had been installed as the forty-second President of the United States, the Secret Service had already given his half-brother Roger a code name: Headache.[60] The path that the Clinton administration took in that first year in office seemingly played out like that of Jimmy Carter—hostility toward the media, immaturity in office, and a "hillbilly" mentality that did not mesh well with the Washington culture.

Roger Clinton would fit perfectly into this image due to a number of acts that would seem connected to his brother's perceived inability to govern. In the first year of the Clinton presidency, Roger would verbally chastise an audience member who criticized his attire at a speech he was giving; he would get into a fight with a patron at a New York Knicks game; and he would appear to be using his connection to his brother to cash in on a singing contract and advertising deals. All the while the press was awarding him the moniker: "the biggest embarrassment since the late Billy Carter."[61]

Roger Clinton, ten years younger than half-brother Bill, grew up in the shadow of an intelligent and politically ambitious brother, much the same as Billy Carter did. Roger was arrested in a cocaine bust in Arkansas in the 1980s when his brother, then-Governor Clinton, gave the go-ahead to the bust, causing an understandable rift in their relationship. By the time Bill Clinton ran for president, the relationship between the two brothers had been reaffirmed. However, seeing Roger as a potential liability, Bill Clinton's strategists kept him out of the campaign.[62]

By the time of Clinton's inauguration, Roger was already getting unflattering press. His performance at the inauguration of Sam Cooke's "A Change Is Gonna Come" was so bad it was described as being worse than "George Hamilton's rendition of 'Dock of the Bay' on *The Ed Sullivan Show*."[63] Further, by inauguration, he had signed a recording contract with Time-Warner's Atlantic Records for his band "Politics," had signed on with a talent agent in order to book public appearances in which he would speak on the "triumph of the American spirit," and was shopping for a book deal on his life growing up with an alcoholic father.

By the end of 1993, Roger Clinton's escapades mirrored nicely with political missteps that marked the first year of the Clinton administration. The Clinton administration saw its hopes for a comprehensive health care package go down the drain in the fall of 1993, along with its public approval ratings. Roger, after the inauguration, headed straight downhill as well. For starters, his record deal with Atlantic Records fell apart after executives at Atlantic claimed to be embarrassed by his performance at the inauguration, noting that he was never a "major recording label" talent.[64] His foray into the lecture circuit (at $10,000 a speech) was short-lived, when a January engagement drew negative press over an argument that Roger got into with an audience member. Roger spoke before the Palm Beach Round Table for nearly fifty minutes when he was supposed to give only a thirty-minute speech. During the speech he was cut off by a woman in the audience who claimed: "His hair was unkempt. He was dirty. He should not embarrass his brother that way." Roger came to the speech dressed in a "baggy navy blue jacket, white shirt, Uncle Sam tie, blue jeans and brown hush puppies."[65] Roger responded to his critic mockingly, noting that her dress style was a relic of the "Fifties or Sixties" and that he could have worn something that met her approval by "sewing little rainbows" on his pocket that resembled those worn by her.[66] Roger was only able to make ten out of forty scheduled speeches. Rather than comparing Roger with his eloquent big brother, one column summed him up nicely: "a rude oaf."[67]

During a trip to New York to perform with his band at a nightclub, the younger Clinton was back in the headlines with more negative press. The day after his performance, the reviews from the New York city presses were largely negative, with one calling his performance "the equivalent of Billy Beer."[68] Shortly after his bad music reviews, Roger was getting more press, this time for getting into a shouting match with a photographer from the *New York Post* who was trying to take his picture while Roger was shopping at Bloomingdales.[69] Then there was the incident at a New York Knicks basketball game in May 1993. Roger became angry at a fan who had been taunting him throughout the game. There is some dispute as to what actually transpired. On tape, there was Roger in what looked like a chokehold on the fan, while Roger claims that it was merely a shoulder squeeze. Roger claims that the fan had been taunting[70] him throughout the game, which lead to the altercation. In the end, Roger was dragged out of Madison Square Garden by a body guard, with Roger screaming "I'll kick your ass" at the fan.[71] The next day, the tabloid paper the *New York Post* ran the following headline: "RAGIN' ROGER: FIRST BRO WRINGS FAN'S NECK AT KNICKS GAME."[72]

In June 1993, Roger gave a prime-time television interview with Connie Chung—an interview that proved embarrassing to both Roger and to Chung, and that gave rise to the nickname "Bubba" for Bill Clinton.

In the interview, clips were used to provide background. In one clip, Roger is asked if he has ever "done it" in the White House. Roger's reply: "No. I'd rather go outside where there's some privacy—the Rose Garden, perhaps—something like that."[73] In another clip, Roger is shown at "Farm Aid" being dressed down by singer Neil Young, who is openly critical of the Clinton administration's farm policy. Roger promises to contact his brother about the concerns of farmers. The next scene shows Roger on the phone with his brother Bill. Roger asks: "Hey Bubba, what's up?" He then asks him why an official did not show up at the event. When asked if he represents the president, Roger replied that "whenever my brother's not somewhere, and if I'm in the public, I'm my brother's representative." When Chung asked him if this is his position or the White House's position, Roger replied: "Nothing I do is according to the White House."[74] In the final portion of the interview, Chung quizzed Roger on the incident at the Knicks game. In the exchange, which brought criticism to Chung, she asked whether the incident was embarrassing to Bill Clinton. Roger said that he did not think it was, to which Chung and Clinton engaged in verbal Ping-Pong, with Chung asking if he really believed he was not embarrassing the President and Clinton reaffirming that the incident was not an embarassment.[75] It ended with Chung concluding that it was embarrassing to President Clinton and with Roger making a statement that would have likely earned nods of approval from Billy Carter, had he been alive to see it. When asked about being in the negative limelight, Roger responded that there is no preparation to be the first brother.[76]

In December 1993, Roger again made headlines that had the potential of embarrassing his brother. The press asked, and Roger reluctantly confirmed, that his live-in girlfriend, Molly Martin, was pregnant. Bill Clinton, sensitive to attacks on him regarding family values, began to pressure Roger to get married, even resorting to not inviting him to the White House for the first Christmas. To make matters worse, Roger began to take bids to pay for a wedding, giving the media outlet who pledged the most money exclusive coverage of the wedding.[77] In the end, Roger would marry Molly in March 1994, and she would give birth two months later to a son, Tyler. The wedding would take place in Dallas, not the White House, and brother Bill would serve as best man.

Roger ended 1993 on a far different note than he started it. In the beginning, there were the promises of a recording deal, speaking engagements, and movie contracts. As 1993 closed, the best Roger could do was to star in a couple of B movies and infomercials, where he hawked "collectibles signed by historical figures ranging from George Washington to John F. Kennedy."[78]

It was not difficult to make the connections, as many did, to Billy Carter. Where Billy's escapades played out over the course of the four years that Jimmy Carter was in office, Roger managed to pack all of his into the first year of the Clinton presidency. What is notable about the Billy Carter–Roger Clinton connection is that this similarity, for the most part, ended in 1993. After 1993, Roger became a model citizen, and more important, he kept out of the public eye.

Over the course of the next seven years of the Clinton presidency, Roger reverted to his old way of making embarrassing headlines just once. And this one instance had the haunting feel of a similar action taken by Billy Carter during the Carter presidency.

In December 1999, Roger Clinton agreed to play a "unification" concert in North Korea. Roger had played in South Korea two times prior (1993 and 1995). During the second visit, Roger was invited by the North Koreans to play a concert on their side of the Korean Peninsula. At that time, Roger rejected the offer. However, in 1999, Roger agreed to play a concert for peace between the two nations. He would be a part of an ensemble that included Korean performers from both the North and South.

While in North Korea, Roger visited the ceremonial head of state, Kim Yong Nam and also bowed at the tomb of Kim Il Sung, the founder of North Korea. Roger told the North Korean state media that he would "convey all of my feelings, all of my lessons and all the information I have got [sic] from brave people to our people and to my brother."[79]

Back home, the Clinton administration was having to deny any connection with Roger's activities in North Korea, noting that he had gone to North Korea as a private citizen. The State Department issued a statement that it did not oppose "cultural exchanges" but was emphatic in making the point that there was no official connection between the Clinton administration and Roger's visit.[80] Further, in a press briefing by White House Press Secretary Joe Lockhart, the question was raised as to whether Roger's visit complicated the relationship between the United States and Pyongyang. Lockhart responded that he did not think it had any bearing on the relationship and that it was nothing more than a "cultural exchange."[81]

Aside from criticism in predictable areas,[82] the Clinton administration did not suffer from the kind of fallout that the Carter administration had with Billy and the Libyan connection. Even though the two were dissimilar events, the eerie similarity of a president's brother being connected to a country deemed to be a terrorist state by the United States should not escape notice. The Clinton administration, however, was able to frame this visit for what it was—a private citizen engaged in a cultural exchange with citizens of another country.

Roger Clinton did not make headlines again until President Clinton was leaving office. In this case, Roger was among a number of individuals (including Hillary Clinton's brother) who accepted money from individuals in return for a discussion with the president regarding a presidential pardon.

THE RELATIONSHIP BETWEEN THE FIRST FAMILY AND THE PRESS

Carter's Failure

The importance that a modern presidential administration places on communications is key. For most of the twentieth century, an important factor in determining the success or the failure of a president has been the degree of attention and sophistication that each president developed in communicating his message and image directly to the public.

Presidents seek to control their message and their image, and this need to control often defines the nature of the relationship between the president and the press. Modern presidents have found it more convenient to bypass the press (avoiding press conferences, for example) and appeal directly to the public.[83] Appealing to the public has meant that presidential leadership is more than the bargaining[84] that is at the heart of the Neustadt paradigm. It has meant that the president seeks to lead by manipulating public opinion in an elaborate dance between the president, who is attempting message and image control, and the press, which is seeking to filter both the message and the image. Additionally, the appeal to the public has meant that the president and his staff adopt a rhetorical strategy that involves verbal and visual devices[85] meant to "shape the language that Americans use to discuss and evaluate political issues,"[86] as well as to move the public in a direction that the president desires.

The reason that the president wishes to bypass the press is largely a result of the nature of the relationship between the press and the president after Watergate. A number of important studies[87] note that following Watergate, the press more often than not reports on the strategies and motives of presidents rather than their message. Any president seeking to advance his policies is seen as a president who is "up to something." The net result of this change in coverage has been a net negative portrayal of the president and the presidency after his first few months in office—a change that makes it extremely difficult for the president to govern.

To combat this switch in coverage, the modern president must be able to control his message and his image. Even before Watergate, Richard Nixon, for example, tightly controlled information and instituted the "line of the day," a strategy that was masterfully improved during the Reagan administration. The line of the day involves the administration developing a central message, and everyone from staff to Cabinet members repeating that message as often as possible to the press.[88] The difference between the Carter presidency and the Clinton presidency, lies in the ability to battle the press for control over message and over image.

Carter had three problems that he never was able to rectify over the course of his presidency and each impacted his family. First, he was an "outsider" who never learned how to effectively manage the press. Carter made no attempt to control his message, as both Nixon and Ford had done prior to him. In fact, Carter neglected the usefulness of the Office of Communications in setting the agenda for the press, something that Nixon (who created the office) and Ford understood.[1] The Carter style impeded the ability of the administration to speak with "one voice."[89] What resulted, and certainly what remained a caricature up until the last day in office, was a picture of an administration grounded in chaos and incoherence. Second, Carter had set himself up as the "anti-Nixon"—a president so wrapped in virtue and godliness that it made it impossible to wiggle out of circumstances that caused some suspicion. The mess that was "Billygate" fell hard on the Carter presidency because it had set itself on an impossibly high pedestal.[90] And third, Carter did not respect the press and the power it has to "educate" the American public about the presidency. Members of the press felt Carter was too pious and self-righteous, and they often felt his interaction with them was more of a lecture than a conversation between professional adults.

The dysfunctional relationship between Carter and the press is something that predated his election to the presidency. During the primaries, Robert Scheer, in an issue of *Playboy* best known for Carter's gaffe of admitting to having "lust in my heart," told of a fish fry he attended on the farm of Carter's sister, Gloria. As Jimmy was preparing to leave, he approached the steps where Scheer was speaking to Gloria and her husband Walter. Carter acknowledged his sister and brother-in-law, but paid no attention to Scheer. Carter also sneered that the press was afraid he would "choke on a fishbone" and they would not be around to catch it.[91] Further, Scheer writes about how maddening it was to have Carter act so pious toward him and other members of the press—an interaction that made him want to go out and find dirt on the candidate. As former Press Secretary Jody Powell suggests:

> Reporters are not, whatever their faults may be, stupid. In fact, they take pride in being intellectually, as well as morally, superior to most of the people they cover. They do not take kindly to being looked down upon by any politician, especially not a peanut farmer from some piddly-ass little gnat-hole in south Georgia.[92]

Once Carter came into office, his lack of attention to the press proved to be devastating to him and his family. His communications advisers later documented the damage that came from the underdeveloped relationship with the press. They noted that the president "was inattentive to press portrayals of his presidency," that he "resisted slogans and simplifying characterizations," and that he was suspicious of "the presidential speechmaking process."[93]

This inattention to the needs of the press created a hostile environment to work in, something described by Powell. Powell notes that of the several journalists he spoke to for his memoir, all listed a dislike for Carter.[94] Further, Powell links the source of the problem to two points—both the faults of the press. First, he claims that any southerner was not going to get a fair shake from the northern elite press, who viewed anyone from the South as an uneducated redneck. Second, he maintains that Carter was much smarter than the members of the press and they knew it. Because of the intellectual superiority possessed by Carter, the press would write stories that would tear him down.[95]

And since the president gave little attention to his or his family's image, he allowed it to be shaped by others, particularly by members of the press. The importance of image management should not be overlooked. Political communications specialist Rita Whillock writes:

> Political images are ethereal. They are guided by impressions, selected and magnified by the press. Moreover, they are often constructed on the basis of a single event. In theory, one good action or one bad action should not be the measure of leadership. Yet single events affect images by impressing upon the imagination an issue that can be retrieved for anecdotal support of future claims.[96]

By allowing the media to shape his image and that of his family, President Carter allowed a caricature both of a White House overrun by slovenly rednecks as well as an administration that was incompetent. It is because of this "master narrative" that the actions of Billy Carter fit in to the overall style of governing so perfectly, and that Billy Carter was the liability that he was.

As to the charge that the administration appeared to come straight out of Mayberry, members of the president's senior staff did not help to dispel this image. For instance, Carter suffered through allegations that Hamilton Jordan, Carter's Chief of Staff, was using cocaine in the White House. The allegation was never proven, but the moniker—the "Georgia Mafia" was now used to describe the administration. And if this was not bad enough, two stories of boorish behavior surfaced involving Hamilton Jordan. In the first instance, in 1977, Jordan reportedly got drunk during a state dinner in which the Egyptian ambassador's wife was seated next to him. During the course of the dinner, Jordan reportedly pulled at the ambassador's wife's dress and asked to see her "pyramids." Later, he stood up to go to the bathroom and announced, "this administration has to take a piss!"[97] In 1978, Jordan allegedly "twice spat an amaretto and cream on the blouse of a young woman" in a Capitol singles bar after she refused his advances.[98]

These events and stories were used to frame the state of the Carter White House. Meg Greenfield, writing in *Newsweek*, offered this summation of the behavior of Carter's staff and Carter's unwillingness to address the problems:

> And there sits Jimmy Carter in the White House, Mr. Morality himself having to answer questions over the first nineteen months about his close associates' entanglements with the quest for dough, the use of drugs, boozing, whoop-de-doo and blabber mouthing.[99]

Hugh Sidey, writing in *Time*, offered this assessment:

> One of the maladies of the Carter Administration these days seems to be a lack of class. Class is not always necessary for effective leadership . . . The Carter Administration seems to be drifting toward a description favored by the late Peter Lisagor of the Chicago *Daily News* who used to say of the buffoons who brought us Watergate, "class they ain't got."[100]

Mark Rozell, in his book on the press and the Carter presidency, argues that the unflattering narrative was intentional on the part of the press, citing claims in the press of a "yahoo syndrome" in the White House. Rozell offers as an example a picture in *Time* magazine of Jody Powell holding a frog with the caption, "Country Boy Powell and Friend."[101]

While the "slack-jawed southern" narrative was insufferable, it was the other narrative that proved to be the most damaging. The image of incompetence was one that the Carter administration and family could not shake, and it is the one most likely to be remembered today.

Clinton's Success

The "master narrative" that President Carter allowed the press to use to define his administration was a significant part of the reason he lost the election in 1980. It was a narrative that began to be used to define the Clinton administration (media critics framed the administration as "southern yahoos" and incompetents) before the administration acted quickly to turn that image around. Therefore, Roger Clinton was never allowed to be tied into the administration's general approach to governing after the administration moved quickly to reform its image following the 1994 midterm losses.

Bill Clinton suffered a number of image problems that dogged him from the moment of his campaign for the presidency up to the moment he left office, and even after. Dubbed "Slick Willie" and a womanizer, Bill Clinton was able to "craft a new image" both to promote his candidacy for the presidency as well as to recover from his horrific start as president.

Bill Clinton and Jimmy Carter were similar in many respects. Both were southern governors. Both had a brother that was an issue to their presidencies. And both disliked the press. For Bill Clinton, the press had been a chronic source of tension since his days as governor. It did not get any easier for him on the campaign trail, where charges of infidelity drove him and his wife to the CBS newsmagazine *60 Minutes* to explain, vaguely, that there was pain in their marriage but that both loved each other. When Bill Clinton was elected president, he at first tried to bypass the media by governing much as he campaigned—speaking in townhall meetings, inviting talk radio to the White House lawn, turning to a relatively new technology, the "Internet" as a means to speak directly to "the people."

Bill Clinton's first year in office and Roger Clinton's romp in the press seemed to parallel each other nicely. Roger's behavior was seen as indicative of the problems in the White House. As one writer put it:

> Just how many of his gaffes matter is difficult to gauge. Clearly, unless he follows Billy Carter and does a deal with Colonel Gadaffi, or starts peddling crack from the White House, Roger is not going to bring the house of Clinton tumbling down. But as the president appears increasingly isolated and at a loss in the snake pit of Washington, so the behavior of Roger Clinton as an innocent adrift in America is seen as a telling metaphor for his brother in the White House.[102]

After the catastrophe of the 1994 midterm elections, Clinton brought in Dick Morris to serve in the White House as a political consultant and to reform the damaged presidential image. This new image would portray the president as a "father figure for the American people."[103] Thus, the president began to stress "family issues" such as child support payments, controlling the level of violence on television, and education, all with noticeable success. Further, Clinton went into the budget showdown with Newt Gingrich and the Congress and played it out masterfully, successfully blitzing Gingrich and gaining the upper hand going into the 1996 presidential election.

The communications team under David Gergen also helped to improve the president's image dramatically. According to James Fallows, Gergen repaired the "anecdote crisis" that existed in the White House.[104] The anecdote is a useful tool that helps reporters write stories. Since White House officials have the inside information, their supply of anecdotes can greatly affect the slant of a story. Gergen would restore the relationship with the press by providing useful "color" to their stories. Gergen further brought a measure of discipline to the White House staff, requiring meetings every day to discuss how to minimize damage or how to spin messages to put the president in a favorable light.[105] The communications staff also sought ways to connect the president with the public directly, in an effort to bypass the filtering process of the press. Thus, an e-mail address was set up so that the average American could communicate directly with the White House and receive the president's "public remarks, his daily schedule, White House press briefings, and even photographs" right to their e-mail boxes—at the same time these were all being made available to the press.[106]

David Gergen noted that the presidency was like a campaign, and that the communications people had to work it like a campaign, which would mean moving popular opinion in a direction that was favorable to the president by using a variety of communications methods to do so.[107] And this all proved successful in turning the president's image around and delinking his brother from the actions of the administration. Thus, in three separate instances, President Clinton was able to strategically use his brother's problem with drugs as a rhetorical advantage in speeches highlighting his administration's efforts to fight the War on Drugs. For example, in remarks the President gave launching his youth antidrug campaign, President Clinton stated: "My brother nearly died from a cocaine habit. And I've asked myself a thousand times, what kind of fool was I that I did not know this was going on?"[108] The President is able cast his brother's troubled past in a positive light that shows him to be caring and empathetic.

In the end, despite the scandals that hounded Bill Clinton during his eight years in office, he was fairly successful in manipulating the press and offsetting any unflattering "master narrative" like the one that existed during the Carter presidency. Even though Clinton did not necessarily like the press, he did understand the press. Clinton's obsession with images was likely to have contributed to the delinking of Roger's foibles with that of the administration's ability to govern. Despite a rocky first year, Bill Clinton's understanding of the press and the power of images was the difference between the way Clinton's relationship with his brother Roger was portrayed in the press and the way Jimmy Carter's relationship with his brother Billy was portrayed.

CONCLUSION

This paper has attempted to shed light on how a presidential family member can negatively impact an administration's ability to govern. The argument has been that the nature of the relationship with the press, rather than actions of the family member—in this case a brother—has more to do with the public's perception of the administration than anything else.

Jimmy Carter simply did not understand the press. He did not develop relationships with them. He spoke down to them, and in the end this hurt him because his lack of attention and care allowed the press to portray his presidency as chaotic and incompetent. Thus Billy Carter, whether it was his boozing or his links to the Libyans, fit into that portrayal perfectly. It should be no surprise then that Billy Carter caused problems for his brother right up to the end of his administration.

Bill Clinton, after a rough start, realized the importance of nurturing a relationship with the media. He brought in people whose sole purpose was to rehabilitate the image of his administration. So in the first year, when the administration was floundering to find its voice, Roger Clinton had a role in the negative approval numbers that Bill Clinton was receiving. Yet after this first year, and coinciding nicely with the image reversal, Roger Clinton disappeared insofar as being portrayed as an extension of the administration.

There could, of course, be competing explanations for the effect that both brothers had on governing. It could be that Jimmy Carter simply never stood a chance to prove himself regardless of how he nurtured his relationship with the press. Perhaps Carter's presidency was so close to Watergate that any president, despite who he was, would not have stood a chance. Further, maybe Carter was a victim of circumstances that were beyond his control. The recession, the Soviet invasion of Afghanistan, and the sacking of the United States Embassy in Iran happened to occur on his watch. He did not "cause" these things to happen.

It also could be that Roger Clinton was easier to influence than Billy Clinton. Many in the Carter family noted Billy's strong will and hard head. He should have altered his behavior just because his brother happened to be president? That did not seem to be the "Billy" way. Roger, however, acknowledged on a couple of occasions how much he admired his big brother and wished to do whatever he could to help. When he was acting up, it may have been the case that what influenced him to behave appropriately was a phone call from his half-brother Bill.

As noted at the beginning of this paper, being the relative of a president is much more difficult than being a staff person to the president. The staff may always quit. For the relative, their actions are always potential fodder for the press. As Billy's wife, Sybil, bitterly noted:

> The bottom line is that members of the president's family have no rights. They cannot speak to who they want to, they cannot have friends in their home, they cannot travel to foreign countries. They're supposed to dig a hole and put their heads in the sand. They are not American citizens. They have no rights.[109]

NOTES TO CHAPTER 6

I wish to thank several people for their valuable assistance in helping me to develop this paper. Nicole Spencer at the Kettering Foundation and Betsy Wyatt at Wright State University provided valuable editorial assistance. Ryan Barilleaux, Robert Hans, and Sandy Hans provided valuable feedback on earlier drafts of this paper. James Fallows at the *Atlantic Monthly* was kind enough to return an e-mail seeking clarification of an issue that arose during the research of this paper. Robert Watson has been a tremendous help in providing the opportunity to do this research, and without him none of this would have been possible. Of course, any errors are the sole responsibility of the author.

1. See Martha Joynt Kumar, "The Contemporary Presidency...," 2001.

2. Ann McFeatters, "Plenty of Fruits on Presidential Family Trees," 1994, C6.

3. Ibid.

4. Ibid.

5. See, for instance, Greig Geordie, "Oh Brother!...," 1994, 63–64.

6. Harry F. Rosenthal, "His Brother's Reaper?" 1980.

7. "Raging Roger; Bill Clinton's Younger Brother Roger," Eye to Eye with Connie Chung, June 17, 1993.

8. Giles Whittell, "The First Brother Changes His Tune," 1994.

9. Geordie, 1994, 63–64.

10. Jimmy Carter, *Keeping Faith ...*, 1984, 544.

11. David Finkel, "Billy Comes Home to Plains," 1987, A1.

12. See Rosenthal, 1980.

13. Carter, 1984, 544–545.

14. See Rosenthal, 1980.

15. Arthur Power Dudden, "The Record of Political Humor," 1985, 67–68.

16. Finkel, 1987, A1.

17. Ibid.

18. Ibid.

19. Bob Sipchen, "Billy Carter Is Back," 1988, 1.

20. Ibid.

21. Richard Pearson, "Billy Carter...," 1988, D6.

22. Finkel, 1987, A1.

23. Margot Dougherty and Joyce Leviton, "Holding His Own Against Cancer...," 1988, 42.

24. Sipchen, 1988, 1.

25. See Geordie, 1994.

26. Pearson, 1988, D6.

27. Carter, 1984, 545.

28. Finkel, 1987, A1.

29. Pearson, 1988, D6.

30. Sally Quinn, "Billy Carter Besieged and Beset," 1980, A1.

31. Quinn, 1980, A1.

32. Ibid.

33. Ibid.

34. Ira R. Allen, "Billy Carter Suggests to President . . . ," 1980.

35. Ibid.

36. Martin Schram, "The Troubled Times . . . ," 1979, A1.

37. Ibid.

38. Clyde Haberman, "Koch Stance is Worrying Carter Aides," 1980, A14.

39. Carter, 1984, 550.

40. Ibid.

41. "Chronology on Libya," 1980, A11.

42. Under 22 USC section 611 (the Foreign Agent Registration Act), Bill Carter would have to register as a foreign lobbyist if he received direct payments for the purpose of advancing the Libyan cause before any governmental official or agency.

43. Mark Rozell, *The Press and the Carter Presidency*, 1989, 168.

44. "Chronology on Libya," 1980, A11.

46. Ibid.

47. Ibid.

48. Ibid.

49. Ibid.; these loads had no written agreement regarding repayment obligations.

50. Ibid.

51. "Dark Days at the White House," 1980, 17.

52. "Chronology on Libya," 1980, A11.

53. "Dark Days at the White House," 1980, 17.

54. Ibid.

55. "Chronology on Libya," 1980, A11.

56. Ibid.

57. "Dark Days at the White House," 1980, 17.

58. Rozell, 1989, 170.

59. Quoted in Rozell, 1989, 168.

60. See Geordie, 1994, 63–64.

61. George Gordon, "Clinton's Brawling Brother Accused," 1993, 10.

62. Michael Kelly, "Seizing the Day . . . ," 1993, A12.

63. Anthony Violanti Janza, "Broken Punk," 1993.

64. Chuck Philips, "What a Difference a Year Makes . . . ," 1993, F1.

65. Patrick Coburn, "Big Brother Is Watching . . . ," 1993, 16.

66. Ibid.

67. See Geordie, 1994, 63–64.

68. Larry McShane, "The First Brother Bites . . . ," 1993.

69. Ibid.

70. Geordie, 1994, 63–64. The nature of the abuse stemmed from negative comments the fan, a New York stockbroker, had been making about Bill Clinton and Roger Clinton's fifteen minutes of fame.

71. Gordon, 1993, 10.

72. McShane, 1993.

73. "Raging Brother . . . ," 1993 interview.

74. Ibid.

75. Ibid.

76. Ibid.

77. Ernie Freda, "Washington in Brief," 1994, A11.

78. Philips, 1993, F1.

79. "Roger Clinton Is VIP . . . ," AP 1999.

80. "Don't Confuse 'Entertainer' with 'Envoy,' " 1999, A2.

81. "Transcript of White House Press Briefing . . . ," FNS 1999.

82. The *Washington Times* ran an editorial that argued that the "spectacle of Roger on stage" made one "long for the good old days of Billy Carter." "Swingtime in Pyongyang," 1999, A14.

83. See Samuel Kernell, *Going Public,* 1993.

84. See Richard Neustadt, *Presidential Power and the Modern Presidents . . .*, 1990.

85. See Jeffrey Tulis, *The Rhetorical Presidency,* 1987; see Barbara Hickley, *The Symbolic Presidency . . .*, 1990.

86. Paul Haskell Zernicke, *Pitching the Presidency . . .*, 1994. 5.

87. See Thomas Patterson, *Out of Order,* 1993; Joseph Cappella and Kathleen Hall Jamieson, *Spiral of Cynicism . . .*, 1997.

88. See Timothy E. Cook, *Governing with the News . . .*, 1998; John Anthony Maltese, *Spin Control . . .*, 1994. The tactic of the administration of George W. Bush has refined this to the "line of the week" in which they get a week's worth of coverage out of a single story.

89. Maltese, 1994, 150.

90. Smoller, 1990, 75.

91. Robert Scheer, "Jimmy, We Hardly Know Y'All," 1976, 96.

92. Jody Powell, *The Other Side of the Story,* 1984, 207.

93. Mark Rozell, "President Carter and the Press . . .," 1990, 421; James Fallows, who worked in the White House, wrote in an Atlantic Monthly column that Carter so misunderstood the speech-making process that he once took two diametrically opposed position papers on foreign policy, stapled them together, and read from the text. James Fallows, "The Passionless Presidency," 1979, 38–46.

94. Powell, 1984, 205.

95. Ibid., 207.

96. Rita K. Whillock, "The Compromising Cliton . . .," 1996, 130–131.

97. Quoted in Eric Alterman, *The Sound and the Fury . . .*, 1992, 84.

98. Rozell, 1990, 77.

99. Ibid.

100. Ibid., 78.

101. Ibid., 77.

102. Fallows, 1979, 46.

103. Ibid., 38.

104. Ibid.

105. Ibid.

106. Ibid.

107. Ibid.

108. See Geordie, 1994, 63.

109. Quinn, 1980, A1.

Seven

First Sons versus First Daughters: A Gender Bias in News Media Coverage?

Lori Cox Han

INTRODUCTION

P
residents and their family members have always fascinated
Americans. Even from the early days of the republic, during
the first presidential administration of George Washington,
members of the first family attained celebrity status and "thrust
upon them immediately were the responsibilities of social exem-
plars and political symbols."[1] While many first ladies have played
an important role in their husband's administrations, especially
from a public relations standpoint,[2] first children have also earned
their share of media attention and public scrutiny throughout the
years. While many children of presidents have managed to live
more "normal" lives than their parents, the public pressure to be
successful "can sometimes prove daunting . . . [since] how they live—
and are raised—remains potent fodder for the media and the opposition party as well as for internal presidential public relations."[3]

   In 1981, political scientist and presidential scholar Barbara
Kellerman examined the political significance of presidential family members, who she believed had been neglected by scholars and
journalists alike by taking presidential family members "at face
value, as a pleasant bit of background" and assuming that their
only role was to "decorate, embellish, and entertain."[4] According
to Kellerman, the only presidential family members during the
twentieth century to be taken seriously as political players in

Washington were first ladies Eleanor Roosevelt and Rosalynn Carter (written obviously before Hillary Rodham Clinton's tenure as first lady), and Robert Kennedy (who served as U.S. Attorney General during his brother's administration). Otherwise, the president's kin had been relegated as figures within "popular culture" whose lives were found most often chronicled in the pages of women's magazines such as *McCall's* and *Ladies' Home Journal.*[5] However, Kellerman observed that since 1960 presidential family members had played a much more significant role in the day-to-day operation of an administration due to several factors: the decline of political parties and increased number of presidential primaries, the increased importance of television's role in the political process, and the personalization of the presidency (all tied to what is commonly referred to as the candidate-centered era of politics).[6]

PRESIDENTIAL CHILDREN IN THE SPOTLIGHT

America's Royalty

Several presidential children throughout the years, for better or worse, have found themselves in the national spotlight. Through the administration of George W. Bush, 42 men have held the office of the presidency; six had no children and the remaining 36 fathered a total of 159 children (2 were adopted and 8 were accepted as illegitimate offspring). In their book *America's Royalty: All the Presidents' Children*, Sandra L. Quinn-Musgrove and Sanford Kanter write that children of presidents enjoy a life that is "somewhat larger than the ordinary." However, they remind us that "first" children enjoy a unique position within American society since they "hold a special intrigue perhaps merely by virtue of their infrequency" and that "such attention reflects a constant curiosity, indeed even fascination, about children of powerful and successful leaders."[7]

E. H. Gwynne Thomas, who has also studied presidential families, notes that presidents and their wives endure some of the same trials and tribulations of raising their children as do ordinary Americans, and that sometimes being the first son or daughter exacerbates the challenges of child rearing. Many presidential children have been "unimpressed" by their special status and often "have overtly displayed . . . resentment and anger against the White House goldfish bowl experience, by which every minor character idiosyncrasy or irrelevant behavior is accorded nationwide scrutiny, exposure, and publicity, to the embarrassment and humiliation of children and parents alike."[8]

Perhaps no presidential child garnered more public attention in her day than did Alice Roosevelt Longworth, eldest daughter of Theodore Roosevelt. Considered in her youth a "female version of the man about town" and later as the "grande dame" of Washington, D.C. society, she married Ohio congressman Nicholas Longworth, who would later become Speaker of the House of Representatives, during a White House ceremony in 1906. Known for her sharp wit and candid political observations, she continued as a public fascination until her death at the age of ninety-six in 1980.[9]

First Sons

Alice Roosevelt notwithstanding, presidential sons remained a more important topic for press, pundits, and scholars throughout most of American history. For example, in 1947, historian J. J. Perling wrote *First Sons*, a book in which he sought to provide a better understanding of the impact of being the male offspring of a United States president. Perling stated, "Even in a democracy there is prestige of name," and proceeded to offer his scholarly account of the careers and accomplishments of all presidential sons from the administrations of George Washington (who had one stepson and step-grandson by wife Martha's first marriage) through the Franklin Roosevelt administration. Perling concluded that James, Elliott, Franklin, Jr., and John Roosevelt, the four surviving sons of FDR (one son died before his first birthday), had raised the public interest in presidential sons to new heights, since "no other sons whose fathers occupied the White House have aroused so much curiosity, comment, or criticism; every episode in their careers has kindled nationwide interest—their marriages, their money-making, their medals, their dividends, their divorces, their dogs."[10] He also noted that the then-current record must end with FDR's sons since the "only child of his successor, Harry Truman, is a daughter," and that "certain it is that their names will often appear in public print—they are a President's sons."[11]

While nearly six decades old, Perling's study nonetheless raises an intriguing question—Do "first sons" receive more public attention through news media coverage than do "first daughters?" This chapter analyzes how the news media has covered children of presidents during the television age of politics. Specifically, it addresses the issue of how first sons are covered in comparison to first daughters, and considers whether or not there is a substantive difference, a quantitative difference, or both based on gender. Among the questions considered are: Do first sons more often make news from the perspective of following in dad's footsteps into the real world—academic, business, and/or political ambitions? And do first daughters more often make news from the perspective of the society page—engagements, weddings, fashion, having children? Or does the pattern of news coverage of first children more often reflect the personalities of not only the individual son or daughter, but that of the president as well?

Analyzing Presidential Children

This chapter will consider the children of seven recent occupants of the White House, beginning with the children of Lyndon Johnson and ending with Chelsea Clinton, the only child of Bill Clinton. This study begins in the 1960s, a decade when the television age firmly took hold of its role in chronicling the president's political and personal daily life. However, the analysis does not begin with the children of John F. Kennedy—Caroline and John, Jr.—who are considered to be "members of the most photographed family in American history."[12] The lives of the Kennedy children from their earliest days—Caroline would turn six and John, Jr. three within days of their father's assassination on November 22, 1963—have been well documented by both the national and international news media. Subsequent first children have not reached the same level of celebrity status and have all been older than the Kennedy children during their fathers' respective administrations. Therefore, the study begins at the start of the Johnson administration in late 1963, and will assess news media coverage of first children during the time period that their father served in the White House.

A content analysis and case study approach is used to analyze coverage of first children in two news mediums: a national newspaper (the *New York Times*) and television network news (ABC, CBS, and NBC newscasts beginning in 1969 through available data in the Vanderbilt Television Archives). The stories were content analyzed by topic and included the following categories: Education; Honors/Awards; Jobs/Careers; Religion; Travel; Security; Health; Holidays/ Special Events; Official/Political Appearances; Fashion; Weddings; Births; Dating/Engagements; Arrests/ Investigations; and Miscellaneous.

THE JOHNSON DAUGHTERS

The Johnson daughters—Lynda Bird (born in 1944) and Luci Baines (born in 1947)—each took turns capturing the attention of the national news media during their father's administration. Lynda, the eldest daughter, graduated from the University of Texas and dated Hollywood heartthrob George Hamilton during her White House years, and later married future Virginia governor and U.S. senator, Charles Robb, in 1967 in the first White House wedding ceremony since Alice Roosevelt's nuptials in 1906.[13] While Lynda had been considered the "smartest one" by her father, younger daughter Luci had a closer relationship with President Johnson.

Luci made more headlines of her own during her father's administration, beginning with the decision in 1964 to change the spelling of her name from "Lucy" to "Luci." In 1965, at the age of eighteen, she converted to Catholicism, and married Patrick Nugent the following year in the National Cathedral on the twenty-first anniversary of the dropping of the atomic bomb on Hiroshima. Both of the Johnson son-in-laws served in Vietnam, and both had been sent to the region in 1968, the year that Johnson announced his decision not to seek his party's nomination for reelection.[14] Johnson once turned to Luci "for momentary solace during the Vietnam War . . . Late at night, in the middle of one crisis, he asked her . . . to take him to a local church where he knelt with her in prayer for strength, and sought guidance from local monks who knew Luci."[15]

The lives of both Johnson daughters were regularly chronicled in the pages of the *New York Times* between late 1963 and January 1969. A total of 237 stories about Lynda and 200 stories about Luci appeared in the newspaper during their father's administration. Most stories for both daughters focused on similar topics: whom they dated, their respective engagements and weddings, travel plans, and details of their married lives. Luci's wedding, which occurred one year prior to her sister's wedding, received extensive coverage on all aspects of the planning, leading up to the actual event at the National Cathedral. Lynda's wedding received half the number of stories in comparison, but still made headlines as the first White House wedding in six decades. (See Tables 7.1 and 7.2.)

Table 7.1. *New York Times* Coverage of Lynda Bird Johnson

Lynda Bird Johnson	1963–64	1965	1966	1967	1968–69
Education	2	1	5	0	0
Honors/Awards	0	1	0	0	1
Job/Career	1	0	11	3	0
Religion	1	0	0	0	0
Travel	2	14	26	7	12
Security	4	1	1	2	0
Health	0	1	2	0	0
Holidays/Events	1	2	9	7	0
Political appearances	6	3	2	4	1
Fashion	0	2	2	3	1
Weddings	0	0	0	26	0
Births	0	0	0	0	9
Dating/Engagement	3	5	19	14	0
Miscellaneous	1	3	5	4	7
TOTAL	21	33	82	70	31

Table 7.2. *New York Times* Coverage of Luci Baines Johnson

Luci Baines Johnson	1963–64	1965	1966	1967	1968–69
Education	3	4	2	3	0
Honors/Awards	6	3	0	0	0
Job/Career	1	1	0	0	0
Religion	0	11	2	0	0
Travel	0	1	8	7	7
Security	2	0	0	0	0
Health	3	0	0	0	0
Holidays/Events	1	1	5	3	2
Political appearances	4	3	3	0	0
Fashion	1	0	2	0	0
Weddings	0	0	50	0	0
Births	0	0	0	12	0
Dating/Engagement	3	14	8	0	0
Miscellaneous	0	5	10	7	2
TOTAL	24	43	90	32	11

THE NIXON DAUGHTERS

The Nixon daughters—Patricia (born in 1946 and known as "Tricia") and Julie (born in 1948)—were considered opposites, yet shared one important quality in their loyalty to their father during the Watergate investigation. The Nixon family exhibited "certainly one of the closest of parent-child relationships" of all White House families, evidenced in the months leading up to Nixon's resignation in 1974: "In the darkest last days of his administration, as others began abandoning him, Nixon's daughters had such an unconditional love for him that they accepted his explanation of his role in the cover-up of the scandal and bucked him up emotionally."[16]

Tricia, who sought privacy from the press during her White House years, married Edward Cox in the first-ever outdoor wedding at the White House on June 12, 1971, one day prior to the first installment of the *Times'* stories on the Pentagon Papers.[17] Younger daughter Julie, considered "extroverted, gregarious, and constantly active," had married her college sweetheart in 1968— David Dwight Eisenhower, grandson of President Dwight D. Eisenhower (in whose administration her father served as vice president).[18]

The Nixon daughters received approximately half the coverage in the *New York Times* during their White House years as had the Johnson daughters, yet still provided the national news media an opportunity to chronicle their education, family life, travels, and support of their father's administration. Tricia received slightly more news coverage in both the *Times* and on the three television network newscasts than her sister Julie, due mostly to coverage surrounding Tricia's 1971 wedding (Julie held her wedding on December 22 1968, less than one month prior to her father's inauguration). Julie made news on accepting a teaching position at a Florida elementary school in 1971, first due to the complaints of some teachers in the district that she had received preferential treatment in being assigned to a nonghetto school just blocks from her apartment, and then when she broke her toe on her second day on the job.[19] At various times, particularly during the Watergate investigation, each daughter also spoke openly and publicly about their support for their father; Julie made 150 public appearances in support of her father in 1973. (See Tables 7.3–7.6.)

Table 7.3. *New York Times* Coverage of Tricia Nixon

Tricia Nixon	1969	1970	1971	1972	1973	1974
Honors/Awards	2	2	0	0	0	0
Job/Career	1	1	0	1	0	0
Travel	4	3	4	1	1	0
Security	0	0	0	1	0	0
Health	3	3	1	0	4	0
Holidays/Events	7	5	4	1	2	0
Political appearances	5	4	2	3	3	0
Fashion	2	2	2	0	0	0
Weddings	0	0	28	0	0	0
Dating/Engagement	2	2	3	0	0	0
Miscellaneous	3	3	5	1	2	2
TOTAL	29	25	49	8	12	2

Table 7.4. Network News Coverage of Tricia Nixon

Tricia Nixon	1969	1970	1971	1972	1973	1974
Honors/Awards	0	1	0	0	0	0
Travel	0	0	0	2	0	2
Health	7	1	0	0	0	0
Holidays/Events	6	3	1	5	1	0
Political appearances	3	5	1	10	0	3
Weddings	0	0	11	0	0	0
Dating/Engagement	1	3	9	0	0	0
Miscellaneous	0	0	0	0	2	2
TOTAL	17	13	22	17	3	7

Table 7.5. *New York Times* Coverage of Julie Nixon Eisenhower

Julie Eisenhower	1969	1970	1971	1972	1973	1974
Education	2	4	0	0	0	0
Honors/Awards	0	0	0	0	0	2
Job/Career	2	0	5	0	1	2
Travel	4	3	7	5	3	0
Health	0	2	2	3	0	10
Holidays/Events	7	5	3	1	2	0
Political appearances	0	6	0	3	1	0
Fashion	0	1	0	0	0	0
Weddings	1	0	0	0	0	0
Miscellaneous	3	3	4	1	3	1
TOTAL	19	24	21	13	19	15

Table 7.6. Network News Coverage of Julie Nixon Eisenhower

Julie Eisenhower	1969	1970	1971	1972	1973	1974
Education	0	1	0	0	0	0
Job/Career	4	0	3	0	1	0
Religion	0	0	0	0	0	1
Travel	3	0	0	1	2	2
Security	2	0	0	0	0	0
Health	1	1	0	0	2	8
Holidays/Events	2	1	4	2	0	3
Political appearances	0	3	1	7	0	2
Miscellaneous	0	0	0	0	12	1
TOTAL	12	6	8	10	17	17

THE FORD CHILDREN

The Ford children—Michael (born in 1950), John (born in 1952 and known as "Jack"), Steven (born in 1956), and Susan (born in 1957)—were thrust onto the national scene as quickly as their father had been when Gerald Ford became vice president in October 1973 (on Spiro Agnew's resignation) and president in August 1974 (on Nixon's resignation). Susan was the only Ford child to live at the White House for any length of time. She graduated from high school in 1975 and her senior prom was held at the White House. Like previous first daughters, Susan's dating habits were watched in the national news media, although not as closely as Lynda and Luci Johnson or Tricia Nixon (perhaps aided by the fact that she was one of four Ford children). While living in the White House, Susan developed a friendship with White House photographer David Kennerly, which prompted her own interest in photography, including a chance to study with famed photographer Ansel Adams. Susan also traveled to China with her parents in 1975, and was embarrassed by her mother Betty's comments in a 1976 interview with Morley Safer of *60 Minutes* that she would not be surprised if Susan were having an affair. The remark, along with the First Lady's comment that her children had probably experimented with marijuana, caused much public controversy and some embarrassment for all four children.[20]

Susan's three older brothers were not considered as newsworthy; Michael was enrolled in divinity school when his father became president; Jack had studied forestry at Utah State University and worked for the National Forest Service; and Steve worked on a cattle ranch in Montana before pursuing an acting career in the late 1970s. The Ford children were often viewed as "extensions" of their father, having little identity of their own yet important in various public relations roles for the president. During his thirty months in office, Ford was faced with the challenge of bringing the office of the presidency back to the American people following Watergate, and his children were viewed as more typically middle-class than had the Johnson or Nixon daughters, who were perceived more as American royalty. (Susan was noted as being the first presidential daughter to ever wear blue jeans in the White House).[21] As Kellerman observed in 1981, "[T]he Ford offspring lacked their own identity, never did anything that really stood out, and now, a scant few years after their photos dotted the 'People' section of *Time* with what some would insist was depressing regularity, are only rather vaguely recalled."[22]

Susan received much more news media attention than her three brothers, yet much less than the Johnson and Nixon daughters. In total, Susan received thirty-seven stories in the *New York Times* and twenty-nine network news stories during her father's White House tenure. (See Tables 7.7 and 7.8) The Ford sons received the following coverage: Michael garnered a total of two *Times* stories and five network news stories; Jack a total of nine *Times* stories and thirteen network news stories (including his invitations to celebrities like Chris Evert, Bianca Jagger, and George Harrison to the White House); and Steve a total of six *Times* stories and eight network news stories.

Table 7.7. *New York Times* Coverage of Susan Ford

Susan Ford	1974	1975	1976–77
Education	1	4	1
Honors/Awards	0	2	0
Job/Career	1	10	2
Travel	0	1	0
Health	0	1	1
Holidays/Events	0	3	0
Political appearances	1	0	0
Fashion	0	2	1
Dating/Engagement	1	1	0
Miscellaneous	0	1	3
TOTAL	4	25	8

Table 7.8. Network News Coverage of Susan Ford

Susan Ford	1974	1975	1976–77
Education	0	3	0
Job/Career	0	2	0
Travel	1	6	0
Health	0	0	1
Holidays/Events	2	2	0
Political appearances	1	0	4
Fashion	0	1	0
Dating/Engagement	1	3	0
Miscellaneous	2	0	0
TOTAL	7	17	5

THE CARTER CHILDREN

The news media paid little attention to the three Carter sons—John (born in 1947 and known as "Jack"), James Earl III (born in 1950 and known as "Chip"), and Donnell Jeffrey (born in 1952 and known as "Jeff")—during his administration. Jack, a Vietnam veteran, was an attorney and businessman; Chip, the most politically active of the Carter children, worked for the Democratic National Committee and made several public appearances on his father's behalf during the Carter administration (he divorced his first wife in 1978); and Jeff, who maintained the lowest public profile during his father's White House tenure, graduated from George Washington University and began a career in computer consulting.

Each of the sons and their wives campaigned extensively for Carter during the 1976 presidential campaign.[23] Chip received more coverage than his two brothers during their White House years with a total of nine stories in the *New York Times* and fifty-three stories on the network news (due mostly to political appearances on his father's behalf). (See Tables 7.9 and 7.10.) In comparison, Jack garnered only two stories in the *Times* and fourteen network news stories during the four-year period, while Jeff received three stories in the *Times* and only seven network news stories.

Table 7.9. *New York Times* Coverage of Chip Carter

Chip Carter	1977	1978	1979	1980–81
Job/Career	0	1	0	0
Travel	0	4	1	0
Miscellaneous	0	1	0	2
TOTAL	0	6	1	2

Table 7.10. Network News Coverage of Chip Carter

Chip Carter	1977	1978	1979	1980–81
Job/Career	1	0	0	0
Travel	7	2	2	1
Health	2	0	0	0
Holidays/Events	2	0	1	0
Political appearances	9	1	11	6
Dating/Engagement	0	0	0	0
Arrests/Investigations	1	0	0	2
Miscellaneous	1	3	0	1
TOTAL	23	6	14	10

The level of public attention for youngest child Amy (born in 1967) was much different than for her brothers. At first, the presence of a young child in the White House (she was nine when her father was inaugurated) seemed reminiscent of the young Kennedy children and the positive image they created for their father's administration. However, Amy's press coverage was not always positive, and at times seemed to "have merely been the object of press barbs really directed at her father."[24] Issues over Amy's schooling immediately made news— the Carters had wanted Amy to attend a public school, the first time a president's child had done so since the Theodore Roosevelt administration. However, the spectacle of Secret Service agents caused quite a disruption to the school's daily routine. Other stories that fascinated the press and public about Amy included her nanny (a convicted murderer who later received a complete pardon by the State of Georgia), unsolicited gifts from well-wishers (most notably a deluge of chain saws sent to the White House when reporters misunderstood Amy's wish for a train set for Christmas), and her attendance at State dinners where, out of boredom, she read books at the table. Perhaps the low point of Amy's notoriety during her father's administration, at least from the President's perspective, came during the 1980 presidential debates with Republican nominee Ronald Reagan, when Carter stated that in a conversation with then-thirteen-year-old Amy that her biggest political concern was nuclear proliferation. The remark was widely lambasted by reporters and comics alike.[25]

During her father's four years in the White House, Amy was often viewed as a "decoration" in that Americans

> never had a passionate interest in what she—who was, after all, only a child—said, or even specifically in what she did. The appeal was in her little girlishness. And the fascination was with the juxtaposition between this girlishness and the hectic political environment in which it was being displayed.[26]

In total, Amy received forty-three stories in the *New York Times* and sixty-nine stories on the network news, far outpacing coverage of all three of her older brothers during the Carter administration. (See Tables 7.11 and 7.12)

Table 7.11. *New York Times* Coverage of Amy Carter

Amy Carter	1977	1978	1979	1980–81
Education	5	3	0	0
Religion	2	0	0	0
Travel	1	3	0	0
Security	1	1	1	0
Health	0	0	1	0
Holidays/Events	2	1	1	0
Political appearances	1	0	0	1
Miscellaneous	16	1	1	1
TOTAL	28	9	4	2

Table 7.12. Network News Coverage of Amy Carter

Amy Carter	1977	1978	1979	1980–81
Education	6	1	1	0
Religion	3	0	0	0
Travel	4	10	8	2
Holidays/Events	9	8	5	2
Political appearances	1	1	2	1
Fashion	2	0	0	0
Miscellaneous	3	0	0	0
TOTAL	28	20	16	5

THE REAGAN CHILDREN

Ronald Reagan was just shy of his seventieth birthday when he took the oath of office in 1981. As such, his four children were all adults during their father's White House years—Maureen (born in 1941 to Reagan and his first wife, actress Jane Wyman), Michael (born in 1945 and adopted as an infant by Reagan and Wyman), Patricia (born in 1952 to Reagan and his second wife Nancy, known as Patti Davis after she took her mother's maiden name as an adult), and Ronald (born in 1958 and known as "Ron," his previous nickname has been "Skip"). During the Reagan administration, Reagan's children "spoke publicly about a gulf between them and their father" and regular visits to the White House did not occur by any of the children until the second term, most often by Maureen. As has been noted by many Reagan observers, "his bond and reliance were never with [his children] but with his wife—a point even more dramatically illustrated during his presidency."[27]

During their father's eight years in office, only Maureen received any regular attention in the news media. An outspoken advocate for the Equal Rights Amendment in the early 1980s, Maureen nonetheless was an active supporter of her father's presidential campaigns and presidency. After trying her hand in show business, she ran unsuccessfully in the California Republican primary for a U.S. Senate seat in 1982, followed by frequent work in radio and television and eventually a career in the export business. (Maureen died in 2001 following a battle with skin cancer.) Each of her siblings also pursued careers in show business, in addition to other professional pursuits. Michael achieved success as a speedboat racer, achieved notoriety in 1981 when he tried to profit from his father's name to solicit clients while employed as a marketing salesman by an aerospace defense contractor, wrote an autobiography in 1987, and has since enjoyed success as a radio talk show host. Patti's relationship with her parents was often stormy during the White House years. Considered "the family rebel," Patti occasionally made news during the 1980s with disdainful comments about her parents; she married yoga instructor Paul Grilley in 1984 in California and was given away by her father, and wrote a somewhat autobiographical novel titled *Home Front* in 1986. Ron toured as part of the New York Joffrey Ballet in the early 1980s, and made headlines for accepting unemployment benefits in 1982. He has since pursued a successful career in print, radio, and television journalism.[28]

With the exception of Maureen's coverage on television news, the Reagan children received little coverage during their father's eight years in the White House. In the *New York Times*, Maureen received a total of four stories (all in 1981); Michael twelve stories (all in 1981); Patti five stories; and Ron six stories. On the three television networks, Maureen received a total of seventy-three stories, due in part to her political appearances on her father's behalf (see Table 7.13). In comparison, Michael received a total of eighteen stories, Patti fourteen stories, and Ron nine stories on television news.

Table 7.13. Network News Coverage of Maureen Reagan

Maureen Reagan	1981	1982	1983	1984	1985	1986	1987	1988 –89
Job/Career	7	13	0	1	0	0	2	0
Security	0	0	0	0	1	0	0	0
Health	5	0	0	0	3	0	0	0
Holidays/Events	3	0	0	2	0	0	0	0
Political appearances	0	0	11	6	5	4	1	1
Weddings	2	0	0	0	0	0	0	0
Miscellaneous	0	0	0	0	0	0	4	2
TOTAL	17	13	11	9	9	4	7	3

THE BUSH CHILDREN

Like Reagan, the five children of George H. W. Bush were all grown when their father entered the White House in 1989. The four sons and one daughter included George W. (born in 1946), John Ellis (born in 1953 and known as "Jeb"), Neil (born in 1955), Marvin (born in 1956), and Dorothy (born in 1959 and known as "Doro"). George and Barbara Bush also had a daughter, named Robin, who died of leukemia just prior to her fourth birthday in 1953. Despite the future political fortunes of the two oldest Bush sons that would prompt many discussions of a political dynasty, the Bush children received little, if any, national press attention during their father's four years in the White House. During that time, George W., previously an oil and gas executive in Texas, had become a managing partner of the Texas Rangers baseball team (followed by twice being elected Texas governor in 1994 and 1998 prior to his presidential election in 2000). Jeb, a successful real estate developer in Florida, had become active in the Florida Republican Party by 1992 (and ran unsuccessfully for governor of Florida in 1994, but won the office in 1998). Neil, who has pursued various business ventures in oil and gas and banking, received public notoriety due to his involvement with a failed Savings and Loan in Denver along with the rash of S&L failures during the late 1980s. The two youngest Bush children, Marvin and Doro, have rarely been the subjects of press coverage. Both have pursued business careers, and Doro became the first presidential family member to wed at Camp David in 1992.

Of all five Bush children, only Marvin garnered a story (about he and his wife's adoption of a child in 1990) in the *New York Times* during his father's administration. While Neil was mentioned in a variety of stories in the *Times* involving the S&L scandal throughout his father's term in office, no story appeared that focused solely on the president's son. Coverage of the Bush children was also sparse on network television, with the exception of Neil, who was a part of thirty-two stories in 1990 dealing with the S&L scandal, followed by two in 1991 and one in 1992. In comparison, George W. received a total of three network news stories (two of which discussed his role in his father's 1992 reelection campaign); Jeb received five stories (three of which focused on political appearances on behalf of his father); Doro received three stories (two of which focused on her 1992 wedding); while Marvin had no coverage on the network news.

THE CLINTON DAUGHTER

The only child of Bill and Hillary Rodham Clinton, Chelsea (born in 1980) turned thirteen within weeks of her father's inauguration. Determined that Chelsea's White House experience would not be similar to Amy Carter's, her parents were aided in their attempt to shield their daughter from the spotlight when Margaret Truman wrote a March 1993 Letter to the Editor of the *New York Times* about the damage that would be done if the press invaded Chelsea's life as reporters had done to her. Chelsea attended a private school in Washington, and rarely made news until her high school graduation in 1997 when speculation began as to her choice of colleges. She received the most press coverage of her father's eight years in the White House that fall when she entered Stanford University as a freshman. With the exception of a *People* magazine cover story in 1999, which brought a stern rebuke from the White House, Chelsea avoided much of the media spotlight during her father's two terms in office. Chelsea received a total of thirty-two stories in the *New York Times*, and a total of eighty-seven network news stories between January 1993 and January 2001. (See Tables 7.14 and 7.15)

Table 7.14. *New York Times* **Coverage of Chelsea Clinton**

Chelsea Clinton	1993	1994	1995	1996	1997	1998	1999	2000 –01
Education	5	1	0	1	6	0	0	1
Travel	0	0	1	0	3	0	0	0
Security	0	0	0	0	3	0	0	0
Holidays/Events	1	0	0	1	0	0	0	0
Political appearances	0	0	0	0	1	0	0	0
Miscellaneous	3	0	0	0	1	0	3	1
TOTAL	9	1	1	2	14	0	3	2

Table 7.15. Network News Coverage of Chelsea Clinton

Chelsea Clinton	1993	1994	1995	1996	1997	1998	1999	2000 –01
Education	5	0	0	0	15	0	0	0
Travel	0	0	6	10	3	6	2	7
Security	1	0	0	0	3	0	2	0
Health	0	0	0	0	0	2	0	0
Holidays/Events	2	0	1	1	6	0	2	1
Political appearances	0	0	0	0	1	0	0	0
Dating/Engagement	0	0	0	0	0	1	0	0
Miscellaneous	2	0	0	2	2	1	3	0
TOTAL	10	0	7	13	30	10	9	8

Does Gender Bias Exist in News Coverage of First Children?

When considering the overall amount of news coverage in both the *New York Times* and on the three television networks from November 1963 through January 2001 of all twenty-two presidential children, several trends emerge. First, no presidential children rivaled the attention in the *New York Times* of the Johnson daughters during their five-plus years in the White House (television data is not available for this time period), followed by the Nixon daughters, Amy Carter, Susan Ford, and Chelsea Clinton. Chelsea Clinton received the most coverage on television, followed closely by Tricia Nixon, Maureen Reagan, Julie Nixon, and Amy Carter. However, only Chelsea Clinton and Maureen Reagan had time periods that spanned eight years; data on the Nixon daughters includes five years and nearly seven months, while Amy Carter's data includes four years worth of coverage. Chip Carter and Neil Bush are the only first sons that rival first daughters in amount of television news coverage, since Chip was somewhat active in his father's political activities and Neil was part of the S&L scandal and subsequent investigation. (See Table 7.16)

When considering the question of gender bias in news coverage, several trends also emerge. First daughters, at least since 1963, have received an overwhelming amount of news coverage when compared to their male counterparts. This can be attributed to several factors; while of the twenty-two children considered here there were fewer female children (10) than male (12), the daughters were considerably younger on average than the sons. Also, six of the daughters were married while their fathers were in office (Lynda Bird and Luci Baines Johnson, Tricia Nixon, Maureen Reagan, Patti Davis, and Doro Bush), a popular story line for the press to follow. The top-story categories (excluding the miscellaneous category) for first daughters included Travel, followed by Holidays/Social Events, Political Appearances, Weddings, and Dating/Engagements. The top-story categories for first sons (excluding the miscellaneous category) included Arrests/Investigations, followed by Political Appearances, Travel, and Job/Career.

From this collection of data, stories appearing more traditionally on the "women's" pages, "features" pages, or both of newspapers—weddings, engagements, social functions, travel—obviously take precedence when covering presidential children over more traditionally "hard" news stories (with the exception of arrests or investigations, which none of the first daughters considered in this study have had to face). (See Table 7.17) Also, it becomes obvious that younger children tend to generate more news coverage during their father's administration than do older children. Of the ten first daughters, the average age at the start of their father's administration was approximately twenty-one years, while the average age for the twelve first sons was almost twenty-nine years. The youngest daughter was nine-years-old (Amy Carter) compared to the youngest son who was eighteen-years-old (Steve Ford). The oldest daughter was forty-years-old (Maureen Reagan) while the oldest son was forty-two-years-old (George W. Bush).

Table 7.16. News Coverage of Presidential Children 1963–2001

Total Stories per Child	New York Times	TV Network News
(During White House years)		
Luci Baines Johnson	200	N/A
Lynda Bird Johnson	237	N/A
Julie Nixon	102	70
Tricia Nixon	125	79
Jack Ford	9	13
Michael Ford	2	5
Steven Ford	6	8
Susan Ford	37	29
Amy Carter	43	70
Chip Carter	9	53
Jack Carter	2	14
Jeff Carter	3	7
Maureen Reagan	4	73
Michael Reagan	12	18
Patti Davis	5	14
Ron Reagan	6	8
Dorothy Bush	0	3
George W. Bush	0	3
Jeb Bush	0	5
Marvin Bush	1	0
Neil Bush	0	35
Chelsea Clinton	32	87
TOTAL	835	594

Table 7.17. Gender Bias in News Coverage of Presidential Children

Story Topics by Gender	First Sons	First Daughters
Education	4	86
Honors/Awards	0	20
Job/Career	24	76
Religion	0	20
Travel	29	207
Security	1	27
Health	6	69
Holiday/Events	11	152
Political Appearances	47	137
Fashion	0	24
Weddings	0	124
Births	0	21
Dating/Engagement	5	98
Arrests/Investigation	63	0
Miscellaneous	29	149
TOTAL	219	1,210

CONCLUSION

Nearly four decades ago, author Christine Sadler wrote one of the earliest compilations that considered the lives of presidential children. In it, she observed that

> there is no rule by which to measure what the White House "does" to children or by which to determine whether a President's children obtain more sadness than gladness from his tenure in the highest office. It is obvious, however, that tenure in the White House sets the children apart and marks them forever. Some react one way, and some another; but by and large they seem to have become basically the same people they would have been in any event.[29]

However, much has changed politically, culturally, and socially in the past four decades, not the least of which has been the intense media focus on both the president and his family members due to the personalization of the political process and the vast increase in the sheer number of media outlets. And while Chelsea Clinton may have been granted a fairly large zone of privacy, the following administration—that of George W. Bush—and his twin daughters, Jenna and Barbara, raised the issue over whether the children of famous politicians deserve a free pass from the news media. However, when the Bush twins, nineteen-years-old when their father entered office, were cited for underage drinking in June 2001 (the second offense for Jenna), most White House observers agreed that by breaking the law, the girls had given up that zone of privacy enjoyed by Chelsea Clinton.

Presidential children now face mainstream media outlets that often cross over into tabloid-style news "as commercial entities with corporate bottom lines to meet [that] have grown increasingly entertainment driven, blurring traditional journalistic standards."[30] And as *Newsweek* reminded its readers after the Bush twins appeared in court, "the daughter of a president lives in a different world."[31] And in spite of the best efforts of presidential children and their parents, this fact always has, and always will, remain.

NOTES TO CHAPTER SEVEN

Note. The author would like to thank Matt Krov at Austin College for his research assistance with this project.

1. Carl Sferrazza Anthony, *America's First Families* . . . , 2000, 14.

2. See Carl Sferrazza Anthony, *First Ladies* . . . , 1992 and 1993; Robert P. Watson, *First Ladies of the United States* . . . , 2001.

3. Anthony, 2000, 87.

4. Barbara Kellerman, *All the President's Kin*, 1981, ix.

5. Ibid., x.

6. Ibid., 5–19.

7. Sandra L. Quinn-Musgrove and Sanford Kanter, *America's Royalty* . . . , 1995, xxiii–xxiv.

8. E. H. Gwynne Thomas, *The Presidential Families* . . . , 1989, xii.

9. Quinn-Musgrove and Kanter, 1995, 149–151.

10. J. J. Perling, *Presidents' Sons* . . . , 1947, 310.

11. Ibid., viii, 346.

12. Harry Benson, *First Families* . . . , 1997, 59.

13. Quinn-Musgrove and Kanter, 1995, 205–207; Thomas, 1989, 389–397.

14. Quinn-Musgrove and Kanter, 1995, 207–208; Thomas, 1989, 390–396.

15. Anthony, 2000, 91.

16. Ibid., 91.

17. Quin-Musgrove and Kanter, 1995, 211–212.

18. Ibid., 213.

19. Thomas, 1989, 402–404.

20. Ibid., 408–413.

21. Kellerman, 1981, 78–86.

22. Ibid., 79.

23. Quinn-Musgrove and Kanter, 1995, 221–224; Thomas, 1989, 418–420.

24. Quinn-Musgrove and Kanter, 1995, 224.

25. Quinn-Musgrove and Kanter, 1995, 224–225; Thomas, 1989, 420–421.

26. Kellerman, 1981, 56.

27. Anthony, 2000, 56.

28. Quinn-Musgrove and Kanter, 1995, 227–231; Thomas, 1989, 436–444.

29. Christine Sadler, *Children in the White House*, 1967, 13.

30. Alexandra Marks, "First Daughters . . . , 2001, 1.

31. Evan Thomas and Martha Brant, "Busted Again in Margaritaville," 2001, 24.

Part III

Profiles of First Families in the White House

The White House Library (courtesy of the Library of Congress)

Overview:
Calling the White House "Home"

W hen George W. Bush became the forty-third president in
2001 he and his family became only the latest in a long
line of first families to live in the White House. As of the
presidency of George W. Bush, forty-two different families have
called the White House home, as George Washington never served
from the building he helped plan. Washington served his two terms
from residents in New York City and later Philadelphia. Or, as it
might be said, the White House remains the most famous building
Washington never slept in. Grover Cleveland served two nonconsecutive terms (as the twenty-second and twenty-fourth president).
However, the composition of the Cleveland family was different in
each term. The Cleveland household during first term included the
President's sister until Cleveland wed Frances Folsom in office,
while the second term included children.

All these first families were faced with the prospect of some-
how creating a sense of home and normalcy in the President's
House or, as it is now known, the White House. The building
serves both as office and private residence of the president and the
challenge of balancing the public and private realms of life is not
an easy task. Some first families have succeeded, enjoying their
years in the presidency and the building they called home for a few
years, while others were not so fortunate.

The composition of first families has varied considerably
throughout history. Some presidents were alone. For instance, James
Buchanan, the fifteenth president, was a bachelor, although his
adopted niece, Harriet Lane, joined him as presidential hostess.
Grover Cleveland entered the presidency as a bachelor, joined by
his sister who served as his hostess. However, Cleveland married
during his first term and had children while still in office. Thomas

Jefferson, Martin Van Buren, Andrew Jackson, and Chester A. Arthur were all widowers during their presidencies. Jackson, however, was surrounded by members of his extended family and Van Buren's sons joined him in the President's House.

Other presidencies have had several children, grandchildren, and other relatives as part of the first family in the White House. The families of Theodore Roosevelt and Benjamin Harrison were quite large, filling the Executive Mansion with children or grandchildren. James Garfield's mother became the first presidential mother to observe her son being sworn in as president. Garfield's mother, wife Lucretia, daughter Mollie, sons Harry, James, Irvin, and Abram, and other family members and friends joined the president in the home. Sadly, James Garfield's happy family suffered the tragedy of his assassination by Charles Guiteau in 1881, less than one year into the President's term.

Most first families, however, have been smaller than the average size family, although Anna Harrison had ten children. Also, as presidents and first ladies have typically been at least middle-aged, many had children who were already adults. The Polks had no children and the Hardings, Washingtons, Madisons, and Woodrow Wilson and his second wife, Edith Bolling Galt, had no children between them, although Florence Harding, Martha Washington, Dolley Madison, and Edith Wilson all had children from previous marriages. Free of the challenge of raising children in the White House, many presidential spouses channeled their energy to politics and served as political partners in the White House.

Common among most first families is the fact that presidents have generally turned to family members for support, advice, and assistance with the social and official functions of the office and home. Some family members campaigned, others served as personal secretaries, some worked as advisers, and John Kennedy employed his brother, Robert, as Attorney General. For this reason and others, the American public has had a fascination with the first family since George and Martha Washington assumed their role as first presidential couple.

From TV Dinners to Horseshoes: A Sense of "Home"

In creating a sense of home in the building, first families have resorted to a wide variety of social and recreational amenities found in homes across the nation. For instance, in the White House or on the grounds have been tennis courts, a swimming pool, horseshoe pit, movie theater, and other amenities for the enjoyment of the first family. Dwight Eisenhower relaxed by putting golf balls on the lawn, George Bush pitched horseshoes, Bill Clinton jogged on a path around the building, and Eleanor Roosevelt had a swing set installed for her grandchildren. Beginning with the Kennedy family, most recent first families have highlighted the arts and American culture at the White House, hosting musical, theatrical, and other performances both for their entertainment and to promote Americana. The casual, Deep South roots of the Carters were reflected in the informal receptions they hosted, guest lists which included average Americans, and a preference for dinning outdoors, often on a menu highlighted by barbecue. Ronald and Nancy Reagan alternated between hosting some of the most extravagant white-tie formals in the building's history and sitting down to quiet "TV dinners" in their private living quarters.

Thomas Jefferson was torn by the prospect of leaving his beloved home, Monticello, to become the first president to serve an entire term in the President's House. While president, Jefferson tried to re-create some sense of his home life, bringing with him musical instruments, experimenting with the flora on the grounds of the building, and designing additional structures and improvements for the new home, just as he repeatedly had done at Monticello.

When Julia Gardner Tyler, barely out of her teen years, moved into the President's House as the new bride of President John Tyler, she brought her vivacious personality and love of parties to the home. A most capable hostess, the First Lady held grand social events reminiscent of those of the legendary Dolley Madison. At her social galas, which helped boost her husband's sagging popularity somewhat, Julia featured the latest fashions and even introduced a new dance to the home and Washington society—the polka. Other first ladies and first families opted for a less ambitious social agenda in the building. Fewer social events with a more subdued tone and less alcohol marked the presidencies of the Hayes, Polk, and Pierce families. This reflected the personalities and interests of the couples. Lucy Hayes opposed the consumption of alcohol, the Polks were a serious, religious, and hard-working couple with no children, and Franklin and Jane Pierce had just suffered the loss of their only remaining child prior to the inauguration. Other first families such as Millard and Abigail Fillmore and their children preferred quiet family time reading and playing music in their private living quarters to hosting Washington society.

Woodrow Wilson, despite his staid public image, loved to sing and play games with his family and close friends at the White House, all of which helped to take his mind off the pressures of the First World War.

The Eisenhowers, who had moved dozens of times and roughly every year of their lives together—sometimes moving more than once a year—because of Dwight's career in the military, found in the White House the first place they shared as a home for any length of time. There they created a sense of home during their eight years as residents of 1600 Pennsylvania Avenue. Mamie Eisenhower oversaw the kitchen staff, planned menus, and even saw to it that a quiet room for her husband to relax and paint was established upstairs to help him recover from the stress of the job and a weak heart. Befitting a family home, the Eisenhowers also enjoyed visits from their children and grandchildren at the White House.

TRIUMPH AND TRAGEDY

As the everyday events of family life are experienced by first families, difficult times, marital stress, and tragedy have been no stranger to the White House. Andrew Jackson entered the presidency having just lost his wife, Rachel, in the interim between the election and inauguration. Not surprisingly, the President suffered periodic bouts of sadness and loneliness but sought comfort in the visits by his nieces and nephews and their families. Similarly, Franklin and Jane Pierce entered the presidency with the grief of having just lost their eleven-year-old son, Benjamin. To make matters worse, Bennie had died tragically in a train wreck in the short interim between Pierce's election and inauguration, had been the only surviving child of the Pierces, and Jane Pierce had opposed her husband's interest in the presidency. Other first families have suffered similar tragedies. For instance, the Calvin and Grace Coolidge as well as John Quincy Adams and his wife Louisa also lost sons during their presidential years. Such events impacted the tone of the President's House and presidency.

In addition to the challenges of everyday life, come extraordinary experiences unique to living in the White House. For instance, four presidents have been assassinated—Abraham Lincoln, James Garfield, William McKinley, and John F. Kennedy—and a few others escaped assassination attempts. A very stressful office, presidents have aged considerably while serving, suffered an array of health maladies, and four chief executives died in office of natural causes—William Henry Harrison, Zachary Taylor, Warren Harding, and Franklin D. Roosevelt. Letitia Tyler, Abigail Fillmore, Caroline Harrison, and Ellen Wilson all passed away during or at the close of their husband's presidencies.

During times of national crisis, first families have honored the country's dilemmas and causes in the nature of White House events. Lincoln's public receptions during the Civil War, for instance, often became gatherings of officers and soldiers. Joining the Lincolns in caring for wounded soldiers and veterans of wars were Martha Washington, Florence Harding, Lou Hoover, and other members of the first family. During World War I, the Wilsons cut back on social events and even used sheep to "cut the grass" on the White House lawn.

White House Stories

This section of chapters profiles first families, including experiences that were somewhat typical of all first families and others that faced great difficulties or controversies in the White House. The initial chapter profiles the Pierce White House, which is described as "a hell on earth" for both President Pierce and his wife. The Pierce presidency was dour and experienced marital stress and the loss of family member. Not surprisingly, the state of the marriage impacted the presidency in negative ways. The subsequent chapter is quite another story, although the state of this marriage also impacted the presidency, but in positive ways. This chapter profiles the family of Theodore Roosevelt, the largest to inhabit the White House. A rambunctious, vibrant, young family, with a first lady who understood her husband's strengths and weaknesses, the President's family became an asset for him and changed the way the public and press viewed the first family.

The following chapter presents perhaps the most scandalous presidency in history. The Harding marriage was an unlikely yet interesting one. While the Hardings were political partners in many ways, the marriage was a troubled one and was defined by infidelity. Presidential marriages and family life in the White House shaped the nature of each presidency and at times was both beneficial and detrimental for the particular president in office, as you shall soon see.

Eight

"A Hell on Earth": The Pierce Marriage During the White House Years, 1853–1857

MICHAEL J. C. TAYLOR

INTRODUCTION

Marriage is a solemn bond between two people meant to endure the triumphs and tragedies of their lifetimes. In confidence and candor the pair strive toward a shared destiny, learn from past experiences, while dealing with present conditions. When this process has been completed, under the worst of circumstances the partners will have followed separate paths; but under the best of circumstances they will have become one entity. To be successful in marriage one must be mindful of unforeseen happenstance and be able to meet challenges with determination and a shared sense of purpose.

Jane and Franklin Pierce began their journey as a married couple attempting to discover a comfortable median between them. Though the bond of affection was strong, their social and political differences made any compromise tenuous at best. During the Pierce presidency their inconsistencies mirrored the political tensions within Antebellum America itself and, as a result, both the marriage and country fractured. The ambition of one partner when contrasted by the reticence of the other, and coupled with a devastating loss, made life in the White House an impossible place for the Pierces to function as a couple. Thus, the presidency for the Pierces was hell on earth, serving only to exacerbate the differences between them.

A Marriage of Personal and Political Differences (1834–1852)

A Democrat and a Whig

Franklin Pierce was born at his family's homestead in Hillsboro, New Hampshire, on November 23, 1804. At the time of Franklin's birth, his father Benjamin, a devoted Jeffersonian, was a rising political star in the Granite State who had served under General George Washington's command during the American Revolution.[1] The culmination of his father's career was his twice being elected governor of the state.[2] Throughout his childhood young Franklin was exposed to many prominent political figures of the time, one being future president Andrew Jackson.[3] While still a boy, Franklin's elder brothers, Benjamin Kendrick Pierce and John Sullivan Pierce, had served with distinction in the War of 1812.[4] His mother's family also had a unique lineage in that they had descended from John Rogers, the first Protestant martyr of England's Queen Mary.[5]

Benjamin Pierce provided a stellar education for Franklin, who attended the best academies in New Hampshire, and later graduated from Bowdoin College in Brunswick, Maine. The younger Pierce apprenticed in the law, one of his mentors being the future Supreme Court Justice Levi Woodbury, and was admitted to the bar in September 1827 at age twenty-two. Afterward, Pierce's rise in Democratic Party politics was swift and sure: elected to the state legislature and House of Representatives while in his twenties and to the U.S. Senate soon after his thirtieth birthday.

Jane Means Appleton was born on March 12, 1806 in Amherst, New Hampshire, to a clan who were the embodiment of detached New England patricians. Pierce biographer Roy Franklin Nichols described her as "shy, retiring, frail, and tubercular, well-bred in the straightest sect of New England theocracy with a host of substantial and aristocratic connections and very strict ideas of propriety."[6] Jane's father, the Reverend Jesse Appleton, was a Congregationalist minister before assuming the presidency of Bowdoin College in 1807, where he served afterward with distinction until his death from tuberculosis in 1818.[7] The Appletons were dedicated evangelicals in their theology and staunch Whigs with regards to their politics. Thus, when Jane accepted Franklin's marriage proposal, her family was mortified to learn her intended was not only a member of the U.S. House of Representatives, but also a Democrat.

Difficulties from the Start

The couple were married by the bride's brother-in-law at the Appleton family home in Amherst, New Hampshire, on November 19, 1834.[8] The union of the reserved, stoic Jane and the charming, outgoing Franklin was a bond based on a mixture of mutual affection and nearly constant irritation.[9] During the first years of their marriage the couple lived at a boarding house in Washington, D.C. Jane abhorred her husband's profession, as shown in an 1837 letter to her aunt Abigail Means Kent: "Oh, how I wish he was out of political life! How much better it would be for him on every account!"[10] She loathed the capital city for it brought out the worst in her husband, which included immoderate drinking. Finally, after tiring of existence in Washington and Franklin's unruly behavior, Jane moved back to Concord with the intention of never returning.[11]

It was this arrangement that lasted until Franklin resigned from the Senate in February 1842, but with it came personal consequences. Senator Pierce was absent when his first son Franklin, Jr., was born on February 2, 1836. Jane had a difficult birth and the child died three days afterward. By the time Franklin received the word of the child's delivery, his son had been dead for two weeks.[12] The loneliness of Washington caused Franklin's alcoholism to manifest itself to the detriment of his reputation and career. A few months prior to his resignation, the New Hampshire Senator took his seat severely inebriated, fell asleep at his desk, and snored loudly. During the session, he awoke from his slumber screaming "Fire! Fire!" at the top of his lungs. When an unamused colleague asked where the fire was, Franklin laughed, rubbed his stomach, and replied "in here."[13]

Following his resignation from the Senate, Franklin established a thriving law practice. The Pierces bought the only home they would ever own, known today as "The Pierce Manse." Temperance was the cardinal rule of the household, as Jane enforced a strict code of conduct.[14] The couple celebrated the birth of a third son Benjamin, named for his paternal grandfather, on April 13, 1841; suffered the death of Frank Robert, their second son, of typhoid fever on November 14, 1842; and, endured a two-year separation while Franklin served as a brigadier general during the Mexican War.[15] Within that decade, the Pierces enjoyed the most prosperous and stable period of their married lives.

At the center of the Pierce marriage was their son Benjamin, the sole child of three to survive infancy. Bennie was very close to his mother for, according to Roy Franklin Nichols, Jane "occupied herself hovering around her child with doting fondness."[16] Franklin was also quite affectionate toward his son and strived to do for Bennie as his own father had for him—to place at Bennie's disposal all of the necessary elements for a successful life as an adult.[17] As the focus of their relationship grew toward their son, Jane and Franklin found a middle ground that bridged their differences and, so long as that locus remained, the union was both strong and affectionate.

A MOVE TOWARD THE PRESIDENCY (1852–1853)

In all likelihood, Franklin Pierce's move toward the presidency began with his service as brigadier general during the Mexican War. Once hostilities were declared, Pierce enlisted as a private, but was soon elevated to brigadier general by President James Polk.[18] The president viewed Pierce as a man possessing exceptional ability and had wanted to appoint him Attorney General in August 1846.[19] The former senator turned down the position, stating that he did not wish to endure long periods away from his family, "except at the call of my country in time of war."[20] As a commanding officer, Pierce proved himself capable and conscientious. He was at odds with the quartermaster for necessities such as adequate horses, weapons, and decent food for the soldiers. When booty was obtained, such as in one skirmish the seizure of a herd of cattle, the benefits were shared equally among officers and enlisted men.[21] Pierce was wounded at the Battles of Churubusco and Chapultepec, and was a member of a peace delegation that sought to negotiate a settlement during the siege of Mexico City.[22]

From Hero to Candidate

Upon his return to Concord in February 1848, Pierce was hailed as a hero in a public ceremony; afterward, he was elected to a further term in the U.S. Senate and nominated for governor of the state, both of which he declined. However, one position he did accept was Chairmanship of the New Hampshire Democratic party.[23] During the 1850 midterm elections, Pierce came to the attention of Southern Democratic leaders when he publicly disciplined party candidates for both the House of Representatives and Governorship for hedging on the slavery controversy.[24] Though Whigs and Free Soilers castigated Pierce in public for his stance against abolition,

Southerners were impressed by his firm action and the controversy propelled him into the national spotlight.

When Associate Justice Levi Woodbury died unexpectedly in September 1851, Franklin Pierce became the "favorite son" candidate of the New Hampshire delegates.[25] At the party's convention the following year, a glut of first-tier candidates such as James Buchanan, Stephen Douglas, William Marcy, and former nominee Lewis Cass, caused a gridlock in the nominating process. After thirty-five roll-call votes failed to determine a standard bearer, the bosses decided on a compromise candidate—Franklin Pierce of New Hampshire—and on the forty-ninth ballot Pierce was nominated by acclamation.

Though Pierce himself was elated with the news, his wife and son were not. Young Bennie Pierce wrote his mother: "I hope he won't be elected for I shall not like to be at Washington and I know you would not either."[26] It was a gruesome campaign in which the Whigs assailed Pierce's personal character—including publicly castigating him as "the hero of many a well fought bottle." Pierce and his running mate, William King, chose the high road, dedicating their administration to healing the sectionalism that ran rampant in the country. When all the shouting was over, the people elected Franklin Pierce to the presidency by both a wide electoral and popular vote margin.[27]

Bittersweet Victory

It was a victory he savored, for not only had he gained the nation's highest office, but had also procured for his son Benjamin a status that would bode well for his future. The Pierce family spent the 1852 Christmas holiday with Jane's cousin, Amos Lawrence, in Boston. Though the president-elect's relationship with his wife's family had been tolerable at best, he had reason to celebrate: as President of the United States his in-laws were cordial, thankful for the connection with the future chief executive—the only such time during his marriage they showed such respect.[28] But during what should have been a time of celebration, Jane voiced her misgivings over her husband's new charge and her suspicions that Franklin had carefully and consciously positioned himself for the nomination. As a result, tension permeated throughout the time the Pierces spent in Boston.

Following the holidays, the Pierces planned to return to Concord and prepare for the move to Washington, D.C. Franklin, Jane, and young Benjamin Pierce boarded the train station at Boston for the noon return trip on January 6, 1853. However, a few minutes after leaving the station, the coupling device of the Pierce's passenger car broke apart at the spot where Bennie was sitting. His parents could only watch in horror as their son was violently thrown from the wreckage. Careening out of control, the compartment derailed and somersaulted into a stony field deceptively covered in fresh snow. Within a few horrible seconds it was all over.[29]

The President-elect was the first to emerge from the wreck, suffering only scrapes and bruises. Viewing the sheet of white, Pierce located his son lying motionless before him 100 yards away. As Franklin reclaimed his son from the ground, the cap Bennie was wearing fell from his head. Blood then flowed freely and revealed the child's crushed skull. Within a few moments, his mother viewed her son in this state and promptly fainted. Young Benjamin Pierce was the accident's only fatality.[30]

The grief following his son's tragic death was overwhelming for the President-elect. In a letter to close friend Jefferson Davis, Pierce wrote: "How shall I be able to summon my manhood and gather up my energies for the duties before me, it is hard for me to see?"[31] But if Bennie's tragic death depleted his father's courage and stamina, it had more dire consequences for his mother and their marriage—as Franklin himself wrote, his wife was "crushed to the earth by fearful bereavement."[32] Franklin alone arranged and attended his son's funeral in Concord, a touching memorial in which Bennie's coffin was borne by his schoolmates.[33] Jane, on the other hand, chose to lock herself in her room either praying aloud for hours or silently writing letters to her "beloved dead." When she did emerge, Jane sat in a rocking chair, clasping a box containing locks of hair from all three of her sons. Though Franklin did what he could to comfort her, in most instances his wife berated him. She blamed Bennie's death on her husband, claiming God had taken their son to keep Franklin from distraction during his presidential term.[34] As a result, Jane initially refused to journey to Washington to assume her duties as first lady.

There is no question that this single event diminished what could have been a productive presidency. Franklin relied on his family for moral support and from this relationship he drew emotional strength. His prime ambition for seeking the presidency had been to provide an easier path to success in life for his son; but, after Bennie's death, Franklin's impetus for holding the office had been taken from him. Thus, at the pinnacle of his career, the Presi-

dent of the United States found himself immersed in a dark cloud
of mourning. Life in the executive mansion was for Franklin Pierce
a lonely existence.

THE LONELY REALITY OF GRIEF (1853–1857)

Separate Lives in the White House

The Pierces dealt with the presidency in two entirely different
ways: whereas Franklin had the varied duties of the office that he
held to occupy his time, Jane chose to dwell within the confinement
of her own grief. A few weeks following the funeral of their son,
the President-elect traveled to Washington to ready his administration; but, blaming Franklin's presidential ambitions for Bennie's
tragic demise, Jane vowed never to set foot in the capital city.
Later, she relented and sojourned to join her husband; yet, when she
arrived at the Baltimore home of her aunt, Abby Means Kent, Jane
decided she could go no farther and placed herself in seclusion.[35]
Though Franklin pleaded with his wife to return to Washington
with him, she refused, and would stay with the Kent family throughout the spring of 1853. This decision would have dire consequences.
    Prior to his inaugural, President-elect Franklin Pierce and
President Millard Fillmore had become friends and spent many
hours in each other's company. When the Fourth of March arrived,
due to Jane Pierce's absence at the podium, Abigail Fillmore stepped
in and held the Bible for the oath of office. During the proceedings,
a cold rain turned into a thick, wet snow, which caused Mrs.
Fillmore to catch a cold. Throughout March 1853 the former First
Lady developed pneumonia. The president often inquired of Mrs.
Fillmore's health, placing the use of the Executive Mansion and his
personal physician at her family's disposal.[36] Within moments after
Abigail Fillmore's death on March 30, 1853, Franklin wrote a heart-
felt letter to her family, insinuating blame on himself for her passing: "I beg you to accept the assurance of my earnest condolence
in this great bereavement."[37]
    Upon his inaugural, Franklin Pierce was arguably the most
popular man in the country and throughout his initial year he
moved boldly on public policy. The president tendered territorial
purchase offers to the governments of Mexico, Russia, and Spain.
He proposed a stringent reform of the civil service, basing employment on competence rather than loyalty, much to the dismay of

party leaders who called him an "ingrate." His treasury opened
vast amounts of public land for sale, the bulk of the proceeds were
then used to bring down the national debt—which decreased from
over $69 million in 1853 to $30 million by 1857. The Pierce administration enlarged the federal district court system and, with
regards to filling a vacancy on the nation's highest court, the president consulted the sitting justices as to a suitable nominee—a precedent unheeded by his successors.[38]

Despite his expert hand in governing the nation, all hell broke
loose in the capitol with the introduction of the Kansas-Nebraska
Act, which held within it a clause allowing for the citizens of the
territories to determine whether to allow slavery. The President
had wanted the Supreme Court to be the agency of the federal
government to overturn the Missouri Compromise line, negotiated
in 1819 by Kentucky senator Henry Clay. It had remained a viable
boundary between slave and free states, although several thousand
square miles of new territory gained from Mexico had brought
forth challenges from both sides of the slavery issue. Many opposed
such a measure on the grounds that it would encourage the spread
of slavery throughout the country.[39]

One of those who believed this to be the case was Jane Pierce.
During the early spring of 1854, the First Lady temporarily put
away her grief over son Bennie's death and channeled her efforts
toward defeating the measure, regardless of whether or not her
husband supported it. According to historian Carl Anthony, Jane
consulted opponents of the bill in private conferences held at
both at the capitol and the executive mansion. Among those invited to these coteries were antislavery activists, the most notable being Charles Robinson, the man who would later be elected
as the governor of the Kansas Territory under the antislavery
Topeka constitution.[40] The First Lady's actions served to add more
tension to the dilemma the president faced: If he signed the Kansas-Nebraska bill it meant protests from the North, the end of his
political career, and further estrangement from his wife; however,
if he vetoed it the repercussions could be southern secession and
civil war. It was while his wife was horseback riding on the executive mansion's south lawn that Franklin Pierce signed the
controversial act into law.[41]

Following the passage of the Kansas-Nebraska Act, the New
England Emigrant Aid Society was formed by a group of ardent
abolitionists solely to encourage free-soil settlement in Kansas and,
by sheer numbers, keep the territory from becoming a pro-slavery

state. The primary financier of the organization was Amos Lawrence, a close cousin of Jane Pierce.[42] Boston Congressman Robert Appleton, another close member of Jane's family, was a leading spokesman in the House of Representatives for the defeat of the Kansas-Nebraska Bill, and often rebuked the president in his many floor speeches.[43] Violence erupted in Kansas between free-soil and pro-slavery settlers, as demonstrated in armed brawls and voting fraud. By the time Jane Pierce made her debut as White House hostess in January 1855, her husband's presidency was in serious trouble—much of it at the behest of his family-by-marriage.

In the assessment of White House historian William Seale, "Jane Pierce built her own hell on earth and took it with her to the White House."[44] Other than her efforts to thwart the passage of the Kansas-Nebraska Bill, the First Lady remained secluded in her room on the second-floor living quarters of the Executive Mansion.[45] The planning and implementation of social functions were left to the president and his secretary, Sidney Webster. The job of hostess at official dinners were assumed by either Jane's aunt and closest confidant, Abigail Means Kent, or Varina Davis, the wife of War Secretary Jefferson Davis.[46]

In Black Veil

Even with the duties of first lady being carried out by others, Mrs. Pierce remained secluded, with the exceptions being visits to the Davis household, and the sole occasion where she toured Mount Vernon with author Nathaniel Hawthorne, a family friend since Franklin's college days at Bowdoin.[47] And when Jane made her debut as hostess on New Year's Day 1855, she was dressed in a black satin dress accented by a black veil, while the Executive Mansion was trimmed in black crepe to demonstrate mourning for her beloved son.[48] Throughout Franklin's term, Jane isolated herself from both her husband and the social world afforded by his position. Though Franklin treated her with affection and delicacy, Jane rarely, if ever, reciprocated, as noted by Roy Franklin Nichols:

> She had never been happy for long; disease or death or her husband's interest and failings had been constant sources of anxiety and melancholy from which she never learned to free herself . . . He, realizing the fundamental incompatibility of their backgrounds, temperaments, and interests, had sought to recompense for that fact by all the tenderness,

consideration, and affection which his sentimental nature could shower upon her.[49]

One of the very few activities the first couple engaged in together were visits to the homes of close friends, their most intimate being Varina and Jefferson Davis. Varina was known throughout official Washington for creating a lively atmosphere whenever she entertained guests. The Pierces' enjoyed their company and often stayed for hours on end. Furthermore, the Davises' infant son, Samuel, intrigued Jane and Franklin. The first couple spent many hours playing with the Davis child. In a letter to her mother, Varina Davis wrote that when President Pierce unexpectedly stopped in for a visit little Sam "ran around the chair and looked, and called out 'pretty man, pretty man.' "[50] When young Samuel Emory Davis died of an unidentified ailment on June 13, 1854, the President was present at both the funeral and burial at Oak Hill Cemetery in the Washington suburb of Georgetown.[51] Jane, too, was devastated by the loss, but did what she could to console the distraught parents.[52]

A Changed Man

Franklin often sought refuge away from the executive mansion, his favorite form of respite being horseback rides to the outskirts of Washington and back.[53] One incident caused so much apprehension within official Washington that his aides sought to limit this practice due to potential danger for the president. During the second Christmas of his administration, Franklin went riding along the country roads north of the capitol with an unnamed friend from Maryland. Following two hours of riding, their horses took fright, and threw the two men into a snowbank; later, the two men were found by a Maryland farmer at his stable door. The President explained to the farmer his situation; but, rather than loaning Pierce one of his horses, the farmer sent one of his sons to the Executive Mansion with a note written by the President. On receiving the news, Sidney Webster, Pierce's personal secretary, concluded that returning to Washington in an open sleigh was unwise, particularly since the President would be soaked from the experience. As a result, the president of the United States spent the night on the floor of a farmer's house north of the Soldier's Home, before returning the following day.[54]

Franklin also enjoyed fishing on the Potomac River adjacent to Washington accompanied by a small group of friends. He was also an expert card player who hosted regular poker games, in the company of key congressmen and close friends at the executive mansion. Of those who regularly gathered at these games, only one got the better of the president—Clement Claiborne Clay. An executive mansion employee described one of the more illustrious games in which President Pierce outsmarted Clay:

> One night he screwed up courage enough to bluff to the extent of $50 on a bob-tail flush. Pierce had an ace full and simply called. "I'm going to quit now," said Pierce, rising and pocketing the money. "I intend to have it said that I came out ahead in at least one game with you" ... Clay was so sick over the loss of his $50 that he staid in bed two days.[55]

After Franklin lost his bid for renomination to Ambassador James Buchanan in June of 1856, the Pierces ventured out of the executive mansion more often as a couple. Though it is educated speculation, perhaps they had recognized the presidency had come between them and, since this burden was coming to an end, they were attempting to heal their differences. There was also no question that the presidency had taken its toll on the Franklin Pierce. He was no longer the charming, pleasant man he had once been, as was noted by the wife of Senator Clement Claiborne Clay:

> I had seen him bound up the stairs with the elasticity and lightness of a schoolboy. He went out after four years a staid and grave man, on whom the stamp of care and illness was ineradicably impressed.[56]

On departing from the White House, Pierce realized the significance the office had on his life. As War Secretary Jefferson Davis was about to take his leave of the soon-to-be former President, Pierce told him, "I can scarcely bear parting from you, who have been strength and solace to me for four anxious years and never failed me."[57] The president's words were definitely in praise of a cabinet member for his extraordinary performance in the administration; however, they can also be interpreted as Pierce's acknowledgment for Davis's unyielding friendship during a time when all the other personal aspects of his life had been destroyed by the position he had struggled with for four long years. Unfortunately, retirement from the presidency would not afford him or his wife a return to a blissful anonymity.

A WANDERING UNTO DEATH (1857–1863)

After the presidency, Jane and Franklin Pierce spent nearly three years abroad—which included nearly a year in Spain in the hope that the dry climate would aid in Mrs. Pierce's health—returning to the United States in the Fall of 1859.[58] As the Pierces were setting up their new home at 52 South Main Street in Concord, a movement lead by Jefferson Davis and Caleb Cushing was underway to renominate Pierce at the next Democratic party convention. After surveying the party's field of candidates, the two former Pierce Cabinet members were convinced the only man capable of keeping the country from fissure was Franklin Pierce. Davis and Cushing lobbied state party leaders in order to secure the nomination for the former president. Though support for Pierce among the delegates was high, the ex-President declined, citing his wife's deteriorating health, and the party nominated Illinois Senator Stephen Douglas—a move that alienated southern delegates. A month later, the southern delegates nominated Vice President John Breckenridge as their standard bearer. A few weeks after this, centrists in the party hurriedly negotiated a deal among the two nominees to step down in favor of a single candidate—Franklin Pierce. When presented the news of this agreement, the former president again declined. The campaign resumed and the divided Democrats lost to the Republican candidate, Abraham Lincoln. [59]

Though he had predicted that sectional animosities would lead to war if left unchecked, Pierce was vehemently against such a conflagration, and became the most vocal critic of the War Between the States. The former president voiced these sentiments when he wrote to Jefferson Davis in January 1860:

> I have never believed that the actual disruption of the Union can occur without bloodshed; and if, through the madness of northern Abolitionists, the fighting will not be along Mason and Dixon's line merely. It will be within our own borders, in our own streets, between the two classes of citizens to whom I have referred. Those who defy law and

scout constitutional obligations will, if we ever reach the arbitration of arms, find occupation enough at home.[60]

In April 1861, Pierce proposed a conference of the five ex-presidents to suggest to President Lincoln alternatives to war. Though all of the former chief executives agreed to attend, the most senior, Martin Van Buren, refused to either call or chair such a meeting and, as such, the plan came to naught.[61] Throughout 1861 and 1862, Pierce made many public speeches denouncing the war, and was the target of a State Department investigation for treason because of it. The former president's ire focused on Lincoln's suspension of habeas corpus and the persecution of dissidents, such as Clement Vallandigham. This stance allowed Pierce to become the front runner for the Democratic party's nomination in 1864.[62] But soon, all the speculation of Franklin Pierce's reentry into presidential politics came to an abrupt and tragic end.

Jane Pierce succumbed to tuberculosis on December 15, 1863 and, with her passing, Franklin's life, so indelibly intertwined with hers, lost all meaning and purpose. "Death continued to afflict him," wrote Roy Franklin Nichols, "weakness overcame him more completely, his constitution, so robust yet so badly used, began to fail in its functions."[63] Following her burial at the Minot enclosure at the Old North Cemetery in Concord, among the children she loved with the very sinews of her being, Franklin poured himself into a bottle of his favored Jamaican rum, and did not reemerge until his baptism in the Episcopal Church during the summer of 1865.

Because of his antiwar activism and critical remarks toward President Lincoln, Pierce became a pariah in the North. When President Lincoln was assassinated in April 1865, Pierce was rebuked by a large mob outside of his home demanding a public display of his patriotism.[64] The previous year, though they had been close lifelong friends, the former president was barred from being a pallbearer at the funeral of author Nathaniel Hawthorne.[65] After the controversy had died down, the ex-President settled into a quiet life riddled with respiratory ailments, shunned by a public to whom he had dedicated so much of his life.

Franklin Pierce died on October 7, 1869, from dropsy and was buried with his family. It took the State of New Hampshire a half a century to recognize their native son's contributions to American history as president of the United States.

CONCLUSION

With few exceptions, the most stable marriages have shaped our greatest leaders. For example, historians cannot render a fully accurate consideration of John Adams's accomplishments without examining the influence of his wife Abigail. Nor would the assessments of presidential successes in the cases of James K. Polk, Theodore Roosevelt, William Howard Taft, or Franklin Delano Roosevelt be complete without a serious consideration of the women who stood by their husbands' side and urged them on to greatness. Other supportive wives such as Abigail Fillmore and Eliza Johnson actually provided their husbands' education. Finally, when President Woodrow Wilson was cut down by a series of strokes, it was his second wife, Edith, who effectively balanced the needs of the country with those of her husband's health and guided the nation with a steady, yet invisible hand.

At its onset, the Pierce marriage was a delicate balance between several disparate elements that managed to coexist. Prior to the presidency, the union of Jane Appleton and Franklin Pierce had survived trials and tribulations that had cut asunder more stable unions; however, in order to make this relationship work, both parties had to concentrate their energies toward either truce or compromise. In the case of Franklin Pierce, it meant walking away from a promising political career he seemed destined for. Prior to the 1852 presidential election, in which Pierce was elected by a wide popular margin, Jane and Franklin had endured the loss of two infant children, distance due to a foreign war, and the turbulence of acute alcoholism. The stoic wife and the charismatic husband, both emotionally brittle, clung to each other as if they both recognized the same dire need for shelter in one another. Thus, historians often ponder a counterfactual alternative: How different the story of his life and presidency would have been had Franklin Pierce chosen a wife whose personality and interests were more compatible with his own.

Following the 1852 presidential election, the common thread in their marriage had been severed, and it sent the couple into an emotional tailspin without the capability of relying on one another. After their son Benjamin's tragic death, Jane displayed her abhorrence of the ambition that gave purpose to her husband's life. In tandem, Franklin found himself at the head of a country that did not want to be governed. In short, it was a vicious cycle that, on a personal level, crippled the mental stability of a man who, in all likelihood, was the most capable and talented leader in the country at the time. Though Franklin Pierce sought to reshape and remake the U.S. government into one based on competence, he found himself swimming in a pool of political sharks without the most trusted and needed weapon in his arsenal: the approval and support of his wife. As such, the accomplishments of the Pierce presidency were marred by "Bleeding Kansas" and the vast crevasse of sectionalism that he was powerless to halt.

The most salient example of what happened to their union during the White House years was the political struggle over the Kansas-Nebraska Bill, in which the couple labored on opposite sides of the popular sovereignty issue. Franklin, while trying to moderate a controversial bill whose passage he viewed as inevitable, was undermined by the efforts of his wife who sought to stop its passage altogether by exerting her influence. As such, the tension became so intense for Franklin, that he often sought relaxation outside the confines of the executive mansion, while Jane locked herself away in her second-floor room and saw no one. Franklin was never to be forgiven by his wife for both winning the presidency and the death of their son and, as a result, the former president spent the rest of his retirement atoning to his wife for these perceived sins, even after her death.

During this critical period in America's history, Franklin Pierce sought to lead his country toward reconciliation. With the country supporting his policies and his family by his side, the new president had every expectation for success. Fate, however, had other plans. Throughout the course of a single term in the presidency, Jane and Franklin Pierce lost their last surviving child and, alas, each other. Afterward, the delicate pieces of the jigsaw puzzle that was their marriage would never again fit together as they once had; as such, after the presidency the Pierces lived together as wedded strangers, bound by an incompatible mixture of dutiful affection and mistrustful guilt. Without question, it is these elements that make the story of the Pierce marriage among the most tragic within the annals of White House history.

NOTES TO CHAPTER 8

1. Roy Franklin Nichols, *Franklin Pierce* . . . , 1931, 5.

2. William A. DeGregorio, *The Complete Book of the Presidents*, 1984, 198.

3. Nichols, 1931, 47.

4. Ibid., 12; in the case of Benjamin Kendrick Pierce, his service during the war proved to be the beginning of both a distinguished military and political career.

5. *Genealogical and Personal Memoirs* ... , 1908, 353–355.

6. Nichols, 1931, 76.

7. Allen Johnsen, "Rev. Jesse Appleton," 1928, 328.

8. DeGregorio, 1984, 199–200; It is perhaps the greatest irony of the Pierce marriage that Jane had been brought up to look down on politics and politicians. Yet, she married one of its best-trained and most effective practitioners. Pierce biographer Roy Franklin Nichols has suggested that though Jane was in love with Franklin, an ulterior motive for marrying this brazen young politician was that she was rebelling against "matriarchal oppression." Nichols, 1931, 75.

9. Nichols, 1931, 524.

10. Jane Pierce, quoted in Nichols, 1931, 104.

11. Ibid., 106.

12. Ibid., 86; Pierce was also absent when his second son Frank Robert was born three years later on 27 August 1839.

13. "The Prince of Good Fellows," originally published in the newspaper the *Memphis Appeal* in 1885, in *It's Still News, Mr. President*, 1969, 44.

14. Nichols, 1931, 115.

15. Tim Taylor, *The Book of the Presidents*, 1972, 157.

16. Nichols, 1931, 171.

17. Ibid., 172; This was at the heart of the bond between father and son and, as Nichols wrote, Bennie "was always eager for his father to come home from his office, and when the latter tarried his son would start down to hurry him up."

18. Bill Severn, Frontier President ... , 1965, 180; The president recognized the potential for a war hero to turn presidential candidate in 1848 and, in Polk's reasoning, if such was to be the case, then that general should be a Democrat.

19. Taylor, 1972, 157; The previous year Pierce had also been selected by the New Hampshire state legislature to serve a further term in the Senate, had been nominated for a term as governor, and appointed U.S. Attorney by President Polk, all of which he declined.

20. Pierce, letter to James Knox Polk, September 18, 1846, in *The Papers of Franklin Pierce* . . . , he was appointed brigadier general on March 1, 1847 under the provisions of the Benton Bill, a commission that he accepted; DiGregorio, 1984, 200.

21. Pierce, Mexican War Diary, in *The Papers of Franklin Pierce.*

22. DeGregorio, 1984, 200.

23. Taylor, 1972, 158.

24. Nichols, 1931, 177–178; Though Pierce himself abhorred the practice of slavery, he viewed it as a constitutionally protected practice, and should be recognized as such until such time it was abolished by federal law.

25. Ibid., 189–190.

26. Benjamin Pierce, quoted in Nichols, 1931, 205.

27. Paul F. Boller, Jr., *Presidential Campaigns*, 1985, 88–89.

28. Nichols, 1931, 224; It was the son and namesake of this Appleby/Means relative that would be the financier of the New England Emigrant Aid Society.

29. "Sad Railroad Accident . . . ," 1853, 1; Nichols, 1931, 224.

30. Ibid.

31. Pierce, quoted in Hudson Strode, *Jefferson Davis* . . . , 1955, 248.

32. Ibid., 247.

33. "Funeral of General Pierce's Son," 1853, 2.

34. William Seale, *The President's House* . . . , 1986, 307–308.

35. Until Jane Pierce assumed her duties as first lady in January 1855, it would be either her aunt, Abby Means Kent, or Varina Davis, wife of Secretary of War Jefferson Davis, who would act in that role; DeGregorio, 1984, 200.

36. Millard Fillmore, letter to Franklin Pierce, March 28, 1853, in *The Papers of Franklin Pierce.*

37. Franklin Pierce, letter to Millard Fillmore, March 30, 1853, in *The Papers of Franklin Pierce*; Afterward, the president ordered all government business to cease in mourning for Mrs. Fillmore.

38. Franklin Pierce, inaugural address, March 4, 1853, in *Speeches of the American Presidents*, 1988, 149–153. Franklin Pierce, initial state of the union address, December 1853, in *A Compilation of the Messages and Speeches of the Presidents*, 1896, 856–857.

39. DeGregorio, 1984, 204–205.

40. Carl Sferrazza Anthony, *First Ladies* . . . , 1990, 157–158.

41. Nichols, 1931, 383; Anthony, 1990, 158.

42. Nichols, 1931, 412.

43. Ibid., 31.

44. Seale, 1986, 307.

45. DeGregorio, 1984, 200.

47. Ibid., 309.

48. Seale, 1986, 308.

49. Nichols, 1931, 524.

50. Varina Davis, letter to Margaret Howell, March 26, 1854, in *Jefferson Davis: Private Letters* . . . , 1995, 76.

51. William J. Cooper, Jr., *Jefferson Davis: American*, 2000, 261.

52. It has been asserted by one of Jefferson Davis' most recent biographers, William C. Davis, that Jane attempted to console the Davises because she, herself, "had almost adopted little Samuel in his stead." Perhaps the first lady had the death of her own son the year before on her mind. William C. Davis, *Jefferson Davis: The Man and His Hour*, 1991, 241–242.

53. The route during most of Pierce's daily rides included a path through Congressional Cemetery, for reasons known only to the president. "Musing of a White House Attendant: President's of Old," originally published in the *Washington Star* (September 1888), in White, 26; In an 1887 interview, a White House courier described the president as "a fine horseback rider." "Presidents as Horsemen: How Chief Magistrates Have regarded Horses," originally published in the *St. Louis Republic* (May 9, 1887), in White, 20.

54. White, 26–27. This is an interesting story that, to this author's knowledge, has not been printed in any of Pierce's biographies.

55. White, 45.

56. Mrs. Clement C. Clay, quoted in Seale, 1986, 328–329.

57. Pierce, quoted in Nichols, 1931, 502.

58. Taylor, 1972, 162.

59. Nichols, 1931, 514–517.

60. Franklin Pierce, letter to Jefferson Davis (January 6, 1860), in *Pierce Papers.*

61. Nichols, 1931, 517–518; Only Roy Franklin Nichols' biography of Franklin Pierce offers any detailed account or assessment of the President's action during the final decade of his life.

62. Ibid., 519–520.

63. Ibid., 524.

64. Ibid., 526.

65. Taylor, 1972, 163.

Nine

TR's White House:
The Biggest First Family

TOM LANSFORD

INTRODUCTION

A ll first families face a variety of adjustments when they enter the White House. For instance, the increased public or media attention often disrupts family life. Concurrently, the actions of family members can be a source of potential political problems for the president. The family of Theodore Roosevelt was the largest to ever occupy the White House. As such, it presented numerous challenges for the first couple. These were complicated by the age range of the Roosevelt children— from infancy to adolescence. While they occupied the White House, the Roosevelts had to arrange social debuts for their daughters and a wedding, and deal with the numerous minor incidents faced by parents.

During the twentieth century and beyond, management and oversight of the public perceptions of the first family have occupied an increasing amount of the president's time. On entering the White House in the aftermath of William McKinley's assassination, Theodore and Edith Roosevelt developed a variety of strategies to manage the growing media interest in their large and high-spirited family as they encountered the inevitable challenges faced by all parents, and those that were particular to first families. By the time they left office in 1909, the Roosevelts had established themselves as one of the most popular and well-known first families in American history.

THE FAMILY

Edith Roosevelt was Theodore's second wife. His first wife, Alice Hathaway Lee, died on February 14, 1884, just two days after the birth of the couple's only child, Alice Lee Roosevelt. Throughout the remainder of his life, Roosevelt's relationship with his daughter was often troubled or, at the very least, strained. Many Roosevelt biographers attribute the problematic relationship to either misplaced feelings of blame or an effort to repress memories of his first wife on the part of the future president. For example, throughout the remainder of his life, Roosevelt refused to call Alice by her first name and instead called her "Baby Lee."[1] One result of the father-daughter relationship was that in many ways Alice would emerge as the most free-spirited of the Roosevelt children and the one that was most often in the contemporary press.

Edith and Theodore were childhood friends and Edith seems to have decided that she would marry Theodore or no one else at a relatively young age.[2] After the death of his first wife, Theodore eventually came back to Edith. The two were married on December 2, 1886. Edith and Theodore would eventually have five children, in addition to Alice. The couple's first child, Theodore, Junior ("Ted"), was born on September 13, 1887, and thereafter, Edith delivered the couple's children in fairly rapid succession. Kermit was born on October 10, 1889, followed by Ethel Carow on August 13, 1891, Archibald ("Archie") Bulloch on April 10, 1894, and Quentin on November 19, 1897.

Room for Family and Friends

When the Roosevelt family moved into the White House on September 23, 1901, following the assassination of McKinley, they were the largest family yet to occupy the executive mansion. This would present special problems since the personal quarters of the White House were quite small and really more suited to an older couple with few or no children, rather than a large household with a number of rambunctious sons and daughters. As a result, the President and First Lady campaigned vigorously for a renovation of the White House. (See chapter 13 for a further discussion of this renovation.) Congress appropriated the funds and the old Executive Mansion underwent one of the most extensive renovations in its history.

The 1902 project resulted in the construction of the West Wing and the subsequent transfer of most of the official offices there. In addition, the renovation freed up space, including the establishment of five bedrooms for the first family. This allowed for reasonable accommodation of the family since at the time the first family entered the White House, Ted had been enrolled in private school at Groton and so did not need a permanent room in the mansion. Edith and Theodore occupied the main southwest suite, while Alice, Ethel, and Kermit had their own rooms, and Archie and Quentin shared a bedroom. Ted would bunk with Kermit on those occasions when he was in the nation's capital during holidays or family events.

Various members of the extended Roosevelt clan were often frequent guests of the White House for overnight visits or both state or family occasions. Roosevelt's sisters Corrine and Anna or "Bamie" and their families often attended dinners and were permanently placed on the guest list for all White House social events (Bamie had a house on N Street in Washington). Thanksgiving and Christmas were usually the major family events that brought together the Roosevelts. However, the stress of planning and overseeing these large gatherings ultimately prompted Edith and Theodore to begin spending more sedate holidays at their property near Charlottesville, Virginia.

Room for Pets and Play

Although many First Families have owned pets of one form or another, few matched the variety or number of the Roosevelt menagerie. In fact, the Roosevelts maintained a virtual zoo that grew dramatically during their time in the White House. As Roosevelt's fondness for animals became widely known, various public officials in the United States and abroad gave the President and the First Family an assortment of new pets. The Roosevelts had dogs and cats, and a range of more eclectic pets, including parrots and a macaw, racoons, flying squirrels, and even a badger.[3] The boys were initially fond of small pets such as guinea pigs since they could be smuggled around the White House in the boys' coats.

During the course of a single year, "Roosevelt received a lion, zebra, hyena, five bears, and numerous birds, snakes, and lizards . . . the more exotic animals were given to the Washington Zoo, but Roosevelt kept one bear and the children retained a variety of strange animals."[4] For instance, Kermit kept a kangaroo rat that had been presented as a gift.[5] In addition, Alice had a green snake, named Emily Spinach, which she routinely carried about in her purse and used as conversation piece at parties or even official functions. One of the most beloved of the Roosevelt pets was Algonquin, a calico pony. Algonquin became part of the lore of the White House one day when the Roosevelt children secretly used the White House elevator to bring the pony to the second-floor bedroom of Archie who was ill with both measles and whooping cough in an effort to lift his spirits.

Besides their intrinsic value to the family, the number and variety of the First Family's pets actually served political ends for the President. Roosevelt's efforts to promote conservation and environmentalism were aided by constant press coverage of his interactions with the White House "zoo." In spite of the exotic nature of many of the family pets, Edith used the creatures as a means to reinforce the egalitarian perceptions of the First Family. For instance, following the death of her dog "Tip," the First Lady procured another canine by simply going to the Washington dog pound and choosing a replacement, an act which the national press widely publicized.

The emphasis on fun and play among the First Family was manifested not only in their zeal for pets, but in their personal interactions. In many ways, the Roosevelt children engaged in antics that would be common among any young children. For instance, they often slid down the staircases on serving trays or played "hide-and seek" throughout the house. However, Edith found that her husband was also just as likely to engage in play and mischief as the children.

Roosevelt himself described one bout of wrestling in October 1901: "Archie and Quentin are just as cunning as can be . . . I had a 'bear' play with them in their room and Kermit and Ethel could not resist the temptation and came in also, and we had a terrific romp on the bed."[6] Such antics were demonstrative of the closeness and affection that Theodore shared with his children. Writing in 1904, Roosevelt stated that

> As I mounted the White House steps, Edith came to meet me at the door, and I suddenly realized that, after all, no matter what the outcome of the election should prove to be, my *happiness* [Roosevelt's italics] was assured, even though my ambition to have the seal of approval put upon my administration might not be gratified,—for my life with Edith and my children constitutes my *happiness* [Roosevelt's italics].[7]

Roosevelt's zeal for the "strenuous life" led him to emphasize the importance of physical activity. He and Edith continued to ride regularly and Theodore once rode 100 miles in one day to demonstrate that a new fitness test for senior officers the Army, which required a 90-mile ride in three days, could be easily done. The President engaged in a variety of other forms of exercise including wrestling, boxing, hiking, and tennis. In fact, as part of the 1902 renovation, he had tennis courts laid at the White House and later organized a group of close friends and diplomats into a loose club that he designated the "Tennis Cabinet."[8] For the boys he had a baseball field created on the South Lawn.

INTERFAMILY RELATIONS

The interpersonal relationships within the Roosevelt clan were complicated and intricate, and extended across several levels of the family. First, Theodore had a close connection with his sisters. In fact, he often turned to Corrine and Bamie for political advice. This often proved to be a source of tension between the President and First Lady. In 1894, Edith was instrumental in convincing Theodore not to run in the New York City mayoral race, a decision that the future President later came to regret.[9] For the remainder of his political career, Theodore consciously avoided political advice from his wife and Edith learned that her input was unwanted. As a result, a 1980, a survey by *Good Housekeeping* found that Edith had basically no political influence on her husband.[10]

Instead of using his wife as a political adviser, the President often turned to his sisters for counsel. When Corrine was in Washington, she and her brother went for rides during which they engaged in political discourse. Roosevelt also often discussed politics and international affairs with Bamie. From time to time, the President would remain awake late into the night talking politics. During one of these sessions in November 1894, Theodore and Corrine stayed up until seven in the morning (Edith went to bed at midnight). Corrine attributed Edith's lack of interest in these marathon sessions to the fact that "she was not born a Roosevelt."

The President's habit of excluding the First Lady from political discussions created some resentment on Edith's part. Although she remained cordial toward Roosevelt's sisters (and indeed the three women remained lifelong friends), on occasion the First Lady demonstrated a capacity for vindictiveness and retribution. Her most common weapon was a biting wit, however, she also undertook a variety of other measures as reprisals. For instance, during the 1905 inauguration of Roosevelt, Edith did not provide enough event tickets for Corrine's children. Roosevelt's sister was sure that the First Lady intentionally planned the incident as an act of vengeance.[11]

"Princess" Alice

Long before the Roosevelts entered the White House, Alice had grown increasingly defiant and determined to be her own person despite the best efforts of her parents to craft a specific vision of the family for the public. Alice acquired a number of habits that proved embarrassing to the President and First Lady, not least of which was smoking. In addition, she adamantly refused to attend school and was instead educated by tutors. Nonetheless, Alice soon came to be one of the media favorites among the family. Her social debut in 1902 was a resounding success and helped restore the White House as the center of the Washington social scene.

Her debut was followed by an invitation to christen the new yacht, *Meteor*, of Kaiser Wilhelm of Germany. Alice's regal demeanor at the occasion led the press to christen her "Princess Alice." There was even a proposal to have Alice represent the United States at the coronation of King Edward of Great Britain.[12] Roosevelt instead dispatched his eldest daughter on a goodwill tour of the Caribbean in 1903, including spots in Cuba and Puerto Rico. This voyage also met with both popular and diplomatic success and it prompted Roosevelt to send Alice on an even more ambitious four-month journey to Asia in 1905. During the trip, Alice visited Japan, China, the Philippines, Hong Kong, and Korea.

When she returned form the trip, Alice became engaged to Republican Congressman Nicholas Longworth from Ohio, who was fifteen years her senior. The wedding was set for February 17, 1906. The President and First Lady hoped that marriage would settle Alice, but meanwhile the planning and management of the wedding were trying times for Edith who assumed all of the responsibility for the wedding ceremony. Alice proved difficult throughout the period leading up to the wedding and even delayed the ceremony. The strain of the process led Edith to exclaim "I want you to know that I'm glad to see you leave. You have never been anything but trouble."[13] The two women reconciled, but relations remained tense throughout Edith's life.

Ethel and the Boys

While Alice proved to be the most troublesome of the Roosevelt children, the boys and Ethel also engaged in their share of high-jinks and rambunctious behavior. Quentin in particular seemed to delight in antics that embarrassed his parents. Quentin led the expedition to smuggle the pony Algonquin into the family quarters of the White House and was even found to have coated the famous presidential portrait of Andrew Jackson with spitballs.[14] In addition, Edith found that her husband often encouraged or even engaged in the same mischievous behavior as the children. His wrestling matches with the boys were legendary and on more than one occasion caused the President to be late for official functions either because he lost track of time or because his clothes became ruffled. Concerning one episode, the President wrote:

> The other night before the diplomatic dinner, having about fifteen minutes to spare, I went into the nursery, where the two small persons [Archie and Quentin] in pink tommies instantly raced for the bed and threw themselves on it with ecstatic conviction that a romp was going to begin. . . . I did not have the heart to disappoint them, and the result was that my shirt got so mussed that I had to change it.[15]

When Theodore was sworn in as President, Ted was already enrolled at the exclusive preparatory school at Groton. One by one, the other boys were enrolled in public schools and then subsequently dispatched to join Ted at Groton when they were old enough.

The President and First Lady insisted that the children be treated the same as any others. The press quickly picked up on the egalitarian nature of the children's initial education. Newspapers were replete with stories and pictures of the children sitting side-by-side with the children of average Americans. The papers and serials also noted the very active role that Theodore and Edith Roosevelt took in their children's education. The President and First Lady often wrote notes to teachers to check on the progress of their children. In one celebrated episode, the President appeared at Quentin's school with a floral bouquet and an official apology for a teacher who had been the target of his son's spitballs the day before. Although Quentin seemed to be the most mischievous of the boys, it was Archie who was expelled from Groton after a disparaging note he had written was confiscated by teachers (he went on to graduate from Andover).

Although Roosevelt had an almost fraternal relationship with his children, he insisted on meting out discipline (Edith often claimed that he was almost useless in all others matters of child-rearing).[16] Over the years, Mrs. Roosevelt had developed a capacity to ignore the minor transgressions of the children. While in the White House, Theodore noted that there was only a single instance in which he had to physically "thrash" one of the children. The incident involved Quentin who left school early without permission and then lied to his parents in an effort to cover his tracks.[17]

DAILY LIFE IN THE ROOSEVELT WHITE HOUSE

Travels and Other Firsts

As President, Theodore Roosevelt accomplished a number of firsts. For instance, Roosevelt was the first president to ride and submerge in a submarine. More significantly, in November 1906, Theodore and Edith Roosevelt became the first president and first lady to travel outside of the United States while in office. The first couple journeyed to Panama to inspect the ongoing construction of the trans–Isthmus Canal. In fact, the Roosevelts were the most widely traveled first family in the nation's history to date. Moreover, Edith traveled more extensively than any other first lady until her niece, Eleanor Roosevelt, occupied the White House almost three decades later.

In addition to Alice's aforementioned journeys, the family also traveled extensively within the United States, including journeys into the West and several extended cruises around the East Coast. For example, Edith took the three youngest children for a cruise through the St. John's River near St. Augustine, Florida, in 1903. Furthermore, each summer, the family journeyed to Sagamore Hill, their estate in Oyster Bay, New York, while they spent the winter holidays at their country house, Pine Knot, in Virginia.

Daily Routine

Nonetheless, during the periods that they were in White House, Theodore and Edith Roosevelt established a daily routine that varied little during the President's tenure. In light of the rambunctiousness of their day-to-day lives, the couple recognized the importance of establishing some degree of stability for the children. They rose at 7:30 A.M., bathed, and dressed for the day. The family ate breakfast together between eight and a quarter after the hour. Edith encouraged conversation during the meal and invariably prodded each of the children to discuss their day while Theodore devoured cup after cup of coffee. Following breakfast, the children were off to school while their parents would usually go for a short walk around the White House grounds. By 9:30 A.M., Theodore was at his desk (except on Sundays). Meanwhile, the First Lady would also begin her official day by sorting through her correspondence and writing the requisite response notes and thank-you cards. Both Edith and Theodore divided their days into what they termed the "official" and "private" times.

The Official Day

Theodore Roosevelt spent his mornings also reading through correspondence and the nation's major newspapers. On average, Roosevelt received approximately 500 letters each day, but the First Lady culled through most of the correspondence. In addition, the President had staffers search through all 350 major newspapers and clip articles for his perusal. From 10:00 A.M. until lunch, at about 1:00 P.M., Roosevelt met with visitors, politicians, and diplomats. On Tuesdays and Fridays, he would meet with the Cabinet officers, usually at 11:00 A.M. Meanwhile, Mrs. Roosevelt would hold meetings with the White House staff to plan or arrange social events. Usually, just prior to lunch, Roosevelt met with reporters.[18] The President and First Lady then dined together for lunch.

Lunch was an adventurous affair since Edith often did not know exactly the time or who would attend. Theodore adopted the habit of inviting those dignitaries or guests with which he was meeting to dine with the First Family. As a result, the topics of the President's meetings often spilled over into lunch. The President tended to dominate the discussions and participants later recounted the great depth and variety of the conversations. For example, Theodore Roosevelt was prone to mixing

> discussions of birds, brief and incisive analyses of political questions, unexpected quotations from Kipling and Swinburne, descriptions of throws he had just learned from his Japanese wrestling instructors, recollections of his Rough

Rider days, and sudden references to Euripides or the lore of the Nibelungenlied.[19]

Although Rosevelt would return to the office on most afternoons, he often used the remainder of the day for exercise or to go riding with his wife. Like the rest of his family, Roosevelt was a voracious reader and often borrowed moments in the afternoon to read popular or scholarly works. It was then time for the First Family to have dinner unless there was a state dinner or other major event planned.

Events and Staff

While the President's staff was well organized before Roosevelt entered office, Edith undertook a number of steps that led to the development of the first official staff for the first lady and further solidified her efforts to institutionalize the office. For instance, she hired Isabelle "Belle" Hagner to be the first official social secretary. Hagner helped Edith with correspondence, planning social events, and dealing with the press. The First Lady would often pen her own stories about the First Family for dissemination to the press in an effort to manage the public perception of the family. Hagner's administrative abilities gained such renown that family friend Archie Butt once stated that "she really is the chief factor at the White House."[20] Hagner would later be employed by other first ladies, including Edith Wilson.

As first lady, Edith Roosevelt believed that one of her chief duties was to restore the White House as the center of the Washington social scene. In order to expand her ability to conduct events, Edith decided to use caterers instead of having the White House staff cook and serve the meals. Ultimately, this resulted in cost savings and increased the efficiency of the service. This allowed the Roosevelts to have a greater number of official events than the President's immediate predecessors had conducted.

Edith also saw herself as a sort of first among equals of the Washington political wives. She met with the wives of the Cabinet officers while their husbands met with the President on Tuesdays and Fridays. Besides being cordial, the First Lady saw these meetings as an opportunity to discuss politics and gather inside information for her husband. For social events, Edith and Hagner developed a master list with separate categories of politicians, family members, and social elites.[21] These lists simplified planning and ensured that there were no mistakes or oversights during the occasions. Edith Rosevelt's attention to detail returned the White House to its former social prominence and events such as Alice's debut and wedding and Ethel's debut were seen as the premier ones of their time.

Family Time

In addition to the family predisposition toward exercise, the second main pastime that bound the Roosevelt family together was reading. The Roosevelt's consistently read to their children throughout their childhood years. As the children grew, each became avid readers. One White House staffer commented that the Roosevelts were

> fiends when it came to reading . . . Never a moment was allowed to go to waste. From the eldest to the youngest they always had a book or magazine before them. The President in particular would just devour a book, and it was no uncommon thing for him to go through three or four volumes in the course of an evening. Likewise we frequently saw one of the children stretched out on the floor flat on his stomach eating a piece of candy and with his face buried deep in a book.[22]

This literary trait served to bring the family closer together and ensure that the children became familiar with both the major literary works of the day and those readings that were important and meaningful to their parents. These works included the writings of Rudyard Kipling, Walter Scott, and Charles Dickens, as well as other classic pieces by noted figures such as Shakespeare. Theodore and Edith Roosevelt also encouraged the children to analyze and discuss these works freely and openly.

One major constraint on the private lives of the Roosevelts was the increased level of security around the First Family. The assassination of McKinley renewed concerns about the safety of public officials and the Roosevelts became the first first family to experience a significant security presence in their day-to-day life. For instance, both Theodore and Edith had a Secret Service agent accompany them on their afternoon horseback rides. The other main limitation on the family was the growing media interest in it. This led the First Lady to insist that the children not speak to reporters without her knowledge or presence and was the foundation for efforts to shape public opinion through astute management of the press.

IN THE PUBLIC EYE

The President and First Lady worked diligently throughout their White House years to cultivate an image of their family that would appeal to Americans, but one that did not necessarily correspond to reality. Both realized the importance of the press. By 1900, the United States was home to more than 2,225 newspapers (an increase of 400 percent since 1870). Furthermore, by the time Roosevelt entered the White House, the precedence had been set for more-or-less continuous coverage of the executive branch, coverage which was heightened during state occasions or national events such as McKinley's assassination.

Consequently, both Theodore and Edith were able to develop close relationships with the national press and employ the newspapers to further their goals. For Roosevelt, this effort was simply part of the broader political campaign to utilize public opinion to sway Congress to his will. In a variety of issue areas, the President sought to use the power of the "bully pulpit" to rally the public behind him. Roosevelt also perceived that he had to aggressively use the press in order to counter negative stories and editorials that ran counter to his position on issues. For instance, he decried the "big reactionaries" who owned many of the major newspapers as his most significant opponents in the 1904 presidential election.[23]

Roosevelt used his office to variously reward or punish reporters depending on their agreement or lack thereof with his views. He established tacit rules about interviews and if reporters violated them, they were punished by the President who denied them access to privileged information (Roosevelt had a name for those reporters that he perceived had betrayed him—"Ananias Club"). On occasion, he even ordered a news blackout from federal sources against specific news organizations.

While her husband often had a confrontational relationship with the press, Mrs. Roosevelt was generally viewed in highly positive light. Her calm demeanor contrasted perfectly with the exuberance of her husband. Edith Roosevelt was also highly conscious of the impact of style and sought to present the First Family in relatively simple and egalitarian tastes. The press would praise "her simple habits and democratic tastes."[24] Throughout her time in the White House, she refused to wear foreign gowns. Instead she used American designers and American clothes.[25]

Edith Roosevelt's main concerns about the press were two-fold: she wanted to preserve the privacy of the First Family to the greatest extent possible; and, because she recognized that press was going to write about the First Family regardless of her efforts, Mrs. Roosevelt wished to ensure that the press was presented with a carefully crafted view of the family. The First Lady understood that both goals could be met through astute management of the media. Hence she and Hagner drafted stories and press releases for public consumption and the First Lady often had carefully staged photographs taken of the First Family in the White House. She even hired a professional photographer, Francis Benjamin Johnson, in order to control the pictures. For his part, Johnson did a masterful job of taking pictures that conveyed a deep sense of intimacy on the part of the family. Edith also tried to avoid public events where the children would be difficult to control.

The Roosevelts' aggressive approach to press management was a sharp departure from that of previous first families. Frances Cleveland had strenuously avoided the public limelight, while Ida McKinley's infirmities prevented her from appearing in public. In contrast, Edith Roosevelt became the first first lady to grace the cover of *Ladies' Home Journal.* [26]

The public image of the Roosevelts was also enhanced by their charitable work. While much of their efforts were through official events or organizations, far greater were their actions in the private sector—away from the public eye. Roosevelt was well-known for his efforts to aid his fellow Rough Riders and Edith engaged in a variety of anonymous donations and charitable work. However, even these "anonymous" actions were soon filtered into the public image of the Roosevelts as reports detailed the actions of the President and First Lady and individuals recounted specific tales of surprise gifts and donations from the White House.

CONCLUSION

The result of these efforts by the President and First Lady was a carefully cultivated public persona for the first family that emphasized egalitarianism and a zest for life. In many ways, average Americans identified with the young first family and their brood of children. Edith Roosevlet symbolized traditional values and simple tastes (despite her privileged upbringing). Margaret Truman wrote that "Edith Roosevelt left the White House in 1909 arguably the most esteemed, beloved First Lady since Martha Washington."[27] Meanwhile Theodore was revered as one of the most successful and influential presidents in American history.

The public and political success of the President and First Lady was directly related to the dynamics of the First Family. Mrs. Roosevelt was a balancer and counterweight to her exuberant husband and kept her husband grounded. Concurrently, the children provided a means for the President to forget the weight of his office and to behave freely. In this manner, the size and complexity of the biggest family that was ever in the White House provided a means of support and comfort to the first president of the twentieth century.

NOTES TO CHAPTER 9

1. H. W. Brands, *TR*, 1997, 194.

2. Tom Lansford, *A "Bully" First Lady*, 2001, 4.

3. The badger was a present from a schoolgirl is Kansas to the Roosevelt children, a gift Theodore Roosevelt accepted while on a tour of the West in 1903; Brands, 1997, 476.

4. Lansford, 2001, 75.

5. Kermit Roosevelt insisted on hand-feeding the pet at breakfast, much to Edith Roosevelt's consternation.

6. Theodore Roosevelt to Theodore Roosevelt, Jr., Washington, D.C., October 19, 1901 in H. W. Brands, *The Selected Letters . . .* , 2001, 272–273.

7. Quoted in Corrine Roosevelt Robinson, *My Brother Theodore Roosevelt*, 1928, 218.

8. Nathan Miller, *Theodore Roosevelt*, 1992, 415.

9. Edith Roosevelt had just given birth to Archie and was concerned about the family's finances (Theodore was relatively well paid at the time as a member of the Federal Civil Service Commission). But, Edith, always the more cautious and practical of the two, was afraid of what would happen if her husband ran for office and lost; Brands, 1997, 266.

10. Cited in Robert P. Watson, *The Presidents' Wives*, 2000, 182.

11. Betty Boyd Caroli, *The Roosevelt Women*, 1998, 184.

12. For Alice Roosevelt Longworth's recollections of the event, see her book Alice Roosevelt Longworth, *Crowded Hours*, 1933, 50.

13. Quoted in Caroli, 1998, 405.

14. Margaret Truman, *First Ladies*, 1996, 311–312.

15. Quoted in Miller, 1992, 414.

16. Ibid., 222.

17. Lansford, 2001, 17.

18. Unless he had a major news event to convey, Theodore Roosevelt usually met only the small group of a half-dozen or so reporters who regularly covered the White House; George Juergens, *News from the White House*, 1981, 14.

19. Kathleen Prindiville, *First Ladies*, 1932, 200.

20. Archibald Butt, *Letters*, 1924, 53.

21. Prindiville, 1932, 198–199.

22. Joan Patterson Kerr, *A Bully Father...*, 1995, 55.

23. In fact, Theodore Roosevelt claimed that "all of the metropolitan newspapers of the largest circulation were against me; in New York fifteen out of every sixteen copies of papers issued were hostile to me," Theodore Roosevelt, *Theodore Roosevelt...*, 1913, 402.

24. Quoted in Edmund Morris, *Theodore Rex*, 2001, 219.

25. Carl Sferrazza Anthony, America's First Families..., 2000, 332–334.

26. Truman, 1996, 307.

27. Ibid., 313.

Ten

The Scandalous Hardings

JAMES S. McCALLOPS

INTRODUCTION

The year 1920 ushered in a new decade and a new sense of optimism for the American public. They elected a new president who promised a "return to normalcy," which to most meant an end to the chaotic reforms of the Progressive Era, a distancing of America from involvement in foreign problems like World War I, and a leader who was common speaking and less idealistic than his predecessor, Woodrow Wilson. Indeed, the image of the 1920s was one of public prosperity and government frivolity, traits largely absent during the previous two decades. President Warren G. Harding stood as the very symbol of the new decade. Along with his wife Florence, the Hardings embraced the twenties' image and attempted to persuade the American public that the future was bright.

Behind the scenes, however, the First Couple was far from the upbeat and optimistic duo they portrayed in public. Petty jealousy, infidelity, illegal drinking, gambling, and corruption plagued the Hardings. Yet, in the two-plus-year period the Hardings lived in the White House, the public was kept in the dark about the First Couples' private lives. Only as the scandals began to surface following Warren Harding's untimely—or perhaps timely— death, did the American people discard their adoration of the Hardings and replace it with scorn and ridicule. To understand how such a situation could have occurred, it is important to understand how Harding gained the office of the presidency and to look more closely at the personalities of the First Couple and their life in the White House.[1]

AN UNLIKELY COUPLE

Warren Gamaliel Harding was elected president of the United States in 1920. A newspaper owner from Marion, Ohio, Harding came from a close-knit family who moved to Marion in 1882 from rural Ohio. Dark-haired and powerfully built, Harding gained the attention of a large number of women in Marion. But the young man also gained a reputation as a womanizer who enjoyed gambling and drinking. At a young age, he bought the *Marion Star*, a small, local newspaper and became its editor, while doing some reporting for the paper.

Florence Kling was fascinated by the strapping newspaper editor and actively pursued him.[2] Her upbringing was quite different than that of her future husband's. The oldest of three children and only daughter of Amos and Louisa Kling, Florence's family was well respected in Marion due to her father's ever-increasing wealth and prosperity. Yet, the Kling home was not a happy one. Amos Kling was extremely controlling, dictating the actions of everyone in the family. Possessing a strong personality herself, young Florence was often at odds with her father and they frequently fought. Finding herself pregnant at nineteen, Florence ran off and married, angering her father and causing him to sever all contact with his daughter.

When her alcoholic husband left her two years later, Florence decided to work and support her child alone. Thus, she moved back to Marion and began teaching piano to support herself and her son, Marshall. The notion that the town's foremost man had a daughter who was a single mother working to pay the rent for a small apartment kept tongues wagging in Marion and further angered Amos Kling.[3]

Eventually, when Florence filed for separation and began the process for divorce, Amos offered to support her son if he lived in the Kling house and took the Kling name. Florence, now faced with the prospect of youthful freedom, gave up her son. She continued to teach piano, becoming close friends with one of her students, Charity Harding. Through this friendship, she met and became acquainted with Charity's older brother, Warren.

Five years his senior and divorced, Florence pursued Warren vigorously. Though initially attracted to his good looks, Florence shared a love of political discussions, animals, and laughter with Warren. But she admitted to her close friends that he lacked a certain drive and must constantly be prodded by her to do more and improve himself.[4] Why the dashing Warren Harding chose ultimately to marry Florence Kling is less clear. Amos Kling adamantly opposed the union and even attempted to thwart it because he believed the rumors that the Hardings had "Negro blood" in their ancestry, a story denied by the Harding family. More likely, Harding married Florence because she was intelligent, perceptive, and driven. While they were dating, she reorganized the subscription collection system for the financially strapped *Marion Star*, at the same time putting it in the black for the first time. In Florence, Warren Harding found a partner and someone to compensate for his weaknesses.[5]

Highly interested in politics from his work in the newspaper business, Warren Harding began his political career as a Republican in a largely Democratic area of the state. Using his charm and party loyalty, Harding advanced up the political ladder, becoming a state senator, lieutenant governor, and U.S. senator before capturing the presidency. At his side and of vital importance to his success was his wife, Florence. In fact, with each election victory, Mrs. Harding became more and more convinced that with her help, there was no limit to what her husband could achieve. In truth, the Hardings remained a team who depended on one another because they trusted each other's judgment. In Florence's case, love also kept her bound to Warren.

PARTNERS IN THE WHITE HOUSE AND PARTNERS IN SCANDAL

It was far from an idyllic union, however. They often fought and argued over a multitude of issues from Harding's extramarital affairs to presidential appointments. Mrs. Harding was very outspoken and unwilling to submit to her husband or a wife's secondary status, during a time when such behavior was frowned on by society. Many a guest at the White House commented on the arguing that could be heard from the Harding's private rooms when Florence summoned Harding to "come here." The First Lady was not averse to speaking her mind to members of the Harding Cabinet either. While the President sat back and observed, the "Duchess" (as he called her) enjoyed engaging in debate with people whose opinions differed from hers. In the end, Harding would make the final decision on an issue, but not surprisingly, he usually sided with his wife.

Descriptions of the Harding's personal life in the White House, however, vary by individual. Those who liked the more common, down-to-earth quality of the Ohioans were laudatory in their praise of the First Couple, while those who viewed them as gauche and garish were harsh in their criticisms.[6] Considering both positions, what emerges is an interesting picture of the First Couple. Clearly they were interested in eliminating the formality that marked previous White House inhabitants. For example, the Hardings shared one bedroom instead of the established pattern of separate sleeping quarters for first couples. They chatted with White House servants and called them by their first names. Mrs. Harding even sometimes snuck into the line for White House tours and hand-picked people who she guided through her private living quarters.

The Ohio Gang

In general, the Hardings wanted the public to love them. They actively sought approval from people and worried over how decisions would affect their popularity. The First Couple had an especially good relationship with the press, which stemmed from their days in Marion running a newspaper. In fact, the Hardings actively sought out what could be called the first "photo ops," orchestrating situations where press photographers would see them in a good light.[7] For both, this was a characteristic trait from their early lives. The President continued to use his ability to charm and gain other's affection to propel both his political career and active social life. Harding made friends easily and was extremely loyal to them. This was evident in his selection of Cabinet officials. High-ranking members of the Senate who helped orchestrate the Harding nomination and election with the belief they could control him, were upset over some of his selections of individuals often referred to as the "Ohio gang."[8]

That characterization, however, was not entirely accurate. Naming Charles Evans Hughes as Secretary of State and Herbert Hoover as Secretary of Commerce were based on qualifications and party loyalty, rather than being from Ohio. But Harding also made some partisan choices by naming Harry Daugherty as Attorney General and Albert Fall as Secretary of the Interior. Neither choice was welcome news to the Senate or the public. Daugherty was a close friend of Harding's who critics claimed received his appointment as payback for support during the campaign. Fall was a poor choice for the Interior position, as critics alleged that a New Mexico oil man he was disinterested in preserving the environment. The President tried to balance his Cabinet, which has been rated as average.[9] The practice of patronage or spoils—a system of political payback—seemed to take place in lesser government jobs. Here, the first couple worked together, with the First Lady helping to name appointments. They both utilized strict friendship and loyalty to award jobs. Many of their appointments were friends and allies from Ohio.

Poker and Alcohol

The appointments were also frequent visitors to the White House, where they would engage in all-night poker games with the President. Harding loved card games and gambling and indulged these interests as often as possible. White House staffers even noticed that the President required little sleep and seemed fully rested after just a few hours of sleep after a night of play. Mrs. Harding did not participate in these gatherings, except to occasionally mix the first round of drinks.

Like many Americans, the Hardings had contradictory views and practices regarding the recent Volstead Act prohibiting the consumption of alcohol. Publically, the first couple never partook of alcoholic beverages and none was served at official White House gatherings. Privately, however, they enjoyed drinking alcohol but were careful only to do it around their circle of close friends. However, once the President arrived at a press conference clearly drunk. In keeping with the manner of reporting at the time, nothing was written about the incident by reporters. For the journalists, there was a clear distinction between the private and the public presidency and they viewed alcoholic consumption as a private matter.[10]

ADULTERY

The press kept Harding's adultery private as well, although it was widely known by the reporters. Once he even commented at a press briefing that "It's a good thing I'm not a woman. I would always be pregnant. I cannot say no."[11] Considered quite handsome and desirable by many of his female contemporaries, he relished the attention he received and continued his extramarital affairs throughout the remainder of his life. Some were short in duration, while others lasted for years. While still in Marion, he became involved with the wife of his close friend Jim Phillips. In fact, Jim and Carrie Phillips spent much time with the Hardings and even took a trip to Europe together. The affair lasted several years and surviving letters illustrate Harding's love for Carrie Phillips. In his rather ribald language, he even describes their sexual acts and names her sexual organs. It seems that Mrs. Harding was unaware of her husband's affair with her friend until 1911 when she intercepted a letter from Carrie to Warren. Though she threatened divorce, in the end Florence and Warren agreed to stay together. Apparently, Mrs. Harding felt that she had invested so much in her husband's career, while Warren realized the importance of his wife in his life.[12] Carrie Phillips did not leave the picture, however, threatening to go public with the candidate's love letters during his presidential campaign. The Republican party established a fund to pay her for the letters, quashing the potentially damaging situation.[13]

Harding continued his dalliances with other women over the years. Of these, Florence Harding appears to have been aware and, while she did not approve, she seems to have been somewhat resigned to them. Yet, to limit Harding's access to other women, his wife began to constantly remain at her husband's side. It was unusual to see Warren without Florence in attendance. Only during her own illnesses did Harding have the opportunity to pursue his love affairs. He once remarked to Carrie Phillips that marital relations had ceased between himself and his wife, and Mrs. Harding was not interested in resuming them. Consequently, Harding, who adored women, found outlets for his passions and affairs. It appears that Florence Harding was hurt by her husband's affairs and worried how they might impact his political career if they were discovered. But, on some level, she felt that men engaged in such things and accepted her own unwillingness to "fulfill his needs."

Still, Mrs. Harding was often jealous of these encounters and did her best to stop them before they occurred. For example, the First Lady had some very loyal secret service agents alert her whenever a particular woman entered the White House. Hurrying down to catch her husband in the act, she was often stopped outside the Oval Office door by a secret service agent loyal to the President, apparently employed by him for that purpose. However, when Mrs. Harding would try to gain entrance to the Oval Office through the adjoining office, the President and his mistress had time to slip out through another door.[14] Warren Harding also began to use the homes of friends such as the McLeans for his romantic encounters so as to avoid his wife. Ned McLean was the owner and publisher of the *Washington Post*, while his wife, Evalyn, was the owner of the famed Hope Diamond. Extremely wealthy, the McLeans owned a mansion outside the capital city called Friendship and another house within the city on I Street, not far from the White House. When possible, Harding preferred to visit and play poker at those two locations because it was easier to conduct his extramarital affairs there. The First Lady was unaware that the McLean's residences were used for such purposes and was extremely hurt when she finally discovered the truth in 1923. Moreover, her friend Evalyn McLean knew of the liaisons but never informed Florence Harding.

Some of the affairs created problems for Harding's presidency. Besides Carrie Phillips, it was rumored that he had fathered at least three children with three different women. There may have been more. The mistresses in question signed affidavits to atest to the affairs and one wrote a book about the affair. The fund established by the Republican party remained active during the length of the Harding presidency, financed by donations and listed under the name Jess Smith, a close friend of Harry Daugherty. Women who made claims against the President were paid off but not before they signed agreements that they would keep the information private. Of those documents that survive, two women claimed Harding fathered children with them: One had a boy who was "adopted out" and the other had her pregnancy terminated (possibly by Harding, but the facts remain uncertain).[15]

The most famous woman in the scandal-ridden presidency was Nan Britton. A resident of Marion, Ohio, her family had been friends with the Hardings. Ms. Britton became enamored of the handsome Harding. According to her, she and Harding commenced an affair that resulted in the birth of their daughter. Though half Harding's age, Britton contended that he truly loved her and evidence exists that he did support the baby girl born to Britton, although he apparently never met the girl. Britton even said that Harding and she had a particularly ardent encounter in a small closetlike room next to the Oval Office while he was president. Evidence of Harding's love for her and the White House encounter come from Nan Britton's book, written a few years after the President's death.[16] It shocked the public when it was released. In the 1920s most Americans were not used to exposés that discussed sexual relations, especially by the presidents.

PUBLIC AND PRIVATE LIVES

The Hardings attempted to lighten the mood of the White House to mirror the gay image of the 1920s. They also understood that people often took their cues from the first couple, so they wanted to portray a vibrant and prosperous nation. At times this was difficult, as the nation plunged into a recession in 1921 and unemployment rose. Curiously, the Hardings were not blamed for the economic downturn, but the First Couple stepped up their efforts to assuage the nation's citizens of their fears about continued economic problems. The First Lady, for example, enlisted the "new" Hollywood movie stars to make appearances at the White House, which were photographed and distributed to the public. The Hardings fascination with the movie industry mirrored the nation's interest and efforts were made from the White House to take the public's mind off the economic situation by diverting attention to such matters as movie stars and the Harding's pet dog, an Airedale named Laddie Boy.[17] Laddie Boy was featured in numerous articles and even wrote his own advice column, ghostwritten by the President himself. The First Pet became a celebrity.

The Hardings also hosted more social events, receptions, and teas, encouraged any group visiting the capital city to have their photographs taken on the White House lawn, and generally made themselves available to the press. Woodrow Wilson had disliked the press and such social activities, however, the Hardings understood the importance of and enjoyed interactions with the media. Thus, both Warren and Florence Harding were prominently featured in newspapers across the country, making them perhaps the most recognizable first couple in history at the time.

The First Couple's Health

Energetic and *vibrant* were words often used to describe the Hardings, but both Warren and Florence faced serious health problems. The President had been raised to believe in homeopathic remedies and the First Lady adopted his faith in such cures. Doc Sawyer, a homeopathic practitioner in Marion, Ohio, became their most trusted caregiver during the early days of their marriage and this relationship lasted through the White House years.[18] In fact, after Harding's election to the presidency, he named Sawyer to head up veteran's issues. Even from this post, Sawyer's main role was the health of the First Couple. Warren Harding suffered from periodic bouts of depression and anxiety that resulted in him being hospitalized for a few months in a sanitarium near Marion shortly after his marriage. In addition, he suffered from high blood pressure and heart problems, which were exacerbated by his drinking, smoking, and keeping late hours. Florence Harding had kidney problems, diagnosed during her life as tuberculosis of the kidneys, which ultimately resulted in her death in 1924. Sawyer was their primary physician and tended to downplay the problems, prescribing tonics and other homeopathic remedies. In fact, he only called in specialists for Mrs. Harding when she was close to death. Both consulting doctors recommended an operation, but Sawyer vetoed it, waiting instead for his patient's health to recover naturally. Fortunately, the First Lady recovered somewhat. Regarding the President's high blood pressure and deteriorating heart, Sawyer remained largely silent, attributing Harding's weakness and chest pains to indigestion.

Faith in homeopathic cures was not the only passion of the First Couple. Mrs. Harding also placed great stock in the words of fortune-tellers. Madame Marcia was her most valued psychic during the White House years. The First Lady consulted the psychic frequently and even summoned her to the White House on numerous occasions late at night. Madame Marcia's most dire prediction haunted Florence Harding and contributed to her constant vigil over the President. According to the fortune-teller, the President would not live to finish his term, but would die in office in a sudden, violent, and mysterious way.[19]

Given this prediction and her faith in fortune tellers, the First Lady altered her husband's schedule if she felt he was in any danger. If Madame Marcia told of events that might lead to injury or death for the President, the First Lady canceled them. Although Mrs. Harding consulted the psychic regularly on all important matters, she did not have the fortune-teller consider the administration's Cabinet. It was not until two years had passed in the White House that the First Lady directed her psychic to include the Cabinet in her visions. Florence Harding would later lament her failure to do this sooner.

Fraud and Bribery

Behind the facade of confidence and prosperity, the Harding administration was faced with scandals and other problems that ultimately destroyed the positive image of the first couple. Many of the scandals ended up involving close personal friends of the First Couple. In the Veteran's Bureau, Doc Sawyer's number-two person was Charlie Forbes, who directed the agency when Sawyer was preoccupied with the Hardings' health. Forbes publically expressed his belief that his bureau should build numerous hospitals to accommodate ailing veterans, but Sawyer countered him, arguing that the demand for such hospitals would decline over time and staying with the existing hospitals would make better sense in the long run.[20] According to official accounts, Forbes waited until Sawyer was out of town and absorbed with the First Couples' health to push forward through the bureau's board plans for building new hospitals. Forbes even awarded construction contracts to various contractors around the country.

When this came to light, members of Congress raised concerns about the manner in which the contracts had been awarded. In reality, Forbes's own lifestyle cast suspicion on his actions. Like other members of Harding's administration, he enjoyed wild parties and alcohol. Forbes entertained celebrities and lived far above his financial means. To cover the expenses, Forbes had been taking money offered by businesses eager to secure contracts. The assistant director also inflated the price of some government land sold for hospital construction, taking a cut off the top for himself.[21] While much of this was unknown to congressional investigators at the time, the issue generated interest by the press, who began their own investigation of the matter. Sawyer was concerned about the growing scandal and wanted Forbes fired, but Harding delayed action, finding it hard to believe that his trusted friend had betrayed him. Mrs. Harding felt particularly betrayed because she had always devoted much of her time and energy to veterans, visiting hospitals and inviting veterans to the White House. Public speculation about her true motives in the wake of the scandal greatly wounded her. Forbes was eventually stripped of his position and the bureau's legal counsel committed suicide. The damage had been done, however.

Harding confidantes including the Attorney General were accused of knowing about and giving tacit approval to bribery and payoffs. Most of the accusations stemmed from the use of Jess Smith to run a secret Republican account to pay off Harding's mistresses. There were also other bribes made and a host of illegalities for which Smith was implicated and Daughtery linked indirectly. So too did Congress and the press speculate about the Attorney General's seeming lack of knowledge about Forbes and a variety of other scandals, including the most damaging of Harding's administration—the leasing of oil lands.

Teapot Dome

The government owned land that contained oil reserves. Early in the administration, Secretary of the Interior Albert Fall leased these lands to Edward Doheny and Harry Sinclair. Harding contended that the leases were within the bounds of the law, while the Navy, who owned the land, was suspicious.[22] Even casual observers would have wondered how Fall with his small government salary could afford to, among other things, buy adjoining land to his ranch and begin expensive remodeling of the home. But the Hardings either did not notice or were inclined to ignore such things. Concern by the Navy prompted newspaper investigations that resulted in Fall resigning from his job in 1923 to accept a position with Sinclair's oil company. Florence Harding was upset by Fall's departure, as she felt that his next appointment would be to the Supreme Court.[23] Fall, however, decided to leave public service in an effort to forestall a congressional investigation of the oil leases. That investigation ultimately began after Harding's death and uncovered massive payoffs to Fall from Sinclair and Doheny. Nicknamed the "Teapot Dome Scandal" for one of the locations of the leases, it proved to be the final disgrace for the former president and first lady.

Of these scandals Harding was well aware before his death. In fact, they might have even contributed to his anxiety and untimely passing. Plagued with high blood pressure and a weak heart, the stress of these misdeeds and possibility of them becoming public would assuredly have weighed heavily on the President's shoulders. Harding even remarked frequently that the presidency was not what he expected and perhaps he would have been happier serving as an ambassador.[24] The press, sensing his pessimistic tone and recent purchase of a ranch, wondered whether he was anticipating another term in the White House. Privately, the decision was not discussed. But Mrs. Harding believed Madame Marcia, who began contending that the President would not live to see 1925 and that Florence's own death would follow soon after. While the First Lady appears not to have disclosed these predictions to her husband, it is clear that she was hesitant about a second term. Consequently, Doc Sawyer announced that the President would not seek a second term. When pressed, Sawyer claimed he made the announcement to suppress intraparty fighting and provide the President with space to make his final decision.[25]

CONCLUSION

In the summer of 1923 as the scandals were brewing, the First Couple undertook a western tour by train that would take them all the way to Alaska. Florence Harding had always wanted to see this part of the country and earlier planned trips had been forced to be canceled for a variety of reasons. So, she was adamant that the couple take the trip. The President suffered a bout with the flu in early spring and was still complaining of frequent chest pains and shortness of breath. His physician, Doc Sawyer, however, attributed the problems to remnants of the flu even though others had noted that Harding's skin had a grayish tone and the President looked ill.[26] The First Lady ignored her husband's weaknesses and the couple continued to exhibit confidence in Sawyer's skill.

The presidential train traveled slowly, making many stops so the Hardings could emerge from their private car and speak to gathered crowds. The First Lady addressed the crowds, cementing her image as a partner to her husband. The entire trip was filled with appearances by the President, even though some advisers felt the schedule was too taxing for the ailing man. As far as we know, the Hardings voiced no concerns or complaints and the schedule remained unchanged.

The trip took a toll on Warren Harding's already precarious health. The hot temperatures and numerous public appearances contributed to his chronic exhaustion. He was unable to sleep unless his head and chest were elevated due to what Sawyer diagnosed as chronic heartburn and indigestion. Harding's speeches also lacked their usual charisma because he had trouble breathing and remembering his train of thought. Reporters noted the difficulties and began questioning the President's health, to which Doc Sawyer responded were lingering effects of the flu. Harding's health was further compromised when the entire entourage consumed tainted seafood in Alaska. Finally alarmed, the First Lady ordered the tour canceled, but decided to wait in San Francisco while her husband rested and regained his strength. It was there on August 2, 1923, that Harding suffered an attack that proved fatal. Sawyer attributed it to a cerebral hemorrhage, but more likely it was a heart attack that killed Harding.[27]

The widowed Florence Harding returned with the body of her late husband to Washington, where the President was placed in state. Then, she accompanied the body back to Marion for burial. The nation's outpouring of grief was profound, as thousands lined the tracks of the returning train to show their respect. Through it all, Mrs. Harding attempted to remain composed. Without her husband, she was unsure what would become of her life except that Warren Harding's memory and reputation must be preserved.

Florence Harding returned to Washington, D.C. from Marion and sought out her late husband's associates and advisers, seeking any correspondence with the Hardings they might be in possession of. She claimed that she wanted to compile papers for a biography and to make a donation to a library. People willingly complied. On receiving those papers, Florence Harding began to burn those she deemed potentially damaging to the image of her late husband and herself. The former first lady undertook this endeavor, first at the White House, and later at the McLean home named Friendship. Here, vehicles brought wooden crates full of papers and personal items that were burned in an open fire on the lawn. Eventually, Mrs. Harding returned to their former home in Marion and their office at the *Star* where she continued destroying evidence. When the curator of the Library of Congress met with her and asked that the Harding papers be donated to the museum, she responded that they had been destroyed to protect the President's memory.[28]

While Warren Harding did not live to see the results of the various congressional investigations of the illegal activities of his administration, Florence Harding did live through much of it. In early 1924, intense scrutiny by Congress of the Harding administration revealed the graft and corruption that existed, tarnishing once and for all the image she and her husband had worked to achieve. For the widow, life after the White House entailed moving back to Marion to settle in a cabin on the lawn of Doc Sawyer's sanitarium. Her health further weakened. Depressed over the scandals surrounding her late husband's presidency and the lingering predictions of Madame Marcia that her own death would soon follow, Florence Harding appeared to give up on life.

On November 21, 1924, she succumbed to a weakened heart and kidney problem, dying that evening. With her passing, the Harding presence and secrets were gone, but a tarnished legacy remained.

NOTES TO CHAPTER 10

1. One of the most useful sources on Florence Harding's life and her marriage to Warren G. Harding is Carl Sferrazza Anthony's book, *Florence Harding—The First Lady of the Jazz Age and the Death of America's Most Scandalous President* (New York: William Morrow, 1998).

2. Anthony, 1998, 36.

3. Ibid., 31.

4. Ibid., 41.

5. Robert K. Murray, *The Harding Era*, 1969, 420.

6. Anthony, 1998, 284.

7. Ibid., 278–280.

8. Andrew Sinclair, *The Available Man*, 1965, 229.

9. Ibid., 190.

10. Anthony, 1998, 291.

11. Ibid., 303.

12. Ibid., 97–98.

13. Ibid., 203.

14. Ibid., 374.

15. Ibid., 302.

16. To consider Nan Britton's version of events, her book about the affair is titled *The President's Daughter*, 1927.

17. Anthony, 1998, 279–280.

18. Ibid., 329.

19. Ibid., 175.

20. Murray, 1969, 429.

21. Sinclair, 1965, 261.

22. Anthony, 1998, 305.

23. Ibid., 395.

24. Ibid., 414.

25. Ibid., 398.

26. Ibid., 398.

27. Ibid., 459.

28. Ibid., 488.

Part IV

Preserving the President's House

Complete reconstruction of the White House during the Truman administration (courtesy of the Harry S. Truman Library)

Overview:
A Mansion with a History

Over its 200-plus-year history, the building now known as the White House has been burned, rebuilt, enlargened, gutted and rebuilt again, and restored many times. The need for completely rebuilding the structure and undertaking ambitious renovations has occurred several times throughout history. For instance, the building was burned by invading British troops in 1814 during the War of 1812. Tragically, the building's interior was destroyed and most of the furnishings and artifacts were lost to the fire. If it were not for the heroics of then–first lady Dolley Madison, who wisely and courageously removed several priceless items including the famous full portrait of George Washington painted by Gilbert Stuart, any link to the history of the President's House would have been lost.

After the inauguration of Andrew Jackson in 1829, supporters of the "people's president"—namely frontiersmen—crowded into the home, destroying furnishings, breaking china, tracking mud from boots, and generally wrecking the interior of the Executive Mansion. In fact, the President had to sneak out of the side of the building for fear for his safety. Over 100 years later, when the leg of his daughter's grand piano broke through the floor of the building and floors and ceilings creaked and sagged precariously, President Harry Truman recognized the need to rebuild the White House. This extensive rebuilding was needed to save the White House, which was in imminent risk of collapse owing to its age, extensive use, and poorly planned renovations.

But not all the threats to the integrity of the Executive Mansion have been so dramatic. Most of the damage to the building has come from the daily wear-and-tear from those who work there, countless guests, and the millions of people who have toured the

White House. Historically, the building and its furnishings have also fallen prey to memento-seeking visitors who have cut away, torn out, and stolen souvenirs from the White House, and previous first families, who often gave away or sold off items with little thought to historic preservation.

There is also the need every four years or so for new occupants to bring their own living needs and decorating tastes to the building, especially the private living quarters upstairs in the White House. As such, the building is in a perpetual state of change and has seen dozens of different interior design styles. There has also been the need for expansion, as additional office, entertaining, and living space became necessary to keep up with the growth in the institution of the presidency and national government. Moreover, the original design of the building gave inadequate consideration to actual living arrangements.

Leaving Their Mark

The first presidential spouse to occupy the building—Abigail Adams—complained that only six rooms were completed on her arrival and she had no place for such practical concerns as where to hang the family laundry. To save his servants from lugging water for the home the one-mile distance to the nearest water source, Thomas Jefferson designed a system of wooden pipes and cistern. (Iron pipes eventually replaced Jefferson's system during Andrew Jackson's presidency and Martin Van Buren installed a reservoir.) Jefferson also accommodated his tastes by building a wine cellar and meat house on the grounds and had housing constructed for servants. As the scope and power of the presidency and federal government expanded, the need for additional staff and office space infringed on the private living quarters of the first family. The need for adequate living space resulted in several expansions of the second and third floors of the building and eventual construction of East and West Wings off the original building to house presidential staff.

From John Adams in 1801 through the twentieth century, first families were relatively free to change the building as they saw fit. There was the occasional need to satisfy members of Congress in order to receive an appropriation for decorating or renovating the building, but often the costs of maintaining and decorating the house came out of the pockets of first families. Thomas Jefferson, James Monroe, and other presidents suffered serious financial setbacks resulting in part from the cost associated with living in the

Executive Mansion. Fortunately, while some first families failed to recognize the importance of preserving the building's history, others made this a priority. The task of decorating, managing, and preserving the building fell naturally to the presidents' spouses, on account of existing sex role social norms. Several spouses undertook important and extensive redecorations and restorations of the Executive Mansion, including Dolley Madison, Julia Tyler, Abigail Fillmore, Mary Lincoln, Julia Grant, Caroline Harrison, Edith Roosevelt, and, perhaps most important, Jacqueline Kennedy, who acquired historic furnishings and period settings for the rooms. Thanks to several of these first ladies and first families, the building has been preserved.

Apart from expansions and major restorations under Theodore Roosevelt and Harry Truman, changes in design and style occurring in the twentieth century, however, have been less dramatic than those of the previous century. By the latter twentieth century, the emphasis in decorating has been on restoration to retain the building's authenticity. Traditionally, while little thought had been given to historic preservation, today preserving the historic integrity of the building is the first and foremost goal of any renovation. Curators, art historians, and other professionals assist first families in maintaining the building. All items have been cataloged and preserved, funds are raised for preservation, and the White House has been preserved as a living museum, symbol of democracy, and the people's house.

The White House We Know Today

This—the final section of the book—explores the effort to preserve the White House. The section opens with an overview of the 200-plus-year history of the building and the many efforts to renovate and restore it. These efforts have varied from making accommodations for day-to-day living, to such mundane tasks as changing the drapes, to grand efforts to save the White House. The second chapter in this section discusses the historic efforts to preserve the building and documents the important role of the curator and other professional staff in preserving the White House. The third and fourth chapters examine two of the most important and major renovations in the history of the White House that took place during the administrations of Theodore Roosevelt and Harry Truman. In these chapters, the vision and efforts by Edith Roosevelt and President Truman, respectively, played a significant role in the renovations and integrity of the White House as we know it today.

Eleven

Renovating the White House: A Brief History

Robert E. Dewhirst

Introduction

The name "White House" is well known not only to American citizens but to people throughout the world. However, the residence of the President of the United States was initially named the "Executive Mansion," but more often simply was called "the President's House." By the time of the Lincoln administration in the early 1860s, the building's popular nickname— "White House"—was being used more commonly.[1] However, the building's name was not officially changed from the Executive Mansion to the White House until 1901, during the presidency of Theodore Roosevelt[2] because of the outside walls, which were white-washed during its construction in the late 1790s.

The national landmark has evolved enormously throughout more than 200 years. Although the white exterior walls of the main structure remain essentially the same today as the day they were erected, the interior of the building has been remodeled and even rebuilt in response to the evolving demands of aesthetics, convenience, function, and even safety.

This chapter chronicles the overall evolution of the building at 1600 Pennsylvania Avenue, Washington, D.C., throughout its more than two centuries at center stage of at first American, and more recently, world politics. Indeed, many of the changes made to the White House could be said to parallel the evolution of technological developments in Western civilization. Changes made to the White House also tended to focus on making the building and its surrounding property a more efficient and attractive setting for the president to live, work, and entertain. Renovation and remodeling changes made to the White House are discussed here as they happened and are grouped within each of four 50-year periods. However, this chapter will focus in particular on the structure's developments during perhaps its most important period—the first half of the nineteenth century.

A Beginning and Then a New Beginning (1800–1850)

The Adams Years

John Adams was the first president to occupy the White House, moving into the uncompleted residence with his wife Abigail on November 1, 1800. Living in the new structure the following winter proved to be somewhat of a hardship experience for the couple. The building lacked main and back staircases and had twenty-four unfinished rooms. Likely adding to the Adams's discomfort that winter was the frequently wet plaster clinging from the recently completed walls of the six rooms that had been officially reported livable. In addition, the building had serious water problems of another sort. First, the closest water supply was about a mile away, necessitating the use of chamber pots before an outdoor toilet could be constructed. Then a leaky roof caused the ceiling of the East Room to collapse. The event undoubtedly was doubly troublesome for Mrs. Adams because her early use of that room as the preferred place to hang washed clothes to dry. In sum, the initial efforts of the Adams family were directed primarily toward making the White House a comfortable residence in which to live.

The Jefferson Years

Simply possessing a comfortable living environment would not be enough for the second occupant of the White House, Thomas Jefferson, who moved into the building on his inauguration the following March of 1801. In many ways Jefferson might be said to have been the president most influential on the physical evolution and development of the White House.[3] A prominent architect in his own right, Jefferson appointed Benjamin Latrobe the Surveyor of the Public Buildings and directed him to plan and replace the leaky roof that had caused the Adams family so many problems. Apparently the original slate roof, combined with lead gutters, were far too heavy for the outer walls, causing them to spread and thereby opening cracks through which rain showered the building's interior. Latrobe also finished an additional bedroom and dug a well to replace the original one whose water had become contaminated.

By the start of his second term Jefferson's architectural enthusiasm came to the forefront. He was eager to make more significant changes to the White House. The President, working with Latrobe, drew up plans for constructing lengthy ground-story office wings straight outward from the east and west ends of the building. Abbreviated versions of these wings were constructed in the years 1805–1806. Jefferson and Latrobe also developed plans for a bow portico on the south side of the building and a more extensive *porte-cochere* extending over the entrance on the building's north side. While Jefferson failed to have those plans implemented during his term, he was successful in having a stone wall constructed around the grounds, with visitor access provided through an arched gate facing the capitol.

The Madison Years

The administration of Jefferson's successor, James Madison, endured one of the most catastrophic events in the history of the White House. On August 24, 1814 the British caused what would become the most extensive renovating project in the history of the White House—their army burned the building. After burning the Capitol that morning, the army moved down Pennsylvania Avenue and set fire to the White House. The blaze quickly gutted the roof and interior of the structure but a sudden intense rain storm, accompanied by fierce winds, saved the exterior walls, although large cracks appeared in the stonework on the upper walls on the north and south sides. Earlier, the president's wife, Dolley, had gathered important documents, clothes, and a famous portrait of George Washington, and escaped before the troops arrived.[4] However, she was unable to save important interior furnishings, which either were burned or taken by looters.

Afterward, the Madisons lived in nearby residences throughout most of the remainder of his administration. Six months after the disaster, Congress, following rejection of a proposal to move the capital inland to Cincinnati, authorized funds to rebuild all of the damaged public buildings, including the White House. The order directed that the White House be restored to its exact condition prior to the fire. A three-member commission was named to oversee the reconstruction to begin in late March of 1815. The commissioners immediately hired James Hoban, an Irish immigrant and the winner of the initial contest for the design of the President's House and the builder of the original White House. By 1815, he also clearly was the most respected builder in Washington.[5]

Hoban immediately confronted a significant and unanticipated hurdle. Early estimates of the extent of the damage to the outer walls proved to be understated considerably. Much more of the exterior would have to be reconstructed than initially anticipated. Cleaning the walls in preparation for reconstruction had revealed their extremely weakened condition, stemming primarily from their exposure to harsh winter weather following the excessive heat of the fire and quick cooling from the intense rain that stilled the fire. Hoban found that the second-floor exterior walls on about half of the building would have to be removed down to the first floor while the exterior walls on the rest of the building would have to be extensively repaired up to and including the second floor. In sum, except for most of the foundation and basement, and the lower parts of several exterior walls, the White House would have to be completely rebuilt.

Additionally, Hoban encountered intense pressure to complete the task in a timely manner. President James Madison and congressional leaders alike, humiliated by the burning of the capital, wanted to reconstruct all destroyed public buildings as soon as possible. Hence, reconstruction of the White House proceeded quickly—taking only about three years to complete—far less than the decade required to build the building only a few years prior. Not wanting to raise the ire of Congress about the unanticipated extent of the damage to the building, Hoban had the bulk of the demolition undertaken after Congress adjourned in 1816. He required builders to endure long workdays of ten to twelve hours or more throughout the rest of the year. By the fall, a roof had been put on the building and the outer walls were essentially complete by the following February. Hoban accelerated the exterior construction by having stone cutters and carvers working in nearby sheds long before the walls were demolished. Hence, new stone was ready for installation as soon as the damaged blocks were removed. Significantly, Hoban also accelerated the process by substituting timber for brick in constructing many important interior walls. He also saved time by having key materials shipped up the nearby

Potomac River on steam boats, an expediency unavailable for the original construction of the White House.

Erection of the walls and roof meant that construction of the interior could be done throughout the winter. The workers put so much of themselves into the job that carpenters celebrated the enclosing of the building with a party, during which they reportedly consumed large amounts of whiskey, bread, cheese, sugar, and crackers. Interior work continued at a steady pace throughout the winter, with saws and workbenches in use throughout the building.

The Monroe Years

Yet, despite these rapid developments the newest president, James Monroe, put additional pressure on the builders. On his inauguration on March 4, 1817, Monroe announced that he would move into the White House the following fall, only eight months after taking office. Monroe spent most of his first year as president touring the New England states and planned on returning to the capital to occupy and receive guests in the completed White House in October. Construction surged to a frenzied pace as workers laid floors, erected walls and staircases, constructed cabinets, and installed interior doors and fine wood trim. They were kept warm by fires in the fireplaces located throughout the building. Moreover, Hoban's plan for the restored White House included installation of twelve additional fireplaces to accommodate rooms he had added to the building and the need for better heating.[6]

Work on the interior progressed steadily throughout the summer. Wood used on the interior was primarily mahogany, baywood, and yellow pine. In addition, marble and sandstone (obtained primarily from nearby quarries in Maryland) were used for important parts of the house. Four 14-foot Ionic columns made of marble were installed beneath the triple arches in the main entrance hall. All of this was done in preparation for plastering the walls and ceilings and, where required, hanging wallpaper or painting. Meanwhile, the exterior of the building was cleaned thoroughly and covered with white lead paint in a linseed oil base instead of the whitewash that covered the original structure.[7] The new heavier white paint better covered the black stains and repairs made from damage caused by the fire.

However, much to President Monroe's dismay, the building was not completed when he returned to Washington. He was greeted with a building featuring the odors of drying plaster and prime-painted woodwork and the sight of freshly installed but unfinished pine floors. Outside, much work also remained. Important finishing work needed to be completed on both the roof and the north and south sides of the building to greatly improve its appearance and also remove the unsightly temporary boards and covers used to protect the White House during the construction of its interior.

The work also included the start of construction of porticos on the north and south sides of the building. Completed by this time were the bases of both porticos. The smaller south portico was planned to feature six Ionic columns and capitals but would lack a pediment, thereby making it a porch. However, funds to complete the porticos were diverted to other more pressing projects, so that the South Portico was not completed until early 1824. Meanwhile, work on the public entrance, the more extensive North Portico—actually a *port-cochere* because it extended over the driveway—was not completed until 1829. This front faced the nearby President's Park which, since 1822, was bordered on its north by Pennsylvania Avenue which had been extended westward from Capitol Hill.

Undoubtedly disappointed by the workers' failure to complete the building, the Monroes moved into the White House in October. The couple was confined to living in a few rooms on the second floor and eating meals prepared by cooks working in a nearly complete kitchen in the basement. Life on the largely unfinished first floor centered on the oval saloon facing the south.[8] Clearly, while enormous progress had been made since Monroe had come to power, much work remained before the building would be completed. However, once in the building, the Monroes pursued their next goal of making the White House sufficiently presentable to renew the tradition of holding an open house on New Year's Day.[9] Hence, efforts centered on making the large first floor rooms at least presentable for featuring a reception for foreign diplomats, to be followed by an open house for the American public.

Because of the limited time available to the craftsmen, interior decorating work tended to focus on making temporary and expedient improvements. Newspaper accounts of the subsequent festivities reported a major social success, with the furnishing apparently providing an attractive backdrop to the event, which was additionally blessed with mild weather outside.[10] In addition, sheltered from the view of those attending the reception, a party with refreshments similar to the previous celebration, was held for the building's deserving workers.[11] Work on the White House resumed soon thereafter and, depending upon the availability of funds, continued throughout the next several presidencies. The south portico was completed in 1824 and the more extensive north portico in 1829.

The Mid-1800s

Completion of the porticos, which quickly became prominent architectural signatures for the building, ended the most extensive and dramatic construction period in the history of the White House. The next two decades have been viewed as a period of overall neglect for initiating any more major upgrades of the building, as federal funds were allocated to other more pressing government priorities. In the view of William Ryan and Desmond Guinness the "nadir" of the decline of the building in this period was reached during the presidency of John Tyler.[12] Instead, what improvements were made tended to be limited to less dramatic, but nonetheless important changes to the interior of the White House.

In the 1830s, Robert Mills succeeded his teacher, Hoban, as primary architect of federal buildings in the capital city. Mills accelerated the trend of employing technological advances to improve the White House. A central heating system was installed in 1837 to heat the primary public reception and entertainment areas of the central corridors and the East room. Wooden screens were installed to help retain the heat. However, the rest of the building remained heated by the less efficient wood stoves and the attractive, yet even less efficient, fireplaces. On entering the White House in 1845, President James Polk had the heating system upgraded and added four furnaces to expand the heated area to all of the rooms on the first floor plus several rooms in the living area on the floor above. The flow of heated air into the rooms was controlled by valves some of which, particularly in the public entertainment rooms, were plated with either silver or brass, while valves serving rooms of the working areas were made of iron.

President Polk also made other historic changes to the White House. He had a "refrigerator ice box" installed in the White House for the first time. Then, in 1848, the White House was for the first time illuminated inside and out by gas lights. Eighty gas lamps were installed in the areas around the building while all interior lights except one chandelier were replaced with gas instruments. It was Mrs. Polk who directed that one chandelier of candles be retained in the building.[13]

Noteworthy but less dramatic improvements during this period included upgrading the basement work and living areas, featuring dividing the level into eleven rooms plus landscaping renovation to the previously unsightly grounds south of the White House.

Improvements to the White House made during the first half of the nineteenth century concluded with the administration of Millard Fillmore, whose most noteworthy contributions were to have a new stove installed in the kitchen to replace the open fireplaces in which all meals had been prepared and the installation of a small library whose books were purchased with public funds.

IMPORTANT CHANGES ARE MADE (1851–1899)

Minor Improvements

The second half of the nineteenth century featured the continuation of comparatively small improvements to the White House, which largely focused on the installation and implementation of new technological innovations as they were introduced to American society. Improvements made in 1853 during the administration of Franklin Pierce included installing a bathroom — complete with a tub and water closet. He also had much of the first floor entertainment areas remodeled in accord with the prevailing styles of the time, including the rebuilding of the fireplaces and the installation of iron-framed glass panels to increase natural light for the first floor corridors. Next, President James Buchanan had a coach house and stable erected east of the White House and a large glass conservatory to the west of the building.

Years of Neglect

President Abraham Lincoln, besieged by the burdens of financing the Civil War, did even less to improve the White House. He had a passage made between his office to the reception room to help him escape to privacy during the depths of the war and the emotional depression that plagued him throughout his life in the White House.[14] Unfortunately, the most noteworthy effort to refurbish the White House during the Lincoln administration occurred when Mrs. Mary Lincoln accumulated massive debts when purchasing numerous expensive pieces of furniture, debts that were unknown by the President.[15] This was all the more interesting when one considers that Lincoln commonly allowed public access to most areas of the White House and often even allowed Union troops to be quartered in the building.

The Post–Civil War Years

The subsequent deterioration of the building presented a significant challenge to the new president, Andrew Johnson. However, his daughter, Martha, oversaw a thorough yet inexpensive refurbishing of the building's interior. In addition, in 1866, the first telegraph office in the White House was installed.

Throughout the nineteenth century, the more private areas on the second floor grew increasingly crowded. The president and his family continued to live in seven rooms on the west end of the second floor. In 1869, a sitting room was added on at the west end of the central hallway. In addition to crowded living quarters, first families had to contend with intrusions on their privacy. To guarantee privacy, family members tended to travel between floors by using a service stairway that connected all the way to the basement.

So too was office space limited. A suite of offices were located on the east end of the second floor. Located primarily over the East Room on the first floor, most second-floor offices were arranged together in one large area that extended out into what was known as the east hall. In addition, workers would occupy the adjacent cabinet room when it was not in formal use. The president himself was the only person to have a private office on this floor and he also could take advantage of an adjoining oval room that was commonly known as the family library. Throughout the second half of the century it appeared that each new president occupying the White House moved into the structure voicing greater complaints than his predecessors about the increasingly crowed living and working conditions on the second floor.[16]

During the 1870s, President U.S. Grant authorized remodeling of much of the first-floor public reception and entertainment areas. By this time, the main-floor visiting area, which had been open to the public since 1801, was available to tourists six days a week. Moreover, during public receptions as many as 6,000 people would crowd into the first-floor rooms. Hence, Grant had large sections of deteriorated floors and ceilings replaced, walls and fireplaces redecorated, and enormous crystal chandeliers, which were

imported from Europe, installed. Outside, a brick stable was constructed before Grant left office and the next president, Rutherford
Hayes, added another large greenhouse. In addition, Hayes was the
first president to have a telephone in the White House—fittingly,
his phone number was "1."

The next technological addition to the Executive Mansion
occurred in 1880 when typewriters were used for the first time.
Finally, Hayes began the tradition of planting commemorative trees
in honor of each president and state.[17] He has several hundred
planted initially.

End-of-the-Century Changes

Perhaps the most aggressive president of this period was Chester
Arthur. He refused to move into the White House following President James Garfield's assassination until the facility could be
cleaned to meet his expectations. Then, after failing to convince
congressional leaders to tear down and replace the White House,
Arthur in 1882 brought in one of the most famous designers of
the era, Louis Tiffany, to redesign the interior of the building. The
subsequent work of Tiffany, most renowned for his stained glass,
featured new panels and stained-glass doors for the entry. Notably, the remodeling featured the installation of two new bathrooms on the second floor and a hydraulic elevator to connect the
floors. Finally, Arthur made still more additions to the extensive
greenhouse complex extending from the west side of the White
House. Also completed during this period was the Ellipse south of
the White House.

The growing problems of crowded quarters on the second floor
reach a climax in 1889 when President Benjamin Harrison entered
the White House accompanied by his wife and numerous children
and grandchildren. Mrs. Caroline Harrison attempted to remedy
the many problems with the design and space of the White House.
For instance, the First Lady narrowly failed in winning congressional approval for her ambitious plan to construct massive additional wings to the east, west, and south of the building.[18] Although
her death in 1892, coupled with apathetic responses from subsequent presidents in the decade, essentially ended her ambitious
plan, pleas for expanding the White House continued throughout
the 1890s. Meanwhile, technological improvements stemming from
the industrial age continued unabated. Electric wiring was installed
in the White House in 1891.

Responding to the Needs of a "Modern" Era (1900–1950)

Expanding the White House

Speculation about the possibility of expanding the White House was in full force in 1900 as the nation prepared to celebrate the centennial of the initial occupation of the executive mansion. The leading advocate of expanding the building was Colonel Theodore Bingham of the Army Corps of Engineers. His massive and ambitious expansion plan was similar to the one advocated earlier by Mrs. Harrison. President William McKinley, after postponing a decision on the plan until after the Spanish American War, was murdered in September of 1901.[19] The large family of the new president, Theodore Roosevelt, assured that he would be extremely interested in any plan to increase the size of the mansion's living and working quarters. However, Roosevelt rejected the massive Bingham plan and retained a prominent New York architect, Charles McKim, to design something less grandiose.

McKim responded with a plan that altered much of the building and grounds, but did not threaten the traditional exterior appearance of the White House. From the west side of the main building McKim sought to remove the conservatory and replace it with a new, initially-termed "temporary"—Executive Office Building, which later was popularly dubbed the "West Wing." Secretarial and staff offices were moved from the second floor of the main building into the new West Wing. The second floor then was devoted entirely to living quarters for the first family as bathrooms, sleeping, an living areas were expanded greatly. In addition, McKim redesigned the East Wing into a social entrance and the basement areas of the main building were remodeled extensively to add a large modern kitchen, food storage, and meal preparation areas. Finally, McKim redecorated the main floor and also removed the grand stair, thereby greatly expanding the State Dining Room.

The next administration, of William Howard Taft, featured the expansion of the West Wing southward in 1909 to double the working space. The plan, created by Nathan Wyeth, included a windowed, curved section extending outward along the south wall with the design inspired by the south face of the White House. The West Wing's curved wall enclosed the first famous Oval Office of the President.

Unanticipated Changes

Following a general renovation hiatus during the years of the First World War, the 1920s produced two important changes to the White House. Both developments were imposed on the facility by outside forces. The first noteworthy effort came during the administration of Calvin Coolidge. By the early 1920s, the wood beams supporting the White House roof, installed during the massive rebuilding in 1817, had deteriorated and required immediate replacement. Replacing the roof provided an unanticipated renovation opportunity. The roof was removed and a third floor of rooms was installed to replace the previous attic. The third floor featured guest bedrooms, bathrooms, utility and service rooms, and a new solarium or "sun parlor." Steel beams and a new roof topped the addition which doubled the amount of living space available to the president and his family.

The second unanticipated event in the decade struck on Christmas Eve, 1929, when a fire extensively damaged the West Wing executive offices. President Herbert Hoover continued living in the White House but worked from rooms in the main building, or offices in the nearby State, War, and Navy department buildings.

The Great Depression and World War II

The Great Depression, which soon followed, did not entirely stop efforts to renovate and improve the White House. First, the dramatic growth of the president's staff during Franklin Roosevelt's administration necessitated an enlarged West Wing.[20] Office space was made in the wing's basement while the main floor was expanded southward. Significantly, the Oval Office was moved to the southeast corner of the West Wing near the Rose Garden and a low penthouse was added to the wing. The Cabinet Room was constructed in an eastward expansion of the wing. Overall, the renovation doubled the office space on the West Wing. Second, in 1933 a heated indoor swimming pool was installed in the west terrace area to provide exercise therapy for the President to treat his poliomyelitis.

Just as the Great Depression failed to halt improvements to the White House, the outbreak of the Second World War was also followed by changes to the building. Attention this time was directed toward the east portico where construction included the addition of offices (primarily for the first lady), a reception room, movie theater, expanded facilities for the security staff, and a bomb shelter. On the other hand, President Roosevelt, to the credit of observers at the time and in the years since, immediately rejected a proposal from Civil Defense officials to paint the White House camouflage for the duration of the war.[21]

The end of the war and the arrival of a new president, Harry Truman, preceded the most extensive and dramatic renovations in the history of the White House (discussed in chapter 14). In 1948, the President initiated, despite extensive public opposition, the construction of a balcony on the South Portico. The addition, subsequently known, of course, as the "Truman balcony," was protected from the elements by wood awnings.

FINE-TUNING A NATIONAL LANDMARK (1950–1999)

The Truman Rebuilding

The Truman years experienced a major rebuilding of the interior of the White House. Begun on December 12, 1949, and completed nearly three years later, the renovation (as explained in detail in the last chapter) were spectacular and extensive. The interior was removed entirely and a 660-ton steel frame constructed to support all of the inside walls and floors, which essentially were replaced. In sum, the renovation, described by one analyst as "the most radical in the history of the building," was also controversial.[22] Some critics, while acknowledging the important and necessary engineering improvements, bemoaned the changes for other reasons:

> from a preservationist's viewpoint the rebuilding was the greatest calamity to befall the President's House since the fire of 1814. The lack of attention to archaeological and historical analysis and the callous disposal of important architectural elements is difficult to excuse.[23]

The President and his family, after living nearby in the Blair House throughout the reconstruction, returned to the White House in the spring of 1952.

The Kennedy Years

Post-Truman administration changes to the White House have primarily been in redecorating and adding antiques and other interior furnishings. President John Kennedy had a second-floor bedroom converted into a small family dining room and a nearby bathroom rebuilt into a kitchen. He also won congressional approval for the White House Historical Association in 1961, and Mrs. Kennedy won approval that year for the Smithsonian Institution to hire the first White House curator, Mrs. John N. Pearce, to manage the historic preservation and operation aspects of the building.

CONCLUSION

Numerous families have called the White House home and generations of Americans—and people throughout the world—have looked to the president's home as more than simply bricks and mortar. Thanks to the concern for preservation and proper conduct of the building's residents, much of the history and majesty of the mansion remains. The efforts of first families to preserve the integrity of the White House, through historic renovations, has been balanced by their need to create a sense of home, including additions to the building reflecting the conveniences of each era's notions of modern living. In many ways, the history of the White House reflects the history of art, architecture, interior design, and culture of the country as well as the nation's politics.

While the building has changed considerably since its initial construction during the presidency of George Washington, it has remained as a powerful symbol of democracy. Unlike most official residences of heads of government and heads of state, the White House also remains remarkably accessible to the public, befitting its status as the home for the world's first true experiment in popular government. Indeed, for more than two centuries America's White House has maintained the contradictory goals of remaining a familiar national monument while simultaneously evolving inside its famous walls to meet the changing and increased demands of the public and its occupants alike. No doubt future generations of Americans will continue bridging those conflicting demands. Their forebears likely would expect no less.

NOTES TO CHAPTER 11

1. White House Historical Association interview, 2002, <www.white househistory.org>.

2. Ibid.; L. Aikman, *The Living White House*, 1991, p. 11.

3. See, for instance, H. Howard, *Thomas Jefferson*, 2003; F. D. Nichols and R. E. Griswold, *Thomas Jefferson: Landscape Architect*, 2003.

4. H. C. Shulman, "Dolley Madison," p. 56, 1996.

5. L. Aikman, 1991, p. 10.

6. L. Aikman, 1991, p. 40.

7. W. Seale, "The White House . . . ," 1995, 1–30.

8. L. Aikman, 1991, p. 41.

9. Ibid.

10. W. Seale, *The President's House*, 1986, 146-149.

11. Ibid.

12. W. Ryan and D. Guiness, *The White House*, 1980, p. 132.

13. R. P. Watson, *The Presidents' Wives*, 2000, p. 94.

14. N. Hirschhorn, R. G. Feldman, and I. A. Greaves, "Abraham Lincoln's Blue Pills," 2001, 315–316.

15. W. Garrison, *A Treasury of White House Tales*, 1989, p. 101–106.

16. J. Whitcomb and C. Whitcomb, *Real Life in the White House*, 2000, p. xv–xvii, 200–201.

17. Rutherford B. Hayes Presidential Center interview, 2002, <www.rbhayes.org>.

18. J. Whitcomb and C. Whitcomb, 2000, p. 200–201.

19. T. Irons-Georges, *The American Presidents*, 2000, p. 370.

20. J. Whitcomb and C. Whitcomb, 2000, p. 310–311.

21. W. Seale, 1995, p. 22.

22. Ibid.

23. W. Ryan and D. Guiness, 1980, p. 177.

Twelve

Preserving the President's House: The Office of the White House Curator

MICHAEL E. LONG

INTRODUCTION

S ince its construction in the early 1800s, the White House has served not only as the official residence of the president of the United States, but it has also emerged as the nation's premier historic house museum. As a museum, the White House attracts millions of visitors annually, maintains a permanent collection of approximately 30,000 items, and provides visitor services to help interpret the story of the Executive Mansion and its select group of forty-two American families (counting the Washingtons, although they never lived in the building) as of 2004. While it seemed only natural to appoint a curator to help manage these services, it was not until March of 1964 that Executive Order No. 11145 was signed into law by President Lyndon B. Johnson. The order provided for the appointment of a curator to

> assist in the preservation and protection of the articles of furniture, fixtures, and decorative objects used or displayed in the principal corridor on the ground floor and the principal public rooms on the first floor of the White House, and in such other areas of the White House as the President might designate.[1]

The need for a professionally trained museum curator at the White House must be viewed from several perspectives. The position

245

evolved out of necessity. Over the years, many private sector companies have donated furniture and decorative art items to the White House. A primary responsibility of the White House Curator is the care and preservation of these items. Second, funds for decorations and furnishings, originally made available through the Congress, are now contributed largely through private sources and donations. The Curator provides advice to the first family regarding the acquisition of furnishings for the executive mansion. Finally, as noted in the executive order of March 1964, the Curator is charged with the care, preservation, and presentation of those public areas in the White House open to the general public.

This chapter examines the evolution of the office of White House Curator in preserving the building's history and the accomplishments of the six museum professionals who have held the position. Theirs is an interesting story, coinciding with transitions of power as well as movement of furnishings, and changes in styles from all presidential administrations since the days of John Adams. This essay will also discuss the response of our federal bureaucracy to support this pioneering effort in America's historic preservation movement.

THE LARGEST RESIDENCE IN THE NEW FEDERAL CITY

To understand the significance of the White House as both private residence and public museum, we must look at the structure in relation to its immediate surroundings. In 1800, Washington City, as it was then known, had approximately 600 houses, only about half as many as were actually needed. In late May of 1800, as one observer noted:

> when the sloops carrying government records and the personal belongings of federal officials docked at Lear's Wharf on the Potomac near the mouth of Rock Creek, the new national capital, bore little resemblance to a city. A half-mile below the landing a sluggish little stream, Tiber or Goose Creek, worked its way to the river through tidal flats. Above the marshy estuary rose the painted sandstone Executive Mansion, flanked on one side by the brick building designed for the Treasury.[2]

Although construction of the first major public buildings—the White House and the Capitol—had begun in 1793—seven years before the government moved to Washington—they were virtually built anew after the sack and burning of the capital by British troops in 1814.[3] Historians differ in their descriptions and accounts of early Washington City. One source tells us that, "the capital had 366 houses, 109 of them made of brick and a population of 3,000, including several lawyers, three or four physicians, and about six pastors."[4]

The burning of Washington City by the British in 1814 fueled discussions about the possibility of the federal government relocating. President Madison and several federal officials returned to Washington within a few days after the British withdrawal to address the issue. Since the Executive Mansion was a shell, President and Mrs. Madison moved into the Octagon House on New York Avenue.[5] The *Washington Intelligencer* said "moving the government from Washington City would constitute a treacherous breach of faith with the citizens who had laid out fortunes in the purchase of property in and about the city." President and Mrs. James Monroe would move into a substantially new White House in September 1817.

Unfortunately, general living conditions in Washington City did not improve until after the Civil War. According to one local historian,

> the confusion that followed Lincoln's assassination raised questions of the adequacy of the local police. Moreover, the sickness in the National Hotel caused by poisonous gas from obstructed sewers provoked a sanitation scandal. The fire that destroyed the books of Congress in the room on the west front of the Capitol could not be extinguished because sufficient water could not be obtained. Members of Congress stumbled along the un-graded and unpaved streets, bumped into roving domestic animals, and fell over bridges that lacked guard railings. In summers, the Potomac River became a swamp filled with malaria. The White House became so unhealthy that Presidents Van Buren, Pierce, and Buchanan, along with many other prominent residents, moved each summer to the heights above Georgetown or the hills north of the city to escape the fever.[6]

PRESIDENTS, FURNITURE, AND VISITORS (1801–1865)

Object of Curiosity

In June 1800, John Adams, accompanied by the commissioners of the new District of Columbia, conducted an inspection and visited the White House for the first time, entering the building through the basement. Adams would insist that everything be in order for him to move into the mansion in early November of 1800. In late June, the President's furniture arrived from Philadelphia and was temporarily stored in wooden crates. In the intervening months before the President's arrival, the White House was already "the prime object of curiosity"[7] in the new federal city. The public wandered in and out, creating such confusion that the commissioners closed the doors to all but those with written passes.[8]

It appeared obvious to those in authority at the time that measures would soon have to be taken to control the access of visitors and eventually control security at the executive mansion. On Saturday, November 1, 1800, the commissioners of the District of Columbia conducted another formal inspection of the White House to ensure that everything was in order for the arrival of President John Adams. He had departed Quincy, Massachusetts, on October 13, 1800, and was expected soon, but they could not determine his exact arrival date and time.[9]

At the time of President John Adams's arrival, only half of the White House's 36 rooms had been plastered. Of the three staircases originally planned, only one had been completed. Fires were lit throughout the mansion to accelerate the drying of the plaster.

Placed about the mansion was "the government's furniture, a shabby mixture of French, English, and American pieces. The full-length Gilbert Stuart portrait of George Washington brought from Philadelphia in June was the lone example of fine art in the house."[10]

The White House was not only a curious site from the outside, but as Adams's successors began to occupy the mansion, a number of curious gifts would begin to arrive to honor the chief executive. Additionally, each president would have his own preferences regarding the furnishings for the residence and the public rooms, creating quite a bit a of variety in styles and designs over the years.

Presidential Preferences

On July 4, 1803, Thomas Jefferson opened the White House for visitors at 12:00 noon to celebrate the negotiation of the Louisiana Purchase. Hundreds of excited citizens crowded the halls. "People were more numerous than I have ever before marked it," wrote one guest.[11] Gifts presented to President Jefferson during his administration were numerous and included several items from the Lewis and Clark expedition, "turning the White House into a museum for the people. This included the delivery of two small bear cubs."[12] When Jefferson left the White House as President, he did so taking

most of his personal furniture with him. Jefferson's personal observations on the President's House were that it represented "a great
stone house, big enough for two emperors, one pope, and the grand
lama."[13] President James Madison was left with a sparsely furnished
executive mansion. In response to this situation, "Dolly Madison
invited congressmen to the White House to see the condition of
the rooms for themselves. Congress quickly appropriated $12,000
for repairs and an additional $14,000 for furnishings."[14]

Beginning with the administration of James Monroe, a serious
attempt was made to control the number of visitors to the White
House. For instance,

> Monroe did not allow the public to walk around the man-
> sion unattended, as had the previous administration. Most
> visitors were restricted to the entrance hall. In addition,
> Monroe employed guards, though not in uniform, and in-
> stalled iron fencing to keep people out. Nonetheless, the
> public continued to gain entry, and at a crowded drawing
> room following the election of John Quincy Adams, Gen-
> eral Scott was "robbed of $800 dollars" by a pick-pocket.[15]

President Andrew Jackson officially occupied the White House
on March 4, 1829 following a wild reception. Most guests in attendance characterized the event as "an unprecedented free-for-all, a
near riot."[16] According to one eyewitness:

> a rabble, a mob of boys, negros, women, children, scrambling,
> fighting, romping. What a pity, what a pity! No arrangements
> had been made no police officers placed on duty and the whole
> house had been inundated by the rabble mob . . . Cut glass
> and china to the amount of several thousand dollars had been
> broken in the struggle to get the refreshments.[17]

During the year 1833, the famous East Room was decorated
for the very first time. Congress allocated $50,000 for the executive
mansion, with nearly one-fifth of the total dedicated to finishing
and furnishing the East Room. It was described as "outfitted with
wood paneling, decorative wooden beams, three large cut glass
chandeliers, each with eighteen oil lamps, and for $1,058.25, a
Brussels carpet in fawn, blue, and yellow with a red border. Also,
the East Room had twenty spittoons at $12.50 each."[18]

Subsequent presidential administrations through Dwight D.
Eisenhower would also receive money from Congress for necessary

White House repairs and furnishings: Martin Van Buren received $27,000 for china, rugs, and general refurbishing; John Tyler was given $6,000 for new furnishings with the restriction that they be "of American manufacture so far as may be practicable."[19] President James K. Polk received a total of $14,900, of which only 50 percent would be expended. Prior to the Civil War, President James Buchanan and his niece-hostess, Harriet Lane, replaced many of the 40-year-old furnishings from the Monroe administration with several pieces of the Louis XV revival style, most of which were carved and gilded items from Gottlieb Vollmer, a German furniture manufacturer living in Philadelphia.[20] During the Buchanan administration, Congress would initially allocate $11,000 for upkeep and in June 1858, authorized an additional $12,000 for the building.

Controversy over White House furnishings and decor plagued the administration of President Abraham Lincoln, thanks primarily to his wife Mary Todd Lincoln. Contemporary scholars attribute these problems to mental instability, particularly in regard to her spending habits. For instance,

> She could be stingy, haggling over small change with tradesmen, but she could also be reckless. She reveled in the opportunity to redecorate the White House with government funds. Between August and September of 1861 while the White House was crawling with workmen, the First Lady went on "extended shopping trips" to Philadelphia and New York—eleven trips to New York alone. She bought furniture, carpet, drapes, china, glassware, gold and silver tableware, damask table linens and more. Her most famous purchase was a huge carved rosewood bed for the state bedroom. Known today as the Lincoln Bed, it is the one their son, Willie, later died in and was probably never intended to be President Lincoln's bed.[21]

Another example of the problem follows:

> In December, 1861 President Lincoln was informed that in just nine months his wife had overspent by $6,700 the $20,000 Congress appropriated for refurbishing. He was enraged and stated "it would stink in the nostrils of the American people to have it said that the President of the United States had approved a bill over-running an appropriation of $20,000 for flub-dubs for this damned old house when soldiers cannot have blankets."[22]

LIVING A COMPROMISED LIFESTYLE (1865–1961)

While living in the White House, each president and first family must live in accordance with custom and protocol, not to mention the desires of the electorate. Change is constant, at least every four to eight years. According to one observer, "the White House, from the beginning, has been perceived as the people's house, and it was thought that any of its landlords had the right to come in for a look or confront the president with a problem."[23] Access to the White House has changed considerably from the days of President Martin Van Buren "when a drunk wandered in and slept on the sofa."[24] Up through the assassination of President James A. Garfield by a disgruntled office seeker, which resulted in the establishment of the U.S. Civil Service Commission to handle federal employment, most government jobs—including everything from postman to ambassador—required presidential approval or, more appropriately, presidential patronage.

The White House has evolved as the nation's showcase for the latest technologies and the best of everything, "acquiring a telephone before there was anyone but the Treasury Department to talk to, and being wired for electricity when turning off the switches still yielded an occasional shock. President Benjamin Harrison would often delegate this task to servants."[25]

Renovations

It is within this historic period in American history, 1865–1961, that two major renovations of the White House would occur. The first renovation was in 1902 during the administration of Theodore Roosevelt. Under the leadership of the architectural firm of McKim, Mead & White, this major renovation project was intended to "restore the White House to George Washington's vision."[26]

Edith Roosevelt supported the renovation of a White House immeasurably different from the dark, dank mansion the Roosevelts had inherited from the McKinleys. Thanks to the project:

> Gone were the executive offices crowding the second floor, and the malignant outgrowth of greenhouses on the west façade. Gone were the sagging floorboards that needed to be shimmed up during receptions. Gone too, were the mustard carpets, the dropsical radiators, the sad-smelling

laundry, the vertical wooden pipes that made flatulent noises in wet weather.[27]

In 1908, it was estimated that "to keep the White House and grounds in proper order at the present time requires an outlay of about $1,000 a week."[28]

The second renovation occurred in 1948 during the administration of President Harry S. Truman. (See chapter 14 for a fuller discussion of this rebuilding.) This project involved a complete gutting of the structure requiring the President and First Lady Bess Truman to relocate across Pennsylvania Avenue at Blair House, now a residence for distinguished White House visitors.

The White House Becomes "Historical"

America's historic preservation movement did not begin with the preservation of the White House, but it is important that we note its place in the history of the movement to preserve the past for the benefit of future generations. Independence Hall in Philadelphia, for example, "emerged from a period of neglect with the visit of Lafayette in 1824." It was not until 1831, however that the Assembly Room, site of the signing of the Declaration of Independence, "took on the aspects of a hallowed place."[29]

As early as 1846, many Americans began to petition the Congress for the designation of George Washington's Mount Vernon "as a shrine that ought to be the property of the nation. The U.S. Congress showed little interest. In 1856, the Virginia Legislature would approve a charter for the Mount Vernon Ladies Association of the Union charged with "the perpetual guardianship of Mount Vernon."[30] Under the leadership of Ann Pamela Cunningham, Mount Vernon's preservation would enlist the support of thousands of people across the country and was made possible by a having "regent" designated for each state to assist in the fundraising efforts.

Preserving History

It was not until the administration of President Ulysses S. Grant in 1869 that the White House would be considered truly historical. As noted,

Visitors to the national capital placed it high on their lists of sights to see, and guidebooks told of its past. Weekdays from ten in the morning until three in the afternoon the East Room could be viewed by anyone who called at the north door. Admission to the state parlors could be procured with a note provided by a congressman or senator.[31]

Indeed, America's Gilded Age became a watershed for many of the early historic preservation programs. The first congressional funding for any historic preservation activity occurred in 1902 when Congress appropriated $2,000 for the preservation of the Casa Grande Indian ruins in Arizona.[32]

In 1924, First Lady Grace Anna Coolidge both made and preserved history when she:

> gathered a commission of experts to advise her on appropriate furnishings. Simultaneously, she decided to improve the White House by redecorating and furnishing the family quarters—again! This would be a problem for the Coolidge family as they had always rented either partially furnished houses or furnished apartments in hotels. When President Harding's personal items were moved out, the Coolidge family borrowed so much furniture from other parts of the executive mansion that the central corridor and several bedrooms were actually left bare.[33]

Mrs. Coolidge, an avid collector of antiques, decided to furnish the family quarters on the second floor with "colonial style" items. Most historians today agree that this was no accident. Following World War I, the American colonial style in interior decoration had become the most popular mode in domestic furnishing. Mrs. Coolidge also wanted to leave her mark as first lady for those who would succeed her in that role. As a result, examples of such items poured into the White House from all over the country— wing chairs, camel-back sofas, candle stands, footstools, drop-leaf tables, grandfather clocks, and four-poster beds.[34] Mrs. Coolidge also received some technical assistance from New York's Metropolitan Museum of Art, which opened its American Wing on November 10, 1924.

This was only the beginning for Anna Grace Coolidge. She can be considered the pioneer in White House preservation in that she worked with the Congress to provide for a joint resolution in 1925 permitting the White House to accept donations of furniture and artwork. This was the first legal recognition the President's house also functioned as a museum.[35]

Thanks to First Families

Prior to the appointment of a Curator, individual presidents, first ladies, and several committees were also involved in helping to bring order out of chaos with regard to White House furnishings and decor. These included:

- The establishment of an advisory committee "to evaluate and make recommendations on the decor of the state rooms and review offers of gifts," the first such committee formed to advise presidents and first ladies on White House interiors (1925).[36]

- The White House Committee on Furnishings (1930) that helped to "review and approve furniture acquisitions" through the 1950s.[37]

- Eleanor Roosevelt creates the Sub-Committee Upon Furniture and Furnishings and Gifts for State Rooms of the White House (1941). The responsibilities of this committee were to be focused on the state rooms and not the family quarters.[38]

- The Commission on Fine Arts named by President Franklin D. Roosevelt, "to review presidential items offered to him and establish criteria for their acceptance" (1942).[39]

- Jacqueline Kennedy's announcement to appoint a committee "to work with the Commission of Fine Arts, on how to form a committee to solicit and receive donations of objects" (1961).[40]

- The establishment of a Special Committee for White House Paintings. Formed with art historian James W. Forsburgh as chairman (1961), its goal was to expand the existing presidential and first lady collection and replace copies of presidential portraits with those painted from life.[41]

- Committee for the Preservation of the White House established by President Lyndon B. Johnson by Executive Order in 1964. Building on the philosophy that had guided the Kennedy Fine Arts Committee, "the new committee developed guidelines and goals for White House collecting, emphasizing the acquisition of objects associated with the White House or its occupants and those that reflected the highest tradition of American craftsmanship."[42]

WHITE HOUSE CURATORS

It would be Jacqueline Kennedy who would institutionalize the idea of the White House as a living history museum and eventually appoint the first curator, Lorraine Waxman Pearce. Her responsibilities would include:[43]

- Reporting to the president and first lady on matters relating to the history of the White House and its collections.

- Working closely with the Committee for the Preservation of the White House to preserve and interpret the museum character of the public rooms.

- The care, preservation, and management of the historic collection of more than 30,000 objects.

- Maintaining a research center and repository for White House history.

- Interpreting the White House and its collections.

Lorraine Waxman Pearce (1961–1962)

When she was appointed White House Curator in 1961, Lorraine Pearce was "a petite young Washington mother of a 13-month-old son."[44] She came to the position as an antique collector, yet knowledgeable in museum operations. Having received a B.A. degree in History from the City College of New York, she was also a Fulbright Scholar and held a M.A. degree in Museum Studies from the University of Delaware's Winterthur Museum Program.

Lorraine Pearce's accomplishments as White House Curator included the compilation of the first catalog of all White House furnishings. She also served as the author for the first comprehensive *White House Tour Guide*, published by the White House Historical Association.

Pearce resigned her position in 1962 citing personal reasons. In accepting her resignation, Mrs. Kennedy said, "Mrs. Pearce has performed an immeasurable service in giving so freely of her knowledge,

time, and enthusiasm in the early difficult days of establishing the
restoration program and that the scholarship which she devoted to the
writing of the *White House Guide Book* would be long remembered."[45]

It was during Pearce's tenure that a 1961 Act of Congress
stated that White House objects "when declared by the President
to be of historic and artistic interest shall be considered to be
inalienable and the property of the White House. Thus, for the first
time, there was now legal protection for historic White House objects
that could no longer be sold at auction, disposed of, or given away."[46]

William V. Elder III (1962–1963)

William V. Elder initially served as the first Registrar of the White
House, responsible for the actual cataloging of the collections. Elder's
academic background included a B.A. degree in art history from
Princeton University and graduate study in architecture at the
University of Pennsylvania. During Elder's tenure as White House
Curator, the permanent collection had grown by approximately
1,000 items with an estimated value in excess of $1,000,000.[47]

Elder worked closely with members of the Fine Arts Commission in screening each item for inclusion in the White House permanent collection. James V. Elder, a native of Baltimore, Maryland,
resigned as White House Curator on December 1, 1963, to become
Curator of Decorative Arts at the Baltimore Museum of Art.

James Roe Ketchum (1963–1970)

James R. Ketchum served as White House Registrar in the early
1960s while his predecessor, James Elder, served as Curator.
Ketchum's academic credentials included a Bachelor of Arts degree in History from Colgate University and graduate study at
both Georgetown University and the George Washington University in Washington, D.C., where he specialized in Art History and
American History. He previously worked with the National Park
Service as Tour Director at the Custis-Lee Mansion in nearby
Arlington, Virginia.

Clement E. Conger (1970–1986)

Clement E. Conger had a distinguished record in American decorative arts. He joined the U.S. State Department in 1947 as served
as Assistant Chief and Deputy Chief of Protocol (1955–1961 and

1969–1970). In his capacity as Assistant Chief of Protocol, Conger recommended the inclusion of official reception rooms in the State Department building. He initiated the program of securing prestige furnishings for the rooms by gifts and loans. After an effort of nearly thirty years, the estimated value of these items is $50,000,000. This collection of eighteenth- and nineteenth-century period furnishings is thought to be the most important in the Washington, D.C. Metropolitan Area, and third greatest in the nation.

From 1970 through 1986 Conger "lifted the White House collection from a medium level to the preeminent collection of Americana of the 19th century. He worked closely with First Ladies Pat Nixon, Betty Ford, Rosalynn Carter, and Nancy Reagan to refurbish a total of 27 rooms."[48] Conger's reputation in the American decorative arts community led the *Washington Post* to dub him "The Grand Acquisitor."[49] According to the *Post*, "Conger's flair for tracking down historic furniture, paintings, china, and silver to create a proper setting at the White House and State Department resulted in the loan or outright gifts in the amount of nearly $6,000,000."[50] Conger's persuasiveness resulted in the White House acquiring a pair of Gilbert Stuart portraits of President John Quincy Adams and his wife Louisa Catherine Adams.

In recognition for his years of service to the State Department and the White House, Mr. Conger received an Honorary Doctor of Humane Letters Degree from the College of William and Mary, Williamsburg, Virginia. He is also the recipient of the Ann Pamela Cunningham Award in Heritage Preservation from the Mary Washington College Center for Historic Preservation, Fredericksburg, Virginia.

Rex W. Scouten (1986–1997)

Rex W. Scouten had a diverse background, initially not suited to museums or the decorative arts. In fact, he first joined the White House staff as a Special Agent of the United States Secret Service during President Truman's tenure. In that capacity, he worked for ten presidents in such assignments as Chief Usher and Assistant Regional Director for White House Liaison with the National Park Service.

President Ronald Reagan appointed Scouten Curator in 1986. During the Reagan administration, First Lady Nancy Reagan "solicited contributions from private individuals for an extensive redecoration of the private quarters as well as maintenance of the public spaces. More than 150 items in the White House underwent some type of conservation during Scouten's tenure as Curator. Funds were also obtained to improve the storage facilities for many items in the White House collection."[51] Ironically, the Reagan White House refurbishing "contrasted ill on the nightly news with images of welfare lines in the South Bronx and tents along the Santa Monica Palisades as many Americans showed an increasing tendency to blame President Reagan for the economic recession."[52]

During the administration of President George W. Bush, the White House Preservation Fund was reorganized as the White House Endowment Fund. Under the auspices of the White House Historical Association, the Fund had a goal of raising $25 million for acquisitions, the care and refurbishing of the public rooms, and the conservation of the collection. This was continued under First Lady Hillary Rodham Clinton.

Betty C. Monkman (1997–present)

President Bill Clinton appointed Betty C. Monkman White House Curator in 1997. She began her museum career at the White House, serving as Registrar in 1967. In 1980, she was named Associate Curator. Her current responsibilities include managing the White House state rooms and the White House collections, planning and supervising curatorial and historical projects, working with the Committee for the Preservation of the White House and the White House Historical Association, and interpreting the White House and its collections through lectures, publications, and exhibits.

Ms. Monkman received her B.A. degree in History from the University of North Dakota and a M.A. in American Studies from the George Washington University, Washington, D.C. In 1995 she was selected to attend the Attingham Summer School for the Study of British Country Houses.

During the Clinton administration, and with the assistance of Ms. Monkman, the President and Mrs. Clinton served as "active participants on the Committee for the Preservation of the White House, and were deeply involved in decisions regarding acquisitions for the permanent collection."[53]

President Clinton appointed additional members to serve on the committee and broadened the committee's expertise.

The past and the present have learned to coexist in the White House and the individual who has helped to smooth that relationship since the administration of President John Kennedy is the Curator. Clearly, the service that these individuals have performed throughout the years have had a lasting impact on the history of the White House and its interpretation to millions of Americans.

NOTES TO CHAPTER 12

1. Executive Order # 11145, The White House, March 7, 1964.

2. Constance McLaughlin Green, *Washington . . .* , 1962, 3.

3. Warren J. Cox et al., *A Guide to the Architecture . . .* , 1974, 8.

4. John Whitcomb and Claire Whitcomb, *Real Life in the White House*, 6.

5. Green, 1962, 63.

6. Frederick Gutheim, *The Potomac*, 1968, 255.

7. William Seale, *The President's House . . .* , 1986, 79.

8. Ibid., 79.

9. Ibid., 80.

10. Ibid., 80.

11. Ibid., 96.

12. Ibid., 23.

13. Ibid., xvii.

14. Ibid., 26.

15. Ibid., 44.

16. Ibid., 59.

17. Ibid., 59.

18. Ibid., 63.

19. Ibid., 87.

20. Ibid., 125.

21. Ibid., 131.

22. Ibid., 131.

23. Ibid., xvii.

24. Ibid., xviii.

25. Ibid., xvi.

26. Whitcomb and Whitcomb, xviii.

27. Edmund Morris, *Theodore Rex*, 2001, 174.

28. See Gilson Willets, *Inside History of the White House* . . . , 1908.

29. Charles B. Hosmer, Jr., *Presence of the Past*, 1965, 31.

30. Ibid., 46.

31. Seale, 1986, 472.

32. Norman Tyler, *Historic Preservation*, 2000, 57.

33. Seale, 1986, 863.

34. Ibid., 864.

35. Ibid., 864.

36. Betty C. Monkman, *The White House* . . . , 2000, 204.

37. Ibid., 208.

38. Ibid., 214.

39. Ibid., 214.

40. Ibid., 234.

41. Ibid., 235.

42. Ibid., 235.

43. See Betty C. Monkman, "Office of the Curator," at the White House web site (www.whitehouse.gov) and White House offices, undated.

44. Mark L. Vaughn, *Washington Star*, 1961, no page number indicated.

45. Maria Smith, "White House Curator Resigns . . . ," 1962, C7.

46. Monkman, 2000, 237.

47. Walter Hackett, "News-Shy Architect Directs . . . ," 1962, F10.

48. See biographical sketch of Clement E. Conger at the White House offices or web site.

49. Dorothy McCardle, "The government Curator . . . ," 1961, 1.

50. Ibid., 1.

51. Monkman, 2000, 259.

52. Edmund Morris, *Dutch* . . . , 1999, 451.

53. See Monkman, 2000, 261.

54. Ibid., 261.

Thirteen

Edith Roosevelt and the 1902 White House Renovation

Tom Lansford

Introduction

Edith Roosevelt often acted as a counterbalance for the exuberant personality and tendencies of her husband Theodore. In many ways, Edith was the more practical and efficient half of the presidential couple. Throughout Theodore's political career, Edith served as household manager and oversaw the family's finances. When her husband was elected governor of the state of New York, Edith redecorated the Governor's Mansion in Albany in order to make it more functional for her husband and more accommodating for the large Roosevelt family. After Theodore became president, Edith undertook a broad and sustained renovation of the White House.

The renovation was part of a wider effort to bring the Executive Mansion into the twentieth century. It was Roosevelt that ordered the name of the residence of the first family to be officially changed form the Executive Mansion to the "White House" in order to more adequately reflect the democratic and egalitarian image that he wished to project. Also as a result of the renovation, the personal quarters of the White House were expanded. In addition, the 1902 project resulted in the construction of the West Wing offices.

Significantly, Edith worked to ensure that the renovation would restore the grandeur of the White House and maintain its twin functions as people's museum and home to the first family. For instance, it was Edith that established the portrait gallery of the

261

first ladies and who initiated the first systemic inventory of the furnishings of the White House. In both the interior and exterior renovations, Edith played a pivotal role. The Roosevelt biographer, H. W. Brands, wrote of the project that, although the President "ordered the name change, Edith ordered the curtains, the carpets, and all the other items and alterations that made the gloomy old place lighter and more livable . . . in her own and more literal way, she contributed to her husband's project of adapting the White House to the twentieth century."[1]

THE DRIVE FOR RENOVATION

Following the assassination of President William McKinley, the Roosevelts continued to reside in a rented house in Washington, D.C., for a brief period, in order to allow First Lady Ida McKinley a suitable period in which to recover from her husband's death. Theodore moved into the White House on September 23, 1901. Edith and the children followed him two days later. Given the circumstance under which he became the nation's chief executive and mindful of the perception that his was an inherited presidency, Roosevelt strove to ensure continuity between his administration and that of his predecessor.

Taking Stock of the Building

Nonetheless, the new president found that both practical and political considerations had combined to force him to make a decision about the future of the Executive Mansion. Because of the limited size of the White House at that point, a number of proposals had been put forward to either construct a new complex that would include the president's residence and expanded office buildings or undertake a major renovation of the residence of the first family. Many suggested that the Executive Mansion should be entirely converted to federal office space because of the existing use of the building by executive branch agencies. For instance, by 1889, almost two-thirds of the original private quarters of the White House had been converted to office space. Then first lady, Caroline Harrison, enthusiastically supported a proposed major expansion of the Executive Mansion.[2] She lobbied enthusiastically for the acquisition of funds, but Congress failed to approve the spending and it would be 20 years before the renovation effort culminated in the 1902 project.

During McKinley's tenure, Colonel Theodore Gingham of the Army Corps of Engineers proposed a dramatic enlargement of the Executive Mansion designed to coincide with the centennial of the building. However, increased foreign policy pressure, including the Spanish-American War, diverted the President's attention away from the project. In addition, the McKinleys' two children had died in their youth, so there was little incentive for the President to endeavor to expand the private spaces of the Executive Mansion.

Once in office, Roosevelt renewed the call for renovation and Edith undertook a prominent role in advocating for a thorough refurbishing and redecoration of the White House. However, the First Family faced opposition from politicians and newspapers, which decried the costs associated with renovation and accused Roosevelt of "extravagance."[3] Such criticism was especially bothersome to Roosevelt because of his desire to portray himself and his administration as more democratic and egalitarian than his predecessors. In spite of his elite background, the new president genuinely wanted to be perceived as a true representative of the people. Both Theodore and Edith Roosevelt were committed to remaining in the White House and therefore undertook efforts to secure funding to renovate the residence in spite of the minor political costs. Theodore engaged in a vigorous campaign to justify the renovation by writing editorials and lobbying members of Congress and prominent public officials.[4] The President's offensive effectively silenced most critics and with Republican control of both houses of Congress, Roosevelt was ultimately able to secure approval to proceed with the renovation. Most significantly, Edith's adroit management of the renovation proved pleasing to both the general public and the political pundits of the day.

The Need for Renovation

The family of Theodore and Edith Roosevelt was the largest first family to ever occupy the White House. In addition to Theodore and Edith, the family consisted of: 17-year-old Alice, Theodore's daughter from his first marriage; 14-year-old Theodore, Jr.; 12-year-old Kermit; 10-year-old Ethel; seven-year-old Archie; and baby Quentin, who was just three-years-old. As she had discovered at the Governor's Mansion in Albany, Edith found that the family space in the White House was much too small for the children and their menagerie of pets. Edith also understood that the Executive Mansion would have to be able to accommodate family and friends, as well as foreign dignitaries.

As the size and scope of the executive branch increased in the aftermath of the Civil War, there was a corresponding increase in the amount of space in the White House devoted to day-to-day government functions and offices. The interior space of the Executive Mansion was also limited by the succession of redecorations that had occurred over the past few decades. Through the years, successive presidents and first families had added their own touches and decor, which had further constrained the available space. During the Grant administration, there were extensive renovations that added gilding and ornate furnishings throughout the White House in an attempt at neoclassicism that came to be derisively known as "Steamboat Gothic."[5] In 1882, Chester A. Arthur added a substantial screen to the vestibule, that was made of stained glass by the famed designer Louis Comfort Tiffany.[6] In 1891, there were further renovations that involved the addition of plaster ornamentation to the walls and ceilings. (See chapter 11 for an overview of these renovations.)

First Impressions

As she moved her family into the Executive Mansion on that gloomy day in September 1901, Edith was profoundly disappointed with her new home. She immediately perceived that the living space would not accommodate her large family. The entire first floor of the White House was divided into offices and areas for official functions and ceremonies. The second floor was supposed to be reserved as private areas for the first family, but out of necessity a number of rooms had been converted into offices. As a result, all that remained were six bedrooms, including one guest bedroom, a small library, and a reception area. Edith realized that this space would be cramped quarters for her, Theodore, and the six active children. The only alleviating factor was that Theodore, Jr., the Roosevelt's eldest son would be away for most of the year at a boarding school in Groton, Connecticut.

By its very nature, the bustle and interaction that took place on the first floor proved distracting for the family and often interfered with the attempts of the First Family to pursue a somewhat normal life. The new president wrote that "Edie says its like living over the store."[7] Concurrently, the restless and rambunctious Roosevelt children proved just as capable of causing mischief and problems for the staff and professional bureaucrats. This was especially true in light of the large number of pets and assorted animals that the family had accumulated through the years (and which often escaped only to cause havoc as the children sought to recapture them). The First Lady was also distressed by the fact that there was no work area or office for her. She had always acted as the financial manager of the family and was used to having an area to work and conduct correspondence. Furthermore, Edith wanted a place where she could escape the rambunctiousness of her husband and children. As a result of her experiences as first lady of New York, Edith realized that the large size of the extended Roosevelt family meant regular visitors and she wanted increased guest space among the private quarters for friends and family members to stay overnight at the White House.

The inadequacy of the family space was not the only disappointment Mrs. Roosevelt faced when she entered the White House. She found the mixed styles and decor that had been added through the years created a "a sense of gloom and darkness in the family's new home."[8] In fact, Edith's step-daughter, Alice, stated that the interior spaces of the White House were "both ugly and inconvenient."[9] Many of the rooms were so filled with furniture or presidential mementos that they were no longer serviceable. Edith decided to minimize the clutter and try to establish some order in the White House. She also wanted to brighten up the residence. To that end, the First Lady directed that the staff bring in fresh flowers in the mornings. In order to air out the residence, the First Lady ordered the windows opened and asked the staff to make greater use of natural sunlight in what many perceived to be a "symbolic" act designed to "freshen" the White House.[10]

THE RENOVATION PLANS

As It Originally Was

The President and First Lady advanced the renovation effort on a variety of fronts. Roosevelt's rechristening of the Executive Mansion as the "White House" was one component of this endeavor. The presidential couple decided to pursue a renovation plan that would expand the private areas of the White House and construct new office space outside of, but still part of, the original mansion. More significantly, the Roosevelts wanted to restore the grandeur and style of the old Executive Mansion to reflect its past. They also wanted any renovation to remain true to the original style and decor. The President stated that "the White House is the property of the nation . . . so far as it is compatible with living therein is should be kept as it originally was."[11]

On the inside, Edith particularly wanted the mixed Victorian styles removed and replaced by the traditional neoclassicist federalist style, including some elements of the contemporary Beaux-Arts trends that were popular in Europe. The result of their efforts was nothing less than a thorough remodeling of the interior and the construction of new structures as part of the exterior. Throughout the planning and construction, it would be the First Lady, not the President, who was most closely involved with the architects and builders.

An old family friend of the Roosevelts, Charles F. McKim, was approached by Theodore to undertake the design of the renovation. McKim was considered to be one of the nation's foremost architects and proponents of neoclassicism and early American colonialism. He was a member of the prestigious firm of McKim, Mead, and White and had been responsible for the design of the renowned Boston Public Library. Roosevelt asked McKim to develop plans that would restore the mansion and that would also ensure that the White House would conform to the broader goals of the McMillan Commission, which was charged with maintaining the neoclassical style of the capital city.[12]

Edith met repeatedly with McKim in order to ensure the architect's vision of the White House conformed with her own. The First Lady changed McKim's plans for red draperies in the East Room and instead insisted on yellow ones. Throughout the planning process, Edith was instrumental in the decision making over wallpaper, carpeting, and wall accouterments. She also played an important role in determining the furniture with which to equip the rooms. The First Lady deftly fashioned a mixture of historical and new pieces in a manner designed to evoke the original decor of the White House and maintain continuity of design.

In addition, the architect had planned a separate office building on the grounds (which became the West Wing) in order to allow for the expansion of private space within the White House proper. However, the site chosen was the contemporary location of the White House greenhouses. McKim's original plan called for the demolition of the gardens, but after consultations with Henry Pfister, the head gardener, Edith decided to save the greenhouses. She summoned McKim and Charles Moore, the secretary of the Commission of Fine Arts, to the Roosevelt estate, Sagamore Hill, at Oyster Bay, New York. The resulting compromise was dubbed the "Treaty of Oyster Bay" and it paved the way for the construction of the West Wing by stipulating that the greenhouses and plant life outside of the White House grounds would be relocated elsewhere in Washington.[13] Edith also pledged to create new gardens on the White House grounds.

Work Commences

With Edith's input, McKim's design was quickly approved by the President. Roosevelt's main concern was the timing of the renovation. He specifically requested that McKim ensure that the renovation and redecoration be completed in six months. Once the plans were finalized, Roosevelt gained congressional approval. Congress appropriated $541,361 for both the renovation and new construction. The majority of the funds were to be spent on the renovation (approximately $475,000), while just $66,000 was allocated for the construction of the "West Wing" of offices.

When the renovation began in the spring of 1902, the first family departed the White House. The President moved into temporary quarters in Washington, and established an office at Lafayette Place. Meanwhile Edith and the children returned to the family estate at Oyster Bay where they remained throughout the summer. Roosevelt joined the family toward the end of the summer. In order for work to proceed, most of the interior accoutrements had to be removed from the mansion. The lavish Victorian ornaments (including the Tiffany screen) and the various presidential additions that had accumulated over the decades were taken out, most to be put in storage and never seen by the public again.

In addition, the creation of new rooms on the upper floor meant that the first floor had to be bolstered with new supports while new flooring was added upstairs. Electricity had been added to the White House during the Harrison administration, but on inspection, McKim found that most of the wiring was wholly inadequate and stated that it was "not only old, defective and obsolete, but actually dangerous."[14] As a result, new wiring was installed throughout the house. McKim liberally placed new electric torchère lamps, cast in bronze, throughout the dwelling, which had the effect of increasing the light and adding to the regal style of the interior. In other areas of the house, McKim had gold and silver chandeliers and wall-mounted lights installed. These light fixtures were based on antique French and English designs and reflected the early accoutrements of the White House.

Other interior upgrades included new plumbing and a new heating system. In order to protect against fires, the architects added a standpipe with a hose that ascended from the ground floor to the attic. McKim even arranged to bring the White House into the twentieth century by adding an oak-paneled elevator. The expansion of electrical outlets would also allow for another twentieth-century invention when Theodore screened the first films in the White House (Edith would also show a number of movies).

THE RESULTS

Creating Functionality While Preserving History

By the time the White House was officially reopened in October 1902, the Victorian grandeur had been removed from the interior spaces of the mansion and replaced with the neoclassic lines and features of the original building. McKim added Doric columns and other architectural features that recalled ancient Rome or Greece.[15] Edith was pleased with the continuity that now existed in the White House proper. She was also pleased that the majority of offices had been transferred to the new West Wing. The second-floor family spaces were greatly expanded and now included new bathrooms and other amenities. A laundry room was converted into a "gentleman's anteroom."[16] The State Dining Room, used for formal meals and receptions, was also enlarged to allow for more guests and greater access by servers. This was accomplished by relocating a staircase to the entrance hall. The aging wallpaper of the dining room was replaced by burled oak panels and the President insisted that animal trophies from his hunts be displayed.

The expansion of the dining hall was important because of the increased number of social functions that the Roosevelts initiated. With Edith as first lady, the White House reemerged as the center of Washington society and the centerpiece of the capital's social circles. Each year, she oversaw eight significant state events, including three state dinners. These dinners accommodated anywhere from 30 to 100 people and involved between eight and ten courses.[17]

In addition, the president's Cabinet Room also gained a long overdue expansion in order to accommodate the growth in Cabinet positions and the corresponding enlargement of the staff members present at Cabinet meetings. The small entrance hall of the White House, which had been reduced in size by the Tiffany Screen, was replaced by a new entrance in the East Wing. Fireplaces were removed and large mirrors took their place, adding to the majesty of the hall. In addition, the multicolored tile floor was taken up and replaced by polished stone. These renovations greatly expanded the area that guests saw when they first entered the White House and both prevented overcrowding and reinforced the grandeur of the mansion.

One of the First Lady's goals during the renovation was to establish space for her to conduct official business. Since the first lady was increasingly called on to carry out official duties, Edith wanted to establish a precedent whereby the first lady had physical space within the White House with which to oversee the household and manage other official duties. The renovation allowed Edith to convert the small library upstairs into her personal office. She especially liked the utility of the office since it was connected to her husband's own private office. This allowed her easy access to Theodore while he wrote or worked on state issues. It also made it convenient for her to get Theodore when he inevitably stayed up too late working or when he became so absorbed in some project that he forgot other commitments or meetings.

The First Lady turned the large suite in the southwest corner of the White House into the presidential bedroom and she ensured that the First Couple slept in the Lincoln Bed. In addition to the bedroom proper, the suite also contained a large dressing area. Furthermore, the "Queen's Suite," thus named because of the number of foreign heads of state and monarchs that had stayed there, became a small guest apartment for members of the extended Roosevelt clan or other family friends when they overnighted at the White House. Edith rechristened the room the "Rose Suite."

Edith's Interior Projects

In addition to her role in reshaping the private quarters, the First Lady also exerted a significant influence on two main areas: the East Room, and the Ground Floor Corridor. For instance, Edith had "the velvety, fringed, potted palm look of the East Room . . . replaced by elegant yellow and gold."[18] She ensured that the ornate Victorian decor was replaced by neoclassic features. Specifically, ornamental columns, mosaics on the ceiling and cross beams were eliminated in favor of more simple, subtle stylistic elements that matched the original decor of the room. The greatly increased the open space in the room and the original grandeur of the area.

The expanded space in the East Room allowed Edith to conduct large social events in the area. Following the renovation, each Friday during the winter months, the First Lady sponsored a musical performance in the East Room. These concerts often attracted 600 or so people, of which a small number would be invited to dine with the First Family. The larger East Room also permitted Edith to resume the practice of serving refreshments in the room, even to large crowds such as those that attended the concerts.[19]

In the Ground Floor Corridor, Edith and McKim developed a design that would allow for the creation of a gallery for portraits of the first ladies. The area was very important for Edith because she felt that it provided a means to further institutionalize what would one day become the Office of the First Lady. It also provided a way to reinforce the history of the position. The area had been utilized for office space, but the creation of the West Wing freed the space for new purposes. McKim had the original vaulted ceiling of the corridor, which had designed by James Hoban, restored to its former glory. Along the corridor were hung the portraits of first ladies. There were also busts or small statuettes positioned along the corridor. The portrait gallery remains one of the enduring legacies of Edith Roosevelt.

The White House as Museum

In fact, the First Ladies Gallery was but one of a number of steps that Edith undertook during the renovation or soon thereafter to preserve or enhance the status of the White House as a national historical treasure and functioning museum. Both Theodore and Edith believed in the historicism of the White House and the need to maintain the structure as a symbol of the American presidency and a tribute to past chief executives. Edith's efforts to maintain the style and character of the original Executive Mansion, the First Lady "set the precedent for thinking of the White House as a museum of U.S. history and the presidency."[20]

In one concrete example of this effort, Edith sought to restore the flair of the past by having existing historical White House furniture reproduced. For instance, after the British burned the Executive Mansion in 1814, President James Monroe had acquired furniture designed by the celebrated French designer Pierre-Antoine Bellange. Through the years, many of the original pieces were damaged or sold (currently only nine of the Bellange pieces exist). Edith asked McKim to design a set of furniture for the Blue Room that was based on the Bellange originals. The architect also decorated the rest of the room around the reproductions and replaced the carpets with oak floors and matching wall hangings.

Edith was particularly distressed when she learned that a variety of furniture and other memorabilia was routinely discarded through public auctions or simply thrown away. During the remodeling process, Edith endeavored to use furniture that had been placed in storage, rather than acquiring new pieces if at all possible. However, Edith's practical nature always made her prefer function over form and when appropriate she brought in new furnishings or decor with durability and value in mind. For instance, the First Lady removed the antique beds in the bedrooms of her young sons in order to prevent damage. Instead she brought in modern and sturdy cast iron bed frames which proved invulnerable to the assaults and antics of the children.[21]

Edith faced some criticisms over the expense, but she defended your choice on the grounds that she was preserving the nation's artifacts from the inevitable damage inflicted by young children or Theodore. Writing to his eldest son in October 1901, the President stated that "Archie and Quentin are just as cunning as can be . . . I had a 'bear' play with them in their room and Kermit and Ethel could not resist the temptation and came in also, and we had a terrific romp on the bed."[22]

The First Lady also took a keen interest in preserving the china collections of the White House. She employed the noted journalist Abby Gunn Baker to conduct a thorough and comprehensive history of the previous china patterns used in the White House. This inventory was followed by efforts to procure remaining pieces from presidential descendants or museums. Baker then collaborated with Edith in the development of the White House China Collection that had been begun by Caroline Harrison. Eventually, the results of the collaboration were put on display for the public. In order to maintain the historical pieces, Edith arranged for the White House to procure a new china set. This service set "objectified the restrained elegance" that Edith and Theodore sought to portray to foreign dignitaries and American public officials.[23]

Edith also wanted to make sure that future administrations would not be tempted to auction furnishings or remove items. Therefore she established the first comprehensive inventory of all of the household items of the White House, including furniture and linens, flatware and china, and wall decorations.[24] The First Lady also led an effort for the passage of legislation that forbade the sale of White House items in the future. This effectively ended the practice of auctioning items and reinforced the historical nature of the furnishings.

EXTERIOR CHANGES

The construction of the West Wing of the White House was the most significant addition to the executive mansion since its construction. It removed the main offices from the original building and consequently dramatically expanded the interior spaces of the White House. Significantly, the renovation moved the president's main office from the second floor of the White House to the West Wing. This transition ultimately paved the way for the establishment of the Oval Office, which was completed during the administration of William Howard Taft. This office became one of the most familiar aspects of the White House for the American people as the site of numerous presidential addresses.

The expansion of office space also had dramatic implications for ways in which the media covered the White House. The new areas provided the president with the ability to offer space within the White House for reporters. Once ensconced in the West Wing, reporters had much greater access to the president and government officials. Meanwhile, Roosevelt was able to forge close relationships with White House reporters and utilize them to disseminate information as part of his efforts to employ the "bully pulpit" to sway public opinion.

On the other hand, the construction of the West Wing necessitated the aforementioned removal of the White House greenhouses from the grounds. In order to compensate for their loss, Edith decided to establish new gardens around the White House lawn. The First Lady oversaw the establishment of a large "Colonial garden" designed to replace the more elaborate greenhouse flora.[25] The centerpiece of the garden was a variety of multicolored bulbs and perennials that brightened the exterior of the mansion. Theodore was especially pleased with Edith's garden because the low-cost plants and flowers contrasted significantly with the previous elaborate greenhouses. For Theodore, the garden served as another small demonstration of the egalitarian nature of his family and of his administration. The renovation also provided Theodore with the ability to highlight his mania for physical fitness. For instance, he had tennis courts installed.

Edith also endeavored to maintain the lawn of the White House in pristine fashion. As a result, she disliked the numerous public ceremonies or events held on the lawn. She especially opposed the annual Easter egg–rolling contest. This spectacle had begun during the Hayes administration and proved quite popular with both the public and her family. While Edith realized that she had to accept the tradition, the damage done to the newly renovated lawn of the White House proved irksome throughout her remaining years in the mansion.

CONCLUSION

Edith Roosevelt endeavored to institutionalize an office of the first lady. During her tenure she initiated a number of customs and traditions that provided the basis for the later growth in power and stature of the office of first lady. Her efforts and work during the White House renovation of 1902 was one concrete example of this broader effort. For instance, the First Lady further used the renovation as means to enhance the historical nature of her office by inaugurating the First Ladies' Portrait Gallery. Furthermore, Edith played a major role in both the redesign and decoration of the Executive Mansion.

Mindful of the history and tradition that surrounded the White House, Edith assumed a leadership role in ensuring that the renovation not only remained true to the original style of the mansion, but that it involved steps to restore the grandeur of the house. As much as possible, Edith utilized furnishings that recalled the original neoclassic style of the White House. This was true of both the interior and exterior spaces. Yet she also worked to improve the functionality of the White House by insisting on the expansion of the private, family areas and the construction of the West Wing. Ultimately her work bolstered the status of her office and enhanced the quality of life of her family as well as future first families.

NOTES TO CHAPTER 13

1. H. W. Brands, *T.R.* . . . , 1997, 432.

2. The major renovation did not take place during Harrison's term because of congressional opposition to the costs. However, Caroline Harrison was able to secure $52,000 for four minor projects, including the construction of a "modern" kitchen and the installation of electricity. Ultimately,

Caroline Harrison's lobbying efforts laid the foundation for the 1902 Roosevelt renovations; Edith Mayo, "Party Politics . . . ," 2000, 583–585.

3. James M. Strock, *Theodore Roosevelt on Leadership* . . . ," 2001, 200–201.

4. Ibid., 200–201.

5. Edward Oxford, "The White House . . . ," 1992, 6–8.

6. The Tiffany screen was placed in the White House entrance hall between Ionic columns in order to reduce drafts. It had the effect of reducing the size of the Cross Hall and creating a Victorian theme.

7. Carl Sferrazza Anthony, *America's First Families* . . . , 2000, 33.

8. Tom Lansford, *A "Bully" First Lady* . . . , 2001, 69.

9. Alice Roosevelt Longworth, *Crowded Hours* . . . , 1933, 44.

10. Sylvia Jukes Morris, *Edith Kermit Roosevelt* . . . , 1979, 223.

11. Quoted in Oxford, 1992, 54.

12. The McMillan Commission was named in honor of Senator James McMillan and tasked with renewing the original beauty of Washington, D.C. through redesign and restrictions on new construction.

13. See Sarah Fayen, "Inhabiting an Icon . . . ," 2000.

14. Valerie Jablow, "Presidential Designs," 2000, 49.

15. For a more thorough study of the intricacies of the renovation, see William Seale, *The President's House* . . . , 1986.

16. This anteroom eventually became the White House Library in 1937.

17. May 2000, 585.

18. Betty Boyd Caroli, *The Roosevelt Women*, 1998, 198.

19. K. Smith, *Entertaining in the White House*, 1967, 149–157.

20. Robert P. Watson, *The Presidents' Wives* . . . , 2000, 80.

21. Lansford, 2001, 69.

22. Theodore Roosevelt to Theodore Roosevelt, Jr., Washington, D.C., October 19, 1901, in H. W. Brands, *The Selected Letters of Theodore Roosevelt*, 2001, 272–273.

23. Mayo, 2000, 584.

24. Morris, 2001, 254.

25. Sferrazza, 2001, 63.

Fourteen

The Truman Renovations of the White House: The House that Harry (Re)Built

RAYMOND FREY

INTRODUCTION

Harry S. Truman changed the White House structurally and architecturally more than any other president who occupied the building.[1] A self-proclaimed "architectural nut," Truman was puzzled when his first ventures into expanding, modifying, and improving the Executive Mansion met with considerable public opposition. He knew the symbolic importance of the White House, but he also knew that it was a place where the executive business of the country took place. It therefore needed to be practical, comfortable, and efficient, as well as a place to receive and entertain VIPs and dignitaries. At first, Truman was mostly interested in making the Executive Mansion a more comfortable and orderly place for the president to live and work. The President's keen eye for detail later revealed a building that was in serious danger of collapse, and his quick and decisive actions to save it preserved the White House for generations to come.

THE EXECUTIVE OFFICE EXPANSION

The Poorest Place to Work

The Executive Office contained 225 employees when Truman took office in April 1945. He was immediately concerned with the crowded working conditions. "The burden of the President has increased to such an extent that now the basement of the so-called office wing is full of workers—it is the poorest place in the world for people to work."[2]

Truman directed Lorenzo Winslow, the official White House architect, to draw up plans for an expansion of the Executive Office Building to the south. They would include additional office space, a staff cafeteria, a museum, and a 375-seat auditorium to be used primarily for press conferences. Since the Oval Office was no longer adequate to accommodate the more than 200 reporters and photographers who routinely covered presidential press conferences, the plans also called for a small stage accessible from the Oval Office and space for radio and television equipment.

Seven months after Truman took office, the final touches were being put on a proposed expansion to be presented to Congress. By the end of November 1945, a plan was finalized, which also included some badly needed repairs to the main White House building—among them, replacement of the floorboards in the second-floor living quarters, and a new heating system to replace the one installed in 1902. Truman's formal request to Congress was warmly received, and an appropriation of $1,650,000 was approved on 3 December 1945, giving the President all he had requested.[3]

The "Addition" Controversy

The project received extensive press coverage, resulting in unexpected resistance by the American public. Winslow, the lead architect, unwisely told reporters that the new wing was an "addition" to the White House, firmly fixing the idea in the public's mind. Truman's radio adviser, J. Leonard Reinsch, said

> Unfortunately, the architect announced it was an 'addition' to the White House. If he had said that it was an addition to the President's office or said that an executive office was being built, we would today have this conference room [auditorium] which is badly needed . . . Once it was announced as an 'addition,' all hell broke loose.[4]

By the middle of January 1946, great numbers of protest letters from angry citizens all over the country began arriving at the White House. The American Home Builders Association charged that the addition would use up scarce building materials to build new homes for veterans returning from World War II. The American Institute of Architects claimed that the stewardship of the White House was granted to their organization by Theodore Roosevelt, and therefore the new president had no authority to make any changes without their consent.

Soon the public furor caught the attention of Congress. Both Democrats and Republicans questioned an expansion program that might result in damage to the White House. Congressman Howard W. Smith of Virginia called for a joint resolution to halt construction until Congress had time to examine the plans.[5]

Secretary of the Interior Harold L. Ickes, a holdover from FDR's cabinet, wrote to Truman that "the White House is a shrine, not only because it houses the Chief Executive of the Nation but for what it represents in the hearts of the people." Since Franklin Roosevelt had put the White House and its grounds under the administration of the National Park Service (NPS) in 1933, and the NPS was part of the Department of Interior, Ickes felt personally responsible for its preservation. He urged the President to slow down and contact leading architects for their opinions before proceeding.[6]

Truman was surprised and annoyed by all of the opposition. He knew firsthand how much the White House had been altered while the Roosevelts had occupied it, including the addition of a new East Wing, and no one had criticized them. "I am going forward with this construction," the President wrote back to Ickes, "because it is absolutely necessary."[7] As the controversy continued, fueled by the newspapers, Truman held a press conference on January 24, 1946, where he threatened to move staff into the staterooms of the White House if he could not build his new wing. He angrily commented that people did not seem to want him to have space in which to work.[8] That same day, the House of Representatives voted to remove, by a vote of 110 to 41, the $883,660 allotted for the addition. Truman was astonished by the revolt. He deleted the museum and the cafeteria from the plans, but told workmen to go ahead with the auditorium. White House architect Lorenzo S. Winslow said he would continue "until the President personally tells me to stop."[9]

Various options were suggested to the President. The American Institute of Architects recommended that a second temporary structure be built between the White House grounds and the State, War, and Navy Building across the street. There was, they argued, already talk of constructing a new State Department building across from the State, War, and Navy structure, so perhaps some staff could be housed in close proximity to the Executive Mansion. Truman was not moved by this suggestion, but now that the war was over, Americans seemed determined to thwart any move by their president or anyone else to change the White House in any way.

Finally realizing that no plan would be acceptable to either Congress or the American people, Truman conceded defeat. A large part of the President's staff was moved to the State, War, and Navy Building, and West Executive Avenue was closed to traffic to allow easy communication between the two buildings. Any further White House expansion plans were put to rest.[10]

THE TRUMAN BALCONY

Harry's Back Porch

"All Harry Truman wanted was a back porch—a cool place where he could sit in the evening, as he used to back in Independence, listening to the whir of the sprinkler on the lawn and the sound of neighbors' voices coming clear through the summer air," *Time* Magazine said in 1948. "He consulted an architect; together, they found just the place for it. It would be inconspicuously tucked away behind the pillars of the White House's south portico, at the second-floor level.[11]

In the summer of 1947, following his failure to expand the White House office space, Truman decided that the appearance of the south front of the building and the livability of the second-floor family quarters would be enhanced by the addition of a balcony built behind the columns of the portico.

Already a great fan of porches, the President decided to build one that would open off of the Oval Room, which he used as his study, and his bedroom. Through his reading of history, Truman noted that Thomas Jefferson, who among his many talents was also a skilled architect, had no objection to second-story porches. During a visit to the University of Virginia on July 4, 1947, Truman took note of the upstairs galleries or porches on the columned buildings on the campus that Jefferson had designed.

Inspired by Jefferson's buildings, Truman presented his idea to the White House architect, Lorenzo Winslow, as soon as he returned to Washington. Given the previous objections to any alterations of the Executive Mansion, and the fact that the portico—a major feature of the White House—had remained untouched since it was built in 1824,

Winslow told the President that such a radical alteration of the appearance of the building was sure to stir opposition. Undaunted,
Truman overrode the objections and ordered it to be built.[12]

Letters of protest poured into the Washington papers, and
editorial cartoonists across the country lampooned the idea. Said
the New York *Herald Tribune*: "'Back-porch Harry' is scarcely an
appellation that a man would like to carry into a presidential campaign, even if he were impervious to the odium of violating good
taste, propriety and historical feeling."[13]

Republicans were delighted, as the "Truman Balcony" became
an overnight controversy. "Back Porch Harry," biographer David
McCullough wrote, "(was) accused of meddling with a structure
that not only didn't belong to him, but that he was not likely to
be occupying much longer."[14]

In Defense of His Balcony

Showing his stubborn side, Truman stood his ground. At a press
conference, he was asked if he were going ahead with the balcony.
He *was*, he declared. Truman added that the same opposition had
been made when bathtubs, gaslights, and cooking stoves were put
in the White House.[15]

The President wasted no time. As correspondents departed
the Oval Office, they stopped to take a look at the south portico.
Work had already begun.

The "porch" would be ten feet wide, its front limit being the
inside line of the columns. The forward edge would conform to the
curved arrangement of the columns. The finished balcony would
be forty feet long, with a three-foot iron railing. The $15,000 cost
was to be paid for by funds for the maintenance of the White
House, so congressional approval was not necessary.[16]

The greater the public outcry, the more Truman defended it.
He insisted that Thomas Jefferson had actually intended such a
porch for the White House, but when pressed for specific documen-
tation, he could not cite anything conclusive.[17] It was, he said,
founded on the best grounds of architectural tradition. He scoffed
at the idea that the balcony was being built to provide an outside
sitting area, or that he actually had the time for rocking on a porch.
He gave two main reasons for adding it: first, to break what he
considered the outlandish, disproportionate height of the portico
columns; and second, to aid in shading the windows of the Blue
Room on the first floor. Unsightly canvas awnings had been previously installed that would collect dirt and mildew; they could be

replaced with neat wooden shades that rolled up under the balcony and could be let down when needed.[18]

By March 1948, as the work was nearing completion, the blistering newspaper attacks continued. A *New York Times* editorial said: "The White House is the heritage of the American people and a national monument, even a national shrine . . . we hope that Mr. Truman will finally decide that architectural details which would be appropriate elsewhere might only desecrate the noble old mansion at 1600 Pennsylvania Avenue."[19] Some were concerned with Truman's almost reckless meddling with such a scared and historic structure as the White House, but much of the criticism was directed at Truman himself. To many, his insistence on a balcony symbolized his hardheaded leadership style—his unbending certainty that he was right. Truman continued to insist that the porch had nothing to do with his personal comfort—it was simply an effort to perfect the appearance of the White House. "When the job is finished, he said, "everyone will like it."[20]

Soon the furor died down, and it was not even an issue in the 1948 presidential campaign. Some experts in historical architecture came to agree with Truman that it improved the appearance of the columns. In time the new addition seemed perfectly natural, and Truman's prediction proved prophetic: it has become a favorite spot for presidential families ever since.

THE WHITE HOUSE IS FALLING DOWN

Creaking, Sagging, and Sinking

It was the last straw.

One day in August 1948, the leg of the grand piano of Truman's daughter, Margaret, suddenly broke through the second floor of the White House, sticking out of the ceiling in the family dining room directly below.

Truman had known for quite some time that the White House was literally falling down. While he was a judge in Jackson County, Missouri, he had overseen the construction of both the Independence and Kansas City courthouses, and gained valuable experience in architecture. Driven by his interest in history, Truman wanted to preserve Jackson County's first courthouse, built in 1827, and rehabilitate its successor in Independence, built in 1832. Truman often told friends and members of his staff over the years that had he been forced as a young man to choose a profession other than politics, he would have been either a farmer, a historian, or an architect.[21] Shortly after moving into the White House, the President noticed the telltale signs of a building under serious physical stress. He frequently complained of drafts and unusual popping and creaking noises in the old house. There were plenty of other signs that it was in trouble. Truman noticed that the big East Room chandelier would begin to sway as the White House color guard marched across the floor. The floorboards of the second-floor living quarters sagged badly, and in the upstairs Oval Room, which Truman used as a study, the floor creaked and swayed under his feet. In his big bathroom, the tub even appeared to be slowly sinking into the floor.[22] In January 1948, Truman asked the Commissioner of Public Buildings, W. E. Reynolds, to bring in engineers to check the safety of the Oval Room's floor. The engineers found it to be overstressed, and advised that no more than fifteen people be allowed in the room at one time.

A History of Wear and Tear

The cornerstone of the White House was laid on October 12, 1792. When the British raided Washington on August 24, 1814, they torched the building, gutting the interior and damaging part of the exterior. Reconstruction began in the spring of 1815, supervised by James Hoban, the original architect. Since that time, many changes were made to the original structure. The south portico was built in 1824, the north portico in 1829. Water pipes were installed in 1833, and gas lighting was added in 1848. An elevator was installed in 1881, and electricity in 1891. In 1902, Congress spent $425,000 to renovate the White House and construct the Executive Office Building. In 1927, a new steel-trussed roof and fire-resistant third floor were added, and the ground floor and kitchens were remodeled in 1935. Yet, these improvements provided only temporary relief and in some cases further stressed the building. The house had deteriorated rapidly by the time the Trumans moved in.

The first floor was safe, having been set on steel and concrete during the 1902 renovations, and the third floor was suspended by the steel framing installed in 1927. The problem was that the second floor was still supported by the wooden beams put in place by James Hoban in 1816. Since then, the beams and studs were drilled or notched, some as much as five inches, in order to install indoor plumbing, gas lighting, electric wiring, and heating ducts. Commissioner Reynolds said that the interior of the White House was standing "purely from habit." Only the outer walls were pronounced sound and worthy of preservation.[23]

Assessing the Extent of the Damage

In February 1948, President Truman called in a committee of architects and engineers, including Lorenzo S. Winslow, the official White House architect, to make a quick examination of the entire house. They found several structural weaknesses and serious fire hazards, and decided that a more thorough examination of the building was needed.[24] A committee of distinguished engineers was formed, with a congressional appropriation of $50,000 to make a thorough structural survey. By September 1948, the experts concluded that the problems were not confined to the second floor; the soft clay foundation footings were only eight feet deep and were slowly sinking, and the heavy steel and concrete third-floor structure was overloading the outside walls.

In a letter to his sister in early 1948, Truman told her what the engineers had finally concluded:

> I've had the second floor where we live examined—and it is about to fall down! The engineer said that the ceiling in the state dining room only stayed up from force of habit! I'm having it shored up and hoping to have a concrete and steel floor put in before I leave here. The roof fell in on Coolidge and they put a concrete and steel third floor in to take its place and suggested that the second floor be done the same way. But Old Cal wouldn't do it. He wanted it to fall like the roof did I guess.[25]

Truman was advised to move out of the White House immediately, but being in the middle of a heated presidential race, and given the fact that Bess and Margaret Truman had returned to Missouri for the summer, Harry was reluctant to leave, because he did not want to reveal the White House's structural problems to the public before Election Day. As daughter Margaret wrote: "The whole mess would have been blamed on Harry Truman."[26]

On October 26, 1948, maintenance men found a large amount of fallen plaster on the floor of the East Room, prompting the staff to close the house to the visiting public. On November 7, 1948, five days after his reelection was secure, Harry, Bess, and Margaret returned from Missouri and were told that the White House was unsafe, and they should consider moving across the street to Blair House, a 124-year-old, four-story yellow stucco house one block down from the White House on Pennsylvania Avenue. The house was bought in 1942 by the U.S. Department of State to house visitors from abroad. Truman had previously lived for a time in Blair House immediately after assuming the presidency on the death of Franklin Roosevelt, in order to give Mrs. Roosevelt time to move out of the White House.[27] Truman wrote from Key West, Florida, on November 17, 1948, where he was taking a postelection vacation with his family, that he agreed with the move. By Thanksgiving, the President and his family had relocated to 1651 Pennsylvania Avenue.

Demolition and Reconstruction

At the time Truman thought that it would "take at least ten months to tear the old second floor out and put it back." But by the time the Trumans returned from Key West, "it was decided that nothing could be saved except the outside walls," Margaret Truman later wrote. "The entire house would have to be gutted and rebuilt."[28]

After studying several alternatives, it was decided to retain the exterior walls, replace the weak structural skeleton, and reconstruct the entire interior. The cost was estimated at $5,412,000. Truman asked Congress to establish a Commission on the Renovation of the Executive Mansion to oversee the project, and to ensure that the historical, aesthetic, and sentimental, as well as the architectural and engineering aspects, be protected. Congress approved the commission on April 14, 1949, and work began on December 12, 1949.[29]

The contractor was John McShain, Inc. of Philadelphia, the same firm that built the Pentagon and the Jefferson Memorial. One morning, when walking over from Blair House on one of his many "inspection tours" to see how work was progressing, Truman spotted large sign, hung near the White House fence, which said "John McShain, Inc. Builders." He ordered it to be taken down at once, as such commercialization was improper for the White House.[30]

The demolition and rebuilding of the White House within its stone walls was a remarkable engineering achievement. The building would literally be reconstructed from the inside out. Workmen began by dismantling the interior rooms, saving wood trim, doors, hardware, and other visible details for possible future use. By February 1950, the interior had been completely dismantled, leaving a cavernous hollow space, 165 feet long, 85 feet wide, and 70 to 80 feet high. "They took all the insides out," Truman wrote in his diary. "Dug two basements, put in steel and concrete like you've never seen in the Empire State Building, Pentagon or anywhere else."[31]

Twenty feet below the foundation the ground was firm, so engineers dug 126 pits, four feet square and 25 feet deep, and filled them with reinforced concrete, creating a network of powerful support columns. At one point, engineers asked Truman's permission to break through an original wall to get a bulldozer inside the structure. Truman refused, so they disassembled the bulldozer piece by piece and then reassembled it inside the walls.[32]

Slowly the new steel framing began to rise, filling the vast shell of the White House. In November 1950, the weight of the outer structure was transferred entirely to the new steel skeleton. As construction proceeded into the early summer of 1950, Truman faced the outbreak of war in Korea. The Secret Service and Truman's military advisers, convinced that a third world war was a real possibility, persuaded the President to make the lowest basement level bombproof. An additional $868,000 was allocated, with no questions asked.

In the early months of the project, work proceeded ahead of schedule, but the Korean War slowed the overall progress of construction. By the autumn of 1950, prices for building materials soared and supplies became scarce. Even with an average of 250 men on the job six days a week, the lack of materials slowed down the work. Truman registered his displeasure with the slow rate of progress by frequently visiting the work site. In fact, it eventually became so common to see the President there that the workmen scarcely bothered to take notice of him.[33]

The contractor, John McShain, complained that the shortage of labor and materials would make it impossible to properly schedule and complete the construction work. Truman responded by pressuring the Office of Price Administration to grant the Congressional Commission on the Renovation of the Executive Mansion a limited priority on purchasing materials. Since this was the President's house, and his protection had become an essential feature of the project, the renovation was reclassified as a "defense effort."[34] The sudden availability of rationed building materials helped considerably in moving the project along.

One casualty of the speed of the renovation was the large quantity of original doors, molding, brick, and stone that were not saved. Although the best of the original furnishings, old mahogany doors, window sashes, mantelpieces, hardware, and floorboards were reused, tons of scrap lumber, ancient plumbing fixtures, pine doors, and stone were hauled away in large trucks to a landfill in Virginia, a process that took nearly a month and was done in secrecy to avoid bad publicity. "By standards of latter-day preservation work, this was a needless and tragic loss," Truman biographer David McCullough wrote. "The justification would be the cost and the President's own desire to see the job finished in a reasonable time."[35]

Abbie Rowe, the official White House photographer, had the responsibility of keeping a complete photographic record of the dismantling, renovation, and rebuilding of the White House, a project to which he devoted a major part of his time between 1948 and 1952. He produced hundreds of detailed black-and-white photographs to document almost every aspect of the work.[36]

In spite of last-minute changes and alterations and a shortage of building materials due to the war, construction continued at a rapid rate. Soon the original four floors were replaced, with the addition of two new ones below the old basement. But even with the quickened pace, it became obvious that the original deadline of October 1951 would not be met. Truman was not happy with the news. He would be in office only until January 1953, and wanted to live in the White House as long as possible. He set a new deadline: Christmas 1951.[37]

The Finishing Touch

By the spring of 1951 the interior began to take shape. Parquet flooring was being laid, wood trim was going up, and some mantels had been brought in. However, a severe shortage of trained floor-layers arose because of the war, and it would take several months to complete the installation of the parquet flooring.[38] Teams of plasterers worked even faster than anticipated, although in August 1951 they went on strike and walked off the job for two weeks.

In March 1951, the general plan of the interior decoration had been approved. The Manhattan department store, B. Altman and Company, was chosen to supply furniture, rugs, draperies, accessories, and any other needed furnishings. The president of the Manhattan store, John S. Burke, agreed to supply all of these goods at absolute cost.[39]

It was hoped that the Trumans would be back in the White House by the fall of 1951. Behind schedule and in need of additional funding to complete the project, Truman was told in July that he would not be in the White House by Christmas. Trying to be patient, he asked that work be completed by April 1, 1952. He wanted to occupy the new White House as president, even if only for a few months.

By February 1952, crates of furniture began arriving as workers finished sanding floors, painting walls, and installing tile. By the middle of March, the construction fences and shacks were removed from the White House grounds. Deep in the new sub-basement, engineers tested the electrical systems. The heat and air conditioning were turned on, machinery in the laundry and ironing rooms were tested, the kitchens and pantries were restocked. On March 22, the regular White House staff returned. Dust covers were removed from furniture and pictures, and vacuum cleaners hummed over the carpets and parquet floors while workmen polished the windowpanes.

On March 27, 1952, the Trumans' belongings were moved from Blair House to the White House. Harry Truman was in the presidential plane, returning home from Key West. Two days later, he would announce that he would not seek another term as president.

The New White House

At the White House, a small ceremony was planned to greet the President when he arrived. A small group of staff members, commissioners, and officials were waiting as the presidential limousine pulled into the driveway. Steeping out of the car under the north portico, Truman was presented with a gold key. A large crowd gathered on the sidewalk cheered, and a group of photographers recorded the event. Truman turned and walked briskly through the glass doors. He was home again in the White House.

After spending more than three years living in the smaller quarters of Blair House, the first family returned to the mansion for their first night back in residence. It was some in ways the same home that they had left three years earlier, but it was now a new and larger home as well. The original forty-eight rooms had expanded to fifty-four, not including the entirely new sub-basement levels containing service areas and other support facilities. And now 660 tons of steel strengthened the new concrete inner walls and floors. The final cost of the renovations was $5,832,000—within approximately $500,000 of the original estimate.

On April 22, 1952, the White House was opened for public tours, and 5,444 people went through on the first day. On May 3, Truman gave the three major news networks a television tour. Thirty million Americans watched—the largest audience ever for a house tour.[40]

Shortly after his return, Truman invited Eleanor Roosevelt to the White House for a personal tour. Apparently she was not impressed with the renovations, as she remarked years later that "Mr. Truman showed me around the White House, which he'd just redone, and he was so proud of the upstairs, which looked to me exactly like a Sheraton Hotel."[41]

CONCLUSION

Although it certainly was a different house from the one she and Franklin had occupied, Eleanor's remark may have been an overstatement. The White House may not have been preserved with the regard for historical accuracy that some may have wished, but Truman's renovation saved the building from almost certain collapse, and his awareness of the importance of the White House as a national symbol averted its demolition, which some engineers had strongly suggested.

Today, the building remains true to the vision of George Washington and those who have inhabited it since John Adams. Time, day-to-day use, and even war have taken their toll on the White House, but the numerous efforts to renovate and restore the building have proven successful, most notably the complete reconstruction overseen by Harry S. Truman. Thanks to the keen interest in the building's history and integrity by first families and support for the president's house by the American public the White House is even more important and impressive than ever, and it continues to have symbolism far beyond serving simply as the president's home.

NOTES TO CHAPTER 14

1. See the White House Historical Association's web site (www.whitehousehistory.org) under "White House Architecture."

2. William Seale, The President's House . . . , 1986, 1007.

3. Ibid., 1986, 1008.

4. J. Leonard Reinsch, interview: Atlanta, March 13 and 14, 1967, Truman Presidential Library archives.

5. "Repairs of 1600 Pennsylvania Avenue," 1946, 25.

6. Letter from Harold Ickes to Harry S. Truman, Washington, January 10, 1946, Truman Presidential Library archives.

7. Letter from Harry S. Truman to Harold Ickes, Washington, January 10, 1946, Truman Presidential Library archives.

8. "The President's Hall," 1946, 29.

9. "Repairs at 1600 Pennsylvania Avenue," 1946, 25.

10. Seale, 1986, 1010–1011.

11. "Back Porch Harry, "1948, 17.

12. Seale, 1986, 1012.

13. "Back Porch Harry," 1948, 17.

14. David McCullough, *Truman*, 1992, 593–594.

15. "Back Porch Harry," 1948, 17.

16. "Truman Decides to Have a Porch . . . ," 1948, 15.

17. See "White House Architecture" at www.whitehousehistory.org.

18. Amy LaFollette Jensen, *The White House . . .* , 1965, 251.

19. "White House Porch," 1948, 22.

20. Seale, 1986, 1015.

21. McCullough, 1992, 882.

22. Jensen, 1965, 252.

23. Ibid.

24. Ibid.

25. Margaret Truman, *Harry S. Truman*, 1973, 398.

26. John Whitcomb and Claire Whitcomb, *Real Life and the White House*, 2000, 328.

27. "Fire Trap," 1948, 24.

28. M. Truman, 1973, 399.

29. William Ryan and Desmond Guinness, *The White House . . .* , 1980, 166–167.

30. McCullough, 1992, 878.

31. Ibid.

32. Whitcomb and Whitcomb, 2000, 329.

33. McCullough, 1992, 881.

34. Seale, 1986, 880–881.

36. Abbie Rowe photo exhibit, Truman Presidential Library, February 2002.

37. Seale, 1986, 1046.

38. Ryan and Guinness, 1980, 172.

39. Seale, 1986, 1040–1041.

40. McCullough, 1992, 886.

41. "Reality and Illusion—The White House and Harry S. Truman," available at the White House Historical Association at www.whitehousehistory.org.

Appendix 1

White House Floor Plan

Cutaway view of the White House (courtesy of the White House Historical Association)

Appendix 2

First Families, 1789–2003

1789–1797 **George & Martha Washington**
George Custis   Nellie Custis
[Martha's grandson]   [Martha's granddaughter]

1797–1801 **John & Abigail Adams**
Thomas Adams [son]   Suzannah Adams
                                                  [granddaughter]
Billy Shaw [Abigail's nephew]   Louisa Smith [Abigail's niece]

1801–1809 **Thomas Jefferson**
Martha Randolph [daughter]   Thomas Randolph
                                                  [son-in-law]
Maria Eppes [daughter]   John Eppes [son-in-law]
[several grandchildren visit]

1809–1817 **James & Dolley Madison**
Edward Coles [Dolley's cousin]   [numerous other relatives visit]

1817–1825 **James & Elizabeth Monroe**
Elizabeth Hay [daughter]   George Hay [son-in-law]
Hortensia Hay [granddaughter] [grandchildren, siblings,
                                                     in-laws visit]

1825–1829 **John Quincy & Louisa Catherine Adams**
Abigail Adams [John's niece]   Mary Adams [daughter-in-law]
Mary Adams [granddaughter]   [children, nephews visit]

1829–1837 **Andrew Jackson**
Andrew Donelson   Emily Donelson
  [wife's nephew]   [wife's niece]
[nieces, adopted grandchildren]

1837–1841 **Martin Van Buren**
Abraham Van Buren [son]
John Van Buren [son]
Rebecca Van Buren
[granddaughter]
[other relatives visit]

Angelica Van Buren
[daughter-in-law]
Martin, Van Buren, Jr. [son]
Smith Van Buren [son]

1841 **William Henry Harrison**
[wife, Anna, never made it to the Mansion]
Benjamin Harrison [nephew]
James Harrison [grandson]
Montgomery Harrison
[grandson]
Lucy Taylor [niece]
[other relatives]

Henry Harrison [great-nephew]
Jane Harrison [daughter-in-law]
William Harrison [grandson]
William Taylor [great-nephew]

1841–1845 **John Tyler & Letitia** [1841–1842] **& Julia** [1844–1845]
Alice Tyler [daughter]
John Tyler, Jr. [son]
Mary Tyler [granddaughter]
Robert Tyler [son]
Letitia Semple [daughter]

Elizabeth Tyler [daughter]
Letitia Tyler [granddaughter]
Priscilla Tyler [daughter-in-law]
Tazewell Tyler [son]
[other relatives visit]

1845–1849 **James K. & Sarah Polk**
Marshall Polk [nephew]

John Hayes [brother-in-law]

1849–1850 **Zachary & Margaret Taylor**
Mary Bliss [daughter]
[numerous other relatives visit]

William Bliss [son-in-law]

1850–1853 **Millard & Abigail Fillmore**
Mary Fillmore [daughter]

Powers Fillmore [son]

1853–1857 **Franklin & Jane Pierce**
Abigail Means [Jane's aunt]

[numerous other relatives visit]

1857–1861 **James Buchanan**
Harriet Lane [niece]

Elliot Lane [nephew]

1861–1865 **Abraham & Mary Todd Lincoln**
Thomas Lincoln [son]
Emilie Helm [Mary's half-sister]

William Lincoln [son]
[numerous other relatives visit]

1865–1869 **Andrew & Eliza Johnson**

Martha Johnson [daughter]	Andrew Johnson [son]
Robert Johnson [son]	Andrew Patterson [grandson]
David Patterson [son-in-law]	Martha Patterson [daughter]
Mary Patterson [granddaughter]	Andrew Stover [grandson]
Lillian Stover [granddaughter]	Mary Stover [daughter]
Sarah Stover [granddaughter]	

1869–1877 **Ulysses S. & Julia Grant**

Ellen Grant [daughter]	Jesse Grant [son]
Frederick Dent [Julia's father]	[numerous other relatives visit]

1877–1881 **Rutherford B. & Lucy Hayes**

Fanny Hayes [daughter]	Scott Hayes [son]
[other children and relatives visit]	

1881   **James A. & Lucretia Garfield**

Abraham Garfield [son]	Harry Garfield [son]
Irvin Garfield [son]	James Garfield [son]
Mollie Garfield [daughter]	

1881–1885 **Chester A. Arthur**

Ellen Arthur [daughter]	[numerous other relatives visit]

1885–1889 **Grover Cleveland & Frances** [1886–1889]
Rose Cleveland [Grover's sister]

1889–1893 **Benjamin Harrison & Caroline** [1889–1892]

Benjamin McKee [grandson]	Mary McKee [daughter]
J. Robert McKee [son-in-law]	Mary McKee [granddaughter]
John Scott [Caroline's father]	Mary Dimmick [Caroline's niece]
[other relatives visit]	

1893–1897 **Grover & Frances Cleveland**

Esther Cleveland [daughter]	Marion Cleveland [daughter]
Ruth Cleveland [daughter]	[other relatives visit]

1897–1901 **William & Ida McKinley**
[numerous relatives visit]

1901–1909 **Theodore & Edith Roosevelt**

Alice Roosevelt [daughter]	Archibald Roosevelt [son]
Ethel Roosevelt [daughter]	Kermit Roosevelt [son]
Theodore, Jr. [son]	Quentin Roosevelt [son]
[other relatives visit]	

1909–1913 **William Howard & Helen Taft**
Charles Taft [son]   Helen Taft [daughter]
Robert Taft [son]   [numerous other relatives visit]

1913–1921 **Woodrow Wilson & Ellen** [1913–1914] **& Edith** [1915–1921]
Eleanor McAdoo [daughter]   Helen Bones [cousin]
Jessie Sayre [daughter]   Margaret Wilson [daughter]
[numerous other relatives visit]

1921–1923 **Warren G. & Florence Harding**
[numerous siblings and other relatives visit]

1923–1929 **Calvin & Grace Coolidge**
Calvin, Jr. [son]   John [son]
[parents and other relatives visit]

1929–1933 **Herbert & Lou Hoover**
Allan Hoover [son]   Joan Hoover [granddaughter]
Herbert Hoover [grandson]   Margaret Hoover
                              [daughter-in-law]
Margaret Hoover   [other relatives visit]
   [granddaughter]

1933–1945 **Franklin D. & Eleanor Roosevelt**
[numerous children and relatives visit]

1945–1953 **Harry S. & Bess Truman**
Margaret Truman [daughter]   Madge Wallace [Bess's mother]
[other relatives visit]

1953–1961 **Dwight D. & Mamie Eisenhower**
Elvira Doud [Mamie's mother]
[numerous children and relatives visit]

1961–1963 **John F. & Jacqueline Kennedy**
Caroline Kennedy [daughter]   John, Jr. [son]
[numerous siblings, parents, and relatives visit]

1963–1969 **Lyndon B. & Lady Bird Johnson**
Luci Johnson Nugent [daughter] Lynda Johnson Robb [daughter]
[other relatives visit]

1969–1974 **Richard M. & Pat Nixon**
Tricia Nixon Cox [daughter]   [other relatives visit]

1974–1977 **Gerald R. & Betty Ford**
           Jack Ford [son]   Steve Ford [son]
           Susan Ford [daughter]   [other relatives visited]

1977–1981 **Jimmy & Rosalynn Carter**
           Amy Carter [daughter]   Annette Carter [daughter-in-law]
           Caron Carter [daughter-in-law] Chip Carter [son]
           James Carter [grandson]   Jeffrey Carter [son]
           [parents and other relatives visit]

1981–1989 **Ronald & Nancy Reagan**
           [numerous children and relatives visit]

1989–1993 **George & Barbara Bush**
           [numerous children and relatives visit]

1993–2001 **Bill & Hillary Rodham Clinton**
           Chelsea Clinton [daughter]
           [other parents and relatives visit]

2001–   **George W. & Laura Bush**
           [numerous children, parents, and relatives visit]

Note. This list is by no means exhaustive. Presidents typically enjoyed the company of extended family members in the Executive Mansion, but most only visited temporarily. Some children of presidents lived in the Executive Mansion, while others were grown and only visited. The list above includes those whose primary residence was the Executive Mansion and those who stayed for extended periods of time.

Bibliography

Aikman, Lonnelle, *The Living White House* (Washington, D.C.: White House Historical Association, 1991).

Allen, Ira R., "Billy Carter Suggests to President: Adopt a More Pro-Arab Policy," United Press International (24 October 1980).

Allgor, Catherine, *Parlor Politics: In Which the Ladies of Washington Help Build a City and a Government* (Charlottesville: University Press of Virginia, 2000).

Alterman, Eric, *The Sound and the Fury: The Washington Puditocracy and the Collapse of American Politics* (New York: Harper Perennial, 1992).

Anthony, Carl Sferrazza, *America's First Families: An Inside View of 200 Years of Private Life in the White House* (New York: Touchstone Press, 2000).

——, *Florence Harding—The First Lady of the Jazz Age and the Death of America's Most Scandalous President* (New York: William Morrow, 1998).

—— , *First Ladies: The Saga of the Presidents' Wives and Their Power, 1961–1990* (New York: William Morrow, 2 vols., 1990 and 1991).

Anthony, Katherine, *Dolley Madison: Her Life and Times* (Garden City, N.Y.: Doubleday, 1949).

"Back Porch Harry," *Time* 51 (26 January 1948), 17.

Baker, Abby Gunn, "White House Collection of Presidential Ware," *Century Magazine* 76 (October 1908), 830.

——, "The China of the Presidents," *Munsey's Magazine* 30 (December 1903), 324–328.

Baker, Jean, "Mary Lincoln," in Robert P. Watson, ed., *American First Ladies* (Pasadena, Calif.: Salem Press, 2002), 113–119.

Benson, Harry, *First Families: An Intimate Portrait from the Kennedys to the Clintons* (Boston: Little, Brown, 1997).

"Betty vs. Rosalynn: Life on the Campaign Trail," *U.S. News & World Report* (October 18, 1976), 22.

Black, Allida M., "(Anna) Eleanor Roosevelt," in Lewis G. Gould, ed., *American First Ladies: Their Lives and Their Legacy* (New York: Garland, 1996).

Blumenfeld, Amy, and Richard Jerome, "When Dad Is President," *People* 55 (June 18, 2001), 52.

Bogosian, Theodore, Press Secretary (Alexandria, Va.: Public Broadcasting System, September 17, 2001).

——, *Presidential Campaigns* (New York: Oxford University Press, 1985).

——, *Presidential Anecdotes* (New York: Penguin, 1981).

Bower, Carol Lynn, "Hillary Rodham Clinton: The Rhetorical Examination of the Three Communicative Stages of an Historic First Lady," paper presented at the annual meeting of the Western States Communication Association, Coeur d'Alene, Idaho, February 2001.

Bowling, Kenneth R., *The Creation of Washington, D.C.: The Idea and Location of the American Capital* (Fairfax, Va.: George Mason University Press, 1997).

——, *Creating the Federal City, 1774–1800: Potomac Fever* (Washington, D.C.: American Institute of Architects Press, 1988).

Boyd, Julian P., ed., *The Papers of Thomas Jefferson* (Princeton, N.J.: Princeton University Press, 1954).

Brands, H. W., *The Selected Letters of Theodore Roosevelt* (New York: Rowman & Littlefield, 2001).

——, *TR: The Last Romantic* (New York: Basic Books, 1997).

Brock, David, *Blinded by the Right: The Conscience of an Ex-Conservative* (New York: Crown Publishers, 2002).

Bruni, Frank, "Barbara Bush Joins G.O.P. Women on Stump to Try to Bridge Gender Gap," *New York Times* 150 (October 19, 2000), A30.

Butt, Archibald, *Letters* (New York: Doubleday, 1924).

Calhoun, Charles W., "Caroline (Lavinia) Scott Harrison," in Lewis G. Gould, *American First Ladies: Their Lives and Their Legacy* (New York: Garland, 1996).

Camehl, Ada Walker, *The Blue-China Book: Early American Scenes and History Pictured in the Pottery of the Time with a Supplementary Chapter Describing the Celebrated Collection of Presidential China in the White House at Washington, D.C., and a Complete Checking List of Known Examples of Anglo-American Pottery* (New York: E. P. Dutton, 1916).

Cannon, Lou, "Billy: 'Water Can Be Drank Straight,'" *Washington Post* (April 23, 1979), A1.

Cappella, Joseph and Kathleen Hall Jamieson, *Spiral of Cynicism: The Press and the Public Good* (New York: Oxford University Press, 1997).

Caroli, Betty Boyd, *The Roosevelt Women* (New York: Basic Books, 1998).

——, *First Ladies*, 3rd ed. (New York: Oxford University Press, 1995).

Carter, Jimmy, *Keeping Faith: Memoirs of a President* (New York: Bantam Books, 1984).

Carter, Rosalynn, *First Lady from Plains* (Fayetteville: The University Press of Arkansas, 1994).

"Chip and Caron Break Up Again," *U.S. News & World Report* (November 27, 1978), 11.

"Chronology on Libya," *New York Times* (July 27, 1980), A11.

Claiborne, William, "Chip Carter Moving Out of White House," *Washington Post* (August 14, 1977), A1.

Cockburn, Patrick, "Big Brother Is Watching Any Freeloading Relatives," *The Independent* (London) (January 24, 1993), 16.

Coleman, Elizabeth Tyler, *Priscilla Cooper Tyler and the American Scene: 1816–1889* (Tuscaloosa: University of Alabama Press, 1955).

Conroy, Sarah Booth, "Toward Comfort for Some, Grandeur for All," *Washington Post* (December 3, 1978), H1.

Conway, John A., "Diplomat in the Family," *Newsweek* (May 9, 1977), 21.

Cook, Timothy E., *Governing with the News: The News Media as a Political Institution* (Chicago: University of Chicago Press, 1998).

Cooper, Jr., William J., *Jefferson Davis: American* (New York: Alfred A. Knopf, 2000).

Cordery, Stacy A., "Edith Kermit (Carow) Roosevelt," in Lewis G. Gould, ed., *American First Ladies: Their Lives and Their Legacy* (New York: Garland, 1996).

——, "Helen Herron (Nellie) Taft," in Lewis G. Gould, ed., *American First Ladies: Their Lives and Their Legacy* (New York: Garland, 1996).

Cormier, Frank, James Deakin, and Helen Thomas, "News Management," in *The White House Press on the Presidency: News Management and Co-option*, ed. Kenneth W. Thompson (Lanham, Md.: University Press of America, 1983).

Crook, William, *Memories of the White House: The Home Life of Our Presidents from Lincoln to Roosevelt* (Boston: Little, Brown, 1911).

Cox, Warren J., Hugh Newell Jacobson, Francis D. Lethbridge, and David R. Rosenthal, eds., *A Guide to the Architecture of Washington, D.C.* (New York: McGraw-Hill, 1974).

Cutter, William Richard, ed., *Genealogical and Personal Memoirs Relating to the Families of Boston and Eastern Massachusetts* (New York: Lewis Historical Publishing, 1908).

Cutts, Lucia B., ed., *Memoirs and Letters of Dolley Madison, Wife of James Madison, President of the United States* (Boston: Houghton Mifflin, 1886).

"Dark Days at the White House," *The Economist* (August 2, 1980).

Davis, William C., *Jefferson Davis: The Man and His Hour* (Baton Rouge: Louisiana State University Press, 1991).

DeGregorio, William A., *The Complete Book of the Presidents* (New York: Dembner Books, 1984).

Denton, Robert E., *The Primetime Presidency of Ronald Reagan: The Era of the Television Presidency* (New York: Praeger, 1988).

Dewhirst, Robert, "White House Manager," in Robert P. Watson, ed., *American First Ladies* (Pasadena, Calif.: Salem Press, 2002), 341–348.

"Don't Confuse 'Entertainer' with 'Envoy,'" *The Times Union* (December 2, 1999), A2.

Dougherty, Margot, and Joyce Leviton, "Holding His Own Against Cancer, Billy Carter Savors Life as Quiet Brother," *People* (April 4, 1988), 42.

Downes, Randolph C., *The Rise of Warren G. Harding, 1865–1920* (Boston: Houghton Mifflin, 1943).

Dudden, Arthur Power, "The Record of Political Humor," *American Quarterly* 37 (Spring 1985).

Earle, Alice Morse, *China Collecting in America* (London: Lawrence and Bullen, 1892).

Ellis, Joseph J., *Founding Brothers: The Revolutionary Generation* (New York: Alfred A. Knopf, 2000).

Fallows, James, *Breaking the News: How the Media Undermine Democracy in America* (New York: Pantheon Books, 1996).

——, "The Passionless Presidency," *The Atlantic Monthly* (May 1979).

Fayen, Sarah, "Inhabiting an Icon: First Ladies in the White House," *Blueprints Magazine* (Winter 2000).

Fetterman, Mindy, "Chip and Caron in Church," *Washington Post* (August 15, 1977), B3.

Finkel, David, "Billy Comes Home to Plains," *St. Petersburg Times* (November 22, 1987), A1.

"Fire Trap," *Time* 52 (November 22, 1948), 24.

Fitzpatrick, John C., ed., *The Diaries of George Washington* (New York: Houghton Mifflin, 1925).

Fraker, Susan, "Plains Women," *Newsweek* (July 26, 1976), 39.

——, "Making of a State Dinner," *Newsweek* (March 21, 1977), 30.

Freda, Ernie, "Washington in Brief," *Atlanta Journal and Constitution* (February 4, 1994), A11.

Freidel, Frank, and William Pencak, eds., *The White House: The First Two Hundred Years* (Boston: Northeastern University Press, 1994).

French, Blaire Atherton, *The Presidential Press Conference: Its History and Role in the American Political System* (Lanham, Md.: University Press of America, 1982).

"Funeral of General Pierce's Son," *New York Times* (January 11, 1853), 2.

Furman, Bess, *White House Profile* (Indianapolis, Ind.: Bobbs-Merrill, 1951).

Garrett, Elisabeth Donaghy, *At Home: The American Family, 1750–1870* (New York: Harry Abrams, 1990).

Garrett, Wendell, ed., *Our Changing White House* (Boston: Northeastern University Press, 1995).

Garrison, Webb, *A Treasury of White House Tales: Fascinating, Colorful Stories of American Presidents and Their Families* (Nashville: Rutledge Hill Press, 1989).

Geordie, Greig, "Oh Brother! Clinton Fears the Next Gaffe," *The Sunday Times* (London) (14 October, 1994).

Gerry, Jr., Elbridge, *The Diary of Elbridge Gerry, Jr.* (New York: Brentano's, 1927).

Gordon, George, "Clinton's Brawling Brother Accused," *Daily Mail* (London) (May 15, 1993), 10.

Graustark, Barbara, "The Carters," *Newsweek* (January 15, 1979), 90.

Green, Constance McLaughlin, *Washington: Village and Capital, 1800–1878* (Princeton, N.J.: Princeton University Press, 1962).

Greenberg, Allan, *George Washington, Architect* (London: Andreas Papadakis Publisher, 1999).

Grossman, Michael Baruch, and Martha Joynt Kumar, "White House and the News Media: The Phases of their Relationship," *Political Science Quarterly* 94 (Spring 1979).

Gutheim, Frederick, *The Potomac* (New York: Grosset & Dunlap, 1968).

Gutin, Myra G., *The President's Partner: The First Lady in the Twentieth Century* (Westport, Conn.: Greenwood Press, 1989).

Haberman, Clyde, "Koch Stance Is Worrying Carter Aides," *New York Times* (August 8, 1980), A14.

Hackett, Walter, "News-Shy Architect Directs Restoration of White House," *The Washington Star* (December 2, 1962), F10.

Hendrickson, Paul, "Light and Magic in the East Room," *Washington Post* (February 26, 1979), B1.

Hinckley, Barbara, *The Symbolic Presidency: How President's Portray Themselves* (New York: Routledge, 1990).

Hirschhorn, Norbert, Robert G. Feldman, and Ian A. Greaves, "Abraham Lincoln's Blue Pills," Perspectives in Biology and Medicine 44 (Summer 2001): 315–332.

Hoganson, Kristin, "Abigail (Powers) Fillmore," in Lewis G. Gould, ed., *American First Ladies: Their Lives and Their Legacy* (New York: Garland, 1996).

Holloway, Laura Carter, *The Ladies of the White House* (New York: U.S. Publishing, 1870).

Hoover, Irwin, *Forty-two Years in the White House* (Boston: Houghton Mifflin, 1943).

Hosmer, Jr., Charles B., *Presence of the Past: A History of the Preservation Movement in the United States Before Williamsburg* (G. P. Putnam's Sons, 1965).

Howard, Hugh, Thomas Jefferson: The Built Legacy of Our Third President (New York: Rizzoli, 2003).

Hurd, Charles, *The White House Story* (New York: Hawthorne Publishers, 1966).

Irons-Georges, Tracy, ed., The American Presidents (Pasadena, Calif.: Salem Press, 2000).

Jablow, Valerie, "Presidential Designs," *Smithsonian* 31 (November 2000), 49.

Janza, Anthony Violanti, "Broken Punk," *Buffalo News* (January 29, 1993).

Jensen, Amy La Follette, *The White House and Its Thirty-Four Families* (New York: McGraw-Hill, 1965).

Johnson, Allen, "Rev. Jesse Appleton," in *The Dictionary of American Biography* (New York: Charles Scribner's Sons, 1928), I: 328.

Juergens, George, *News from the White House* (Chicago: University of Chicago Press, 1981).

Kellerman, Barbara, *All the President's Kin* (New York: Free Press, 1981).

Kelly, Michael, "Seizing the Day; New President Brings Opportunity to Cash In," *New York Times* (18 January 1993), A12.

Kennon, Donald, R., ed., *A Republic for the Ages* (Charlottesville: University Press of Virginia, 1999).

Kernan, Michael, "Aswim in the Social Fishbowl: Life in the Washington Fishbowl," *Washington Post* (28 August 1977), K1.

Kernell, Samuel, *Going Public* (Washington, D.C.: CQ Press, 1993).

Kerr, Joan Paterson, ed., *A Bully Father: Theodore Roosevelt's Letters to His Children* (New York: Random House, 1995).

Kirk, Elise Kuhl, *Music at the White House: A History of the American Spirit* (Urbana: University of Illinois Press, 1986).

Klapthor, Margaret Brown, *Official White House China: 1789 to the President*, 2nd ed. (New York: Barra Foundation, 1999).

Kumar, Martha Joynt, "The Contemporary Presidency: The Pressures of White House Work Life: 'Naked in a Glass House,' " *Presidential Studies Quarterly* 31 (December 4, 2001).

Kutz, Howard, *Spin Cycle: How the White House and the Media Manipulate the News* (New York: Touchstone Books, 1998).

Langford, Edna, and Linda Maddox, *Rosalynn: Friend and First Lady* (Old Tappan, N.J.: Revell, 1980).

Lansford, Tom, "Family Life in the White House," in Robert P. Watson, ed., *American First Ladies* (Pasadena, Calif.: Salem Press, 2002), 394–403.

——, *A "Bully" First Lady: Edith Kermit Roosevelt* (Huntington, N.Y.: Nova History Books, 2001).

Lee, Charles, "Two Koreas to have Unification Concert," United Press International (November 26, 1999).

Leonard, Thomas C., *The Power of the Press: The Birth of American Political Reporting* (New York: Oxford University Press, 1986).

Levin, Phillis, *Abigail Adams* (New York: St. Martin's, 1987).

Liebovich, Louis W., *The Press and the Modern Presidency: Myths and Mindsets from Kennedy to Clinton* (Westport, Conn.: Praeger, 1998).

Longworth, Alice Roosevelt, *Crowded Houses: Reminiscences of Alice Roosevelt Longworth* (New York: Charles Scribner's Sons, 1933).

Malone, Dumas, *Jefferson and His Time*, vol. 2 (Boston: Little Brown, 1951).

Maltese, John Anthony, *The White House Office of Communications and the Management of Presidential News* (Chapel Hill: University of North Carolina Press, 1994).

Marks, Alexander, "First Daughters: Legitimate News . . . or Tabloid Topic?" *Christian Science Monitor* 4 (June 4, 2001), 1.

Mayo, Edith, "Party Politics: The Political Impact of the First Ladies' Social Role," *Social Science Journal* 4 (2000), 577–590.

McCardle, Dorothy, "The Government Curator They Call 'Grand Acquisitor,'" *Washington Post* (January 17, 1961), 1.

McColloch, James, *John Adams* (New York: Simon & Schuster, 2001).

McFeatters, Ann, "Plenty of Fruits on Presidential Family Trees," *Cleveland Plain Dealer* (March 6, 1994), C6.

McShane, Larry, "The First Brother Bites the Big Apple—Ouch," Associated Press (May 15, 1993).

Miller, Hope Ridings, *Scandals in the Highest Office* (New York: Random House, 1973).

Miller, Nathan, *Theodore Roosevelt: A Life* (New York: Quill, 1992).

Minor, Elliott, "Irreverent Billy Carter Dead after Battle with Cancer," Associated Press (September 26, 1988).

Monkman, Betty C., "The White House Collection: Research Sources in the Office of the Curator," *White House History* 9 (Spring 2001).

——, *The White House: Its Historic Furnishings and First Families* (Washington, D.C.: White House Historical Association, 2000).

Morris, Edmund, *Theodore Rex* (New York: Random House, 2001).

——, *Dutch: A Memoir of Ronald Reagan* (New York: Random House, 1999).

Morris, Sylvia Jukes, *Edith Kermit Roosevelt: Portrait of a First Lady* (New York: Coward, McCann & Geoghegan, 1979).

McCullough, David, *Truman* (New York: Simon and Schuster, 1992).

Murray, Robert K., *The Harding Era: Warren G. Harding and His Times* (Minneapolis: University of Minnesota Press, 1969).

Nacos, Brigitte Lebens, *The Press, Presidents, and Crises* (New York: Columbia University Press, 1990).

Nelson, W. Dale, *Who Speaks for the President? The White House Press Secretary from Cleveland to Clinton* (Syracuse, N.Y.: Syracuse University Press, 1998).

Neustadt, Richard, *Presidential Power and the Modern Presidents: The Politics of Leadership from Roosevelt to Reagan* (New York: Macmillan, 1990).

Nichols, Frederick Doveton, *Thomas Jefferson, Landscape Architect* (Charlottesville: University Press of Virginia, 2003).

Nichols, Roy Franklin, *Franklin Pierce: Young Hickory of the Granite Hills* (Philadelphia: University of Pennsylvania Press, 1931).

Oxford, Edward, "The White House," *American History Illustrated* 27 (Sept–Oct. 1992), 6–8.

The Papers of Franklin Pierce. Presidential Documents and Diaries. Washington, D.C.: Manuscript Division, Library of Congress.

Patterson, Thomas, *Out of Order* (New York: Alfred A. Knopf, 1993).

Pearson, Richard, "Billy Carter, Ex-President's Brother, Dies of Cancer," *Washington Post* (26 September 1988), D6.

Perling, J. J., *President's Sons: The Prestige of Name in a Democracy* (New York: Odyssey Press, 1947).

Philips, Chuck, "What a Difference a Year Makes for Roger Clinton," *Los Angeles Times* (December 27, 1993), F1.

Podell, Janet, and Steven Anzovin, eds., *Speeches of the American Presidents* (New York: H. W. Wilson, 1988).

Powell, Jody, *The Other Side of the Story* (New York: William Morrow, 1984).

"The President's Hall," *Newsweek* 27 (January 28, 1946), 29.

"The President's News Conference of August 4, 1980," *Weekly Compilation of Presidential Documents* (August 4, 1980), 16: 32.

Prindiville, Kathleen, *First Ladies* (New York: MacMillan, 1932).

Quinn, Sally, "Billy Carter: Besieged and Beset," *Washington Post* (27 July 1980), A1.

Quinn-Musgrove, Sandra L., and Sanford Kanter, *America's Royalty: All the Presidents' Children* (Westport, Conn.: Greenwood Press, 1995).

Radcliffe, Donnie, "Chip and Caron Carter: Moving Back from Georgia," *Washington Post* (October 28, 1977), D1.

"Raging Roger: Bill Clinton's Younger Brother Roger," *Eye to Eye with Connie Chung* (June 17, 1993).

Reagan, Nancy, *My Turn: The Memoirs of Nancy Reagan* (New York: Random House, 1989).

"Remarks at Georgetown University," *Weekly Compilation of Presidential Documents* (July 6, 1995), 31: 27.

"Remarks at the Children's Town Meeting with Peter Jennings," *Weekly Compilation of Presidential Documents* (20 February 1993), 20: 8.

"Remarks on Launching the National Youth Anti-Drug Media Campaign in Atlanta, Georgia," *Weekly Compilation of Presidential Documents* (July 9, 1998), 34: 28.

"Repairs of 1600 Pennsylvania Avenue," *Newsweek* 27 (February 11, 1946), 25.

Richardson, James D., ed., *A Compilation of the Messages and Speeches of the Presidents* (Washington, D.C.: U.S. Government Printing Office, 1896).

Rives, John C., ed., *The Congressional Globe: News Series: Containing Sketches of the Debates and Proceedings of the First*

Session of the Thirty-First Congress, vol. 22 (Washington, D.C.: Blair & Rives, 1850).

Robinson, Corrine Roosevelt, *My Brother Theodore Roosevelt* (New York: Charles Scribner's Sons, 1928).

Roeder, Bill, "The Busy White House Curator," *Newsweek* (February 16, 1981), 19.

"Roger Clinton a VIP in North Korea," Associated Press (December 9, 1999).

Roosevelt, Theodore, *Theodore Roosevelt: An Autobiography* (New York: Charles Scribner's Sons, 1913).

Rosenthal, Harry F., "His Brother's Reaper?" Associated Press (August 2, 1980).

Rozell, Mark, "President Carter and the Press: Perspectives from White House Communications Advisors," *Political Science Quarterly* 105 (1990).

———, *The Press and the Carter Presidency* (Boulder, Colo. Westview Press, 1989).

Ryan, William, and Desmond Guinness, *The White House: An Architectural History* (New York: McGraw-Hill, 1980).

"Sad Railroad Accident: Son of Gen. Pierce Killed," *New York Times* (January 7, 1853), 1.

Sadler, Christine, *Children in the White House* (New York: G. P. Putnam's, 1967).

Scarry, Robert J., *Millard Fillmore* (Jefferson, N.C.: McFarland, 2001).

Scheer, Robert, "Jimmy, We Hardly Know Y'All," *Playboy* (November 1976).

Schram, Martin, "The Troubled Times of a Different Billy Carter," *Washington Post* (April 23, 1979), A1.

Seale, William, "The White House: Plans Realized and Unrealized," in *Our Changing White House*, ed., Wendell Garrett (Boston: Northeastern University Press, 1995).

———. *The President's House: A History* (Washington, D.C.: White House Historical Society, 1986).

Severn, Bill, *Frontier President: The Life of James K. Polk* (New York: Ives Washburn, 1965).

Sheehy, Gail, *Hillary's Choice* (New York: Random House, 1999).

Shulman, Holly Cowan, "Dolley Madison," *American First Ladies: Their Lives and Their Legacy,* Lewis L. Gould, ed., (New York: Garland, 1996), 45–68.

Sievers, Harry J., *Benjamin Harrison: Hoosier President: The White House and After* (Indianapolis, Ind.: Bobbs-Merrill, 1968).

Sinclair, Andrew, *The Available Man* (New York: Macmillan, 1965).

Sipchen, Bob, "Billy Carter Is Back," *Los Angeles Times* (March 7, 1988).

Smith, Carolyn, *Presidential Press Conferences: A Critical Approach* (New York: Praeger, 1990).

Smith, Elbert B., *The Presidencies of Zachary Taylor and Millard Fillmore* (Lawrence: University Press of Kansas, 1988).

Smith, K., *Entertaining in the White House* (Washington, D.C.: Acropolis Books, 1967).

Smith, Margaret Bayard, *The First Forty Years of Washington Society* (New York: Frederick Ungar, 1965).

Smith, Maria, "White House Curator Resigns: Baltimore Man to Replace Lorraine Pearce," *Washington Post* (August 3, 1962), C7.

Smith, Page, *John Adams* (Garden City, N.J.: Doubleday, 1902).

Smith, Richard Norton, *Patriarch* (Boston: Houghton Mifflin, 1993).

Smith, Terrence, "Brothers Carter: A Gulf in the Family," *New York Times* (25 July 1980), A10.

Smoller, Frederic T., *The Six O'Clock Presidency: A Theory of Presidential-Press Relations in the Age of TV* (New York: Praeger, 1990).

Speer, Albert, *Inside the Third Reich* (New York: MacMillan, 1970).

Stoddard, Henry L., *As I Knew Them: Presidents and Politics from Grant to Coolidge* (New York: Harper & Brothers, 1927).

Strege, Dave, "Hail to the Angler," *Orange County Register* (August 14, 1997), D15.

Strock, James M., *Theodore Roosevelt on Leadership: Executive Lessons From the Bully Pulpit* (Roseville, Calif.: Forum, 2001).

Strode, Hudson, ed., *Jefferson Davis: Private Letters, 1823–1889* (New York: De Capo Press, 1995).

——, *Jefferson Davis, 1808–1861* (New York: Harcourt, Brace, 1955).

Stuckey, Mary E., *The President as Interpreter-in-Chief* (Englewood Cliffs, N.J.: Chatham House, 1991).

"Swinging in Pyongyang," *Washington Times* (8 December 1999), A14.

Taft, Helen Herron, *Recollections of Full Years* (New York: Dodd, Mead, 1914).

Taylor, Tim, *The Book of the Presidents* (New York: Arno Press, 1972).

Tebbel, John, and Sarah Miles Watts, *The Press and the Presidency: From George Washington to Ronald Reagan* (New York: Oxford University Press, 1985).

Thacker-Estrada, Elizabeth Lorelei, "The Heart of the Fillmore Presidency: Abigail Powers Fillmore and the White House Library," *White House Studies* 1: 83–98.

Thomas, E. H. Gywnne, *The Presidential Families: From George Washington to Ronald Reagan* (New York: Hippocrene, 1989).

Thomas, Evan, and Martha Brant, "Busted Again in Margaritaville," *Newsweek* (11 June 2001), 24.

Trani, Eugene P., and David L. Wilson, *The Presidency of Warren G. Harding* (Lawrence: University Press of Kansas, 1977).

"Transcript of White House Press Briefing, Dec. 3 by Joe Lockhart," *Federal News Service* (December 3, 1999).

Troy, Gil, "Jacqueline Kennedy," in Robert P. Watson, ed., *American First Ladies* (Pasadena, Calif.: Salem Press, 2002), 250–258.

——, *Mr. and Mrs. President: From the Trumans to the Clintons*, 2nd ed. (Lawrence: University Press of Kansas, 2000).

"Truman Decides to Have a Porch at White House to Cost $15,000," *New York Times* (January 3, 1948), 15.

Truman, Margaret, *First Ladies* (New York: Random House, 1996).

——, *Harry S. Truman* (New York: Macmillan, 1973).

Tulis, Jeffrey, *The Rhetorical Presidency* (Princeton, N.J.: Princeton University Press, 1987).

Twohig, Dorothy, ed., *The Papers of George Washington* (Charlottesville: University Press of Virginia, 1998).

Tyler, Norman, *Historic Preservation: An Introduction to Its History, Principles, and Practice* (New York: W. W. Norton, 2000).

Vaughn, Mark L., *The Washington Star* (Washington, D.C.: Washington Star, 1961).

"Washington Whispers," *U.S. News & World Report* (February 2, 1981), 14.

Waterman, Richard W., Robert Wright, and Gilbert St. Clair, *The Image Is Everything Presidency: Dilemmas in American Leadership* (Boulder, Colo.: Westview Press, 1999).

Watson, Robert P., "Nation's Social Hostess," in Robert P. Watson, ed., *American First Ladies* (Pasadena, Calif.: Salem Press, 2002), 349–356.

——, *First Ladies of the United States: A Biographical Dictionary* (Boulder, Colo.: Lynne Rienner Publishers, 2001).

——, *The Presidents' Wives: Reassessing the Office of First Lady* (Boulder, Colo.: Lynne Rienner Publishers, 2000).

Weisberger, Bernard A., *The District of Columbia: The Sea of Government* (New York: Time-Life Books, 1968).

Willets, Gilson, *Inside History of the White House: The Complete History of the Domestic and Official Life in Washington of the Nation's Presidents and their Families* (New York: Christian Herald, 1908).

Whillock, Rita K., "The Compromising Clinton: Images of a Failure, a Record of Success," in Robert E. Denton and Rachel L. Holloway, *The Clinton Presidency: Images, Issues, and Communication Strategies* (Westview, Conn.: Praeger, 1996).

Whittell, Giles, "The First Brother Changes His Tune," *The Times* (London) (October 14, 1994).

Winfield, Betty Houchin, *FDR and the News Media* (Urbana: University of Illinois Press, 1990).

Whitcomb, John, and Claire Whitcomb, *Real Life at the White House* (New York: Routledge, 2000).

The White House: An Historical Guide (Washington, D.C.: White House Historical Association, 1995).

"White House Porch," *New York Times* (January 16, 1948), 22.

White, Kathleen Kelly, ed., *It's Still News, Mr. President* (Clinton, Mo.: The Printery, 1969).

Wolff, Perry, *A Tour of the White House with Mrs. John F. Kennedy* (Garden City, N.J.: Doubleday & Co., 1962).

Zernicke, Paul Haskell, *Pitching the Presidency: How Presidents Depict the Office* (Westport, Conn.: Praeger, 1994).

Contributors

Carol Lynn Bower returned to college after an award-winning, twenty-year career in journalism and is completing two Ph.D.s in communication and political science at the Hugh Downs School of Human Communication and Department of Political Science at Arizona State University. She investigates the intersection of politics and rhetoric with an emphasis in gendered political discourse. Her work includes examinations of female candidacy, congressional discourse, the historic 1998 Arizona election, first ladies' communication, the White House Press Corps, media analysis, and legal discourse.

Virginia A. Chanley, Ph.D. is a political consultant and research associate with Abacus Associates in Massachusetts. Formerly, she was on the faculty of the Department of Political Science at Florida International University, where she taught courses on American politics, the presidency, political parties, public opinion and electoral behavior, and research methods. Her research has been published in journals such as *American Politics Quarterly*, *Political Behavior*, *Political* Psychology, *Public Opinion Quarterly*, and *White House Studies*. She is currently working on an edited volume of comparative research on the role of public opinion in foreign policy and a book about former first lady Rosalynn Carter. Her Ph.D. is from the University of Minnesota.

Robert E. Dewhirst, Ph.D. is professor of political science at Northwest Missouri State University. His teaching and research have focused on American national and state politics, institutions, and political behavior. He is the author or coauthor of six books on American politics, including *Rites of Passage: Congress Makes Laws*, and has contributed chapters to numerous reference books and edited collections. Dewhirst is currently writing separate biographies of Mamie and Dwight Eisenhower and editing the _Encyclopedia of the American Congress._

Raymond Frey, Ph.D. is associate professor of history and Dean of Faculty at Centenary College in New Jersey. He has written extensively on the Truman administration and is working on a book entitled _Bess Truman: The Reluctant First Lady._

Lori Cox Han, Ph.D. is associate professor of political science at Austin College in Texas. A former journalist, her research focuses on the American presidency and media and politics. She is the author of _Governing from Center State: White House Communication Strategies during the Age of Politics_ and her work has been published in numerous journals. She received the Goldsmith Research Award from the Joan Shorenstein Center for the Press, Politics and Public Policy at Harvard University and is currently completing an edited book titled _In the Public Domain: Presidents and the Challenge of Public Leadership._ Her Ph.D. is from the University of Southern California.

Christopher S. Kelley is currently a doctoral fellow at the Kettering Foundation, a research organization that works to improve democracy and democratic practices. Kelly is ABD in political science at Miami University in Ohio, where he is finishing his dissertation on the development and significance of the presidential signing statement.

Tom Lansford, Ph.D. is associate professor of political science at the University of Southern Mississippi, Gulf Coast. Dr. Lansford is the author of numerous books, including _All for One: NATO, Terrorism and the United States; The Lords of Foggy Bottom: The American Secretaries of State and the World They Shaped; A "Bully" First Lady: Edith Kermit Roosevelt;_ and _Evolution and Devolution: The Dynamics of Sovereignty and Security in Post–Cold War Europe._ He has also edited several books and his articles have appeared in such journals as _Defense Analysis, The Journal of Conflict Studies, European Security, International Studies, Strategic Studies,_ and _White House Studies._ Lansford is a member of the board of the National Social Science Association and a Fellow at the Frank Maria Center for International Politics and Ethics.

Michael E. Long has served as instructor of history and political science at Pasco-Hernando Community College in New Port Richey, Florida since August 2001. Prior to a career in higher education, he served in Virginia local government as assistant city manager and town manager, serving communities participating in the National Main Street downtown revitalization program (1989–1996). He also worked as a museum curator and administrator for the Division of Historic Preservation of the Fairfax County (VA) Park Authority (1973–1975); at Historic Bethlehem, Inc. in Bethlehem, Pennsylvania (1975–1976); and as Executive Director for the Parkersburg Arts Center in Parkersburg, West Virginia (1976–1977).

Russell L. Mahan, J.D. is City Attorney for Bountiful, Utah, a position he has held since 1993, and was Assistant City Attorney from 1981 to 1993. Mahan was editor and publisher of *Presidential History Magazine* from 1998–1999 and editor and publisher of *Revolutionary War Magazine* from 1986–1987, and is a member of the editorial board of the journal *White House Studies*. Mahan has conducted research at numerous historic presidential sites, including the Richard M. Nixon Birthplace and Library, Martin Van Buren Home, Jimmy Carter Presidential Center, Woodrow Wilson Boyhood Home, and others, and is currently completing the book *Capturing History: The First Presidential Photographs.* Mahan completed his B.A. Summa Cum Laude in History from the University of Northern Colorado and his J.D. from Brigham Young University.

James S. McCallops, Ph.D. is an associate professor at Salisbury University in Maryland, specializing in women's history and gender studies. Besides this chapter on the Harding White House, he has a book coming out in 2004 on Edith Wilson, and he wrote essays on both First Lady Florence Harding and First Lady Edith Wilson in *American First Ladies* and a chapter on Mrs. Wilson in *The Presidential Companion.*

Michael J. C. Taylor, Ph.D. is assistant professor of history at Dickinson State University in North Dakota, whose research and publications focus on the Civil War, the presidency, and Franklin Pierce. He is currently writing biographies of Herbert "Zeppo" Marx and Franklin Pierce, and editing a reader titled the Philosophy of History.

Elizabeth Lorelei Thacker-Estrada is the special projects manager at the San Francisco Public Library. She received her Master of Library and Information Studies degree at the University of California, Berkeley. Thacker-Estrada is completing the first scholarly books about Abigail Fillmore and Jane Means Appleton Pierce. Her work has been published in the *Presidential Companion* (University Of South Carolina Press, 2003), *American First Ladies* (Salem Press, 2001), *Laura Bush: The Report To The First Lady* (Nova, 2001), and the journal *White House Studies*.

Robert P. Watson, Ph.D. is associate professor of political science at Florida Atlantic University. He has published 20 books and over 100 scholarly articles, essays, and reviews on such topics as the presidency, first ladies, women in politics, civil rights, campaigns and elections, bureaucracy, and environmental protection, and is the founding editor of the journal *White House Studies*. A frequent media commentator on the first families, Watson has been interviewed by CNN, MSNBC, *USA Today*, and dozens of other media outlets. He also served as a guest for CNN.com's coverage of the 2001 presidential inaugural, appeared on C-SPAN's "Book TV" program, and directed the first-ever "Report to the First Lady," which was presented to Laura Bush and Lynne Cheney after the 2001 inaugural. Watson serves on the boards of several scholarly journals and presidential foundations, and has lectured as a visiting fellow at many universities and presidential sites.

Index